Gold of the Akan from the Glassell Collection

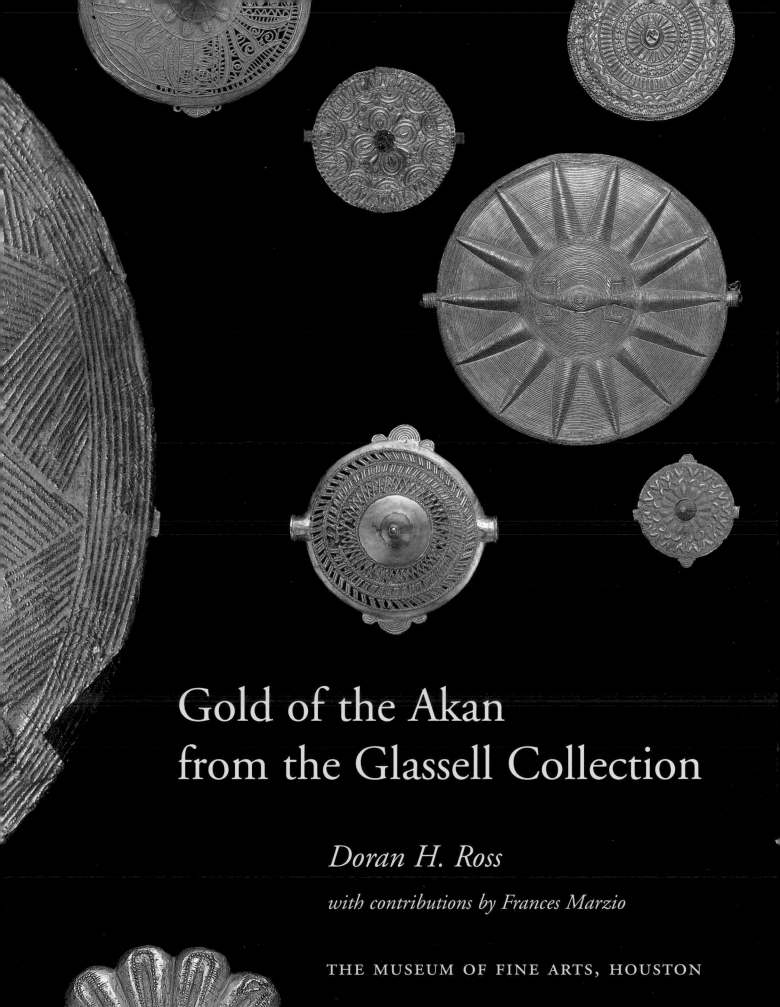

# Gold of the Akan
# from the Glassell Collection

## Doran H. Ross

### with contributions by Frances Marzio

THE MUSEUM OF FINE ARTS, HOUSTON

Lynne Kostman, *Managing Editor*
Danny Brauer, *Designer and Production Manager*
Thomas R. DuBrock, *Principal Photographer*
David L. Fuller, *Cartographer*

The Museum of Fine Arts, Houston
1001 Bissonnet
P.O. Box 6826
Houston, Texas 77265-6826

Requests for permission to reproduce material from this volume
should be sent to the Museum of Fine Arts, Houston,
Publications Department at the above address.

Printed and bound in Hong Kong by South Sea International
Press, Ltd.

ISBN 0-89090-116-3 (softcover edition)
ISBN 0-89090-115-5 (hardcover edition)

Hardcover edition distributed by Merrell Publishers Limited


Library of Congress Cataloging-in-Publication Data

Museum of Fine Arts, Houston.
        Gold of the Akan from the Glassell collection / Doran H.
Ross ; with contributions by Frances Marzio.
            p. cm.
        Includes bibliographical references
ISBN 0-89090-115-5 (hard) — ISBN 0-89090-116-3 (soft)
1. Goldwork, Akan — Ghana. 2. Regalia (Insignia) — Ghana. 3. Akan
(African people) — Ghana — Social life and customs. 4. Glassell,
Alfred C. (Alfred Curry), 1913 — Art collections. 5. Goldwork —
Private collections — Texas — Houston. 6. Museum of Fine Arts,
Houston. I. Ross, Doran H. II. Marzio, Frances. III. Title.

NK7415.G45 M87 2002
739.2'2'089963385 — DC21
                                        2002033702

Cover: Sword hilt of *sankɔfa* bird. Gold leaf, wood. H: 10⅛ in.
97.1390. (See discussion, p. 81.)

Page 304: Staff finial of elephant. Gold leaf, wood. H: 7⅜ in.
97.1291. (See discussion, pp. 39, 40.)

# Contents

# Foreword

In donating his world-famous collection of works of art in gold in 1997, Alfred C. Glassell Jr. made the Museum of Fine Arts, Houston, a center for the appreciation and study of African genius. The permanent galleries of African gold designed to house the collection by curator Frances Marzio established a new style of artistic presentation intended to convey the beauty and visual message of these masterpieces of the Akan peoples of West Africa. During the design process, Doran Ross shared the knowledge derived from his extensive fieldwork in Africa, advising, encouraging, and contributing his invaluable first-person experience. The collection has since attracted the attention of museums throughout the world, and in December of 2001, a selection of 140 works from the Glassell Collection was exhibited before enormous crowds at the Pushkin State Museum in Moscow.

The vision of Alfred C. Glassell Jr. and the efforts of Doran Ross and Frances Marzio have merged in the creation of this book, a visual feast that explores in scholarly fashion the functions and importance of Akan regalia. The text examines the unique relationship that exists between Akan oral tradition and art objects, as well as the diverse sources of Akan designs and imagery. The objects speak vividly of intermingling cultures and the synthesis, mutation, and continuous evolution of forms and meanings.

The trustees of the Museum of Fine Arts, Houston, are forever indebted to Alfred C. Glassell Jr. whose generosity to the Museum is surpassed only by his brilliance as a collector.

The trustees also wish to express their appreciation to Caroline Wiess Law and Alfred C. Glassell III for their support of this project. A final note of gratitude must go to all the staff of the Museum for their work on the permanent installation, conservation, preparation, photography, and publications related to this collection.

*Peter Marzio*
Director
Museum of Fine Arts, Houston

Young chief from Anomabu. Photograph by Herbert M. Cole, 1973.

# Acknowledgments

The visual quality of this volume is in large measure a product of the beautiful and sensitive studio photographs of Museum of Fine Arts staff photographer Thomas R. DuBrock. Equally important is the imaginative and thoughtful publication design of Daniel Brauer whose work continues to amaze. Lynne Kostman edited the text with considerable intelligence, care, and remarkable attention to detail. Maps were skillfully executed by cartographer David L. Fuller. In Houston logistical support was provided by Kathleen Crain, George Zombakis, and especially Winnie M. Youngblood whose close familiarity with the collection kept the project on track. Both colleague and friend, Winnie juggled many tasks and spurred on critical elements of the book ensuring its successful completion. In Los Angeles Betsy Escandor, Linda Lee, and Patrick Fitzgerald were instrumental in getting the book off the ground. Betsy Quick magically transformed ink into electronic text, inserting good critical thinking in the process.

Much of the early research informing this volume was conducted by the principal author with Herbert M. Cole in preparation for the UCLA Fowler Museum of Cultural History's book and exhibition *The Arts of Ghana* (1977). Herbert Cole remains a continuing inspiration. Some of his wonderful photographs appear in this volume along with those of Angela Fisher, Frank Fournier, Raymond Silverman, Monica Blackmun Visoná, and Susan M. Vogel. Many thanks to all. The photography of Eliot Elisofon is courtesy of the National Museum of African Art, Eliot Elisofon Archive, Smithsonian Institution. As with almost all books on the cultural history and artistic heritage of Ghana, we also owe a major debt to the Basel Mission Archive and its director, Paul Jenkins.

The contributions of many Ghanaians have informed virtually all of the text in this volume. In Asante we would like to thank the following leaders, past and present: Asantehene Otumfuo Opoku Ware II, Asantehene Otumfuo Osei Tutu II, Mamponhene Nana Atakora Amaniampong II, Adansehene Nana Kwantwi Barima II, Agonahene Nana Boakye Yiadom II, Asumegyahene Odeneho Oduro Numapau II, Bekwaihene Nana Osei Kwadwo II, Dwabenhene Nana Kofi Siriboe II, Edwesohene Nana Diko Pim III, Kokofuhene Nana Osei Assibey III, Kumawuhene Barima Asumadu Sakyi II, Nsutahene Nana Yaw Sekyere II, and Offinsohene Nana Wiafe Akenten II. From the Asantehene's court special thanks are due to Akyeamehene Nana Nsuase Poku, Nana Kwadwo Nyantakyi III, Sanaahene, and Nana Akwasi Asafo Agyei II, Abanasehene. Nana Abrafi Mansah was especially helpful in elucidating jewelry names and motifs.

Among the southern Akan the following chiefs were particularly helpful: Nana Kwabu Ewusi VI of Abeadze Dominase, Nana Baidoo Bonsoe XV of

Ahanta, Otumfuo Ansa Sasraku VI of Akwamu, Nana Amonu X of Anomabu, Nai Wyetey Agyeman Larbie II of Awutu, Nana Yamfo Ababio of Enyan Abaasa, Nana Adoku V of Mankcsim, Osabarimba Kwesi Attah II of Oguaa, and Tufohene Nana Kodwo Baiden of Mankesim.

Research in Ghana during the 1970s was facilitated by Professor J. H. K. Nketia whose initiative opened many doors. Malcolm McLeod has generously shared his research and provided many courtesies over the years. Transcriptions and translations of notes and tapes were at various times provided by Dr. Yaw Boateng, Frederick Dennis, B. A. Firempong, Elijah Kannatey-Asibu, Nii O. Quarcoopome, and Rebecca Van Dyck-Laumann. Samuel Cophie, Samuel Adams, Kwame Labi, Joseph Nkrumah, and Francis Duah have been important colleagues over the years.

Most significantly, we would like to thank Alfred C. Glassell Jr. for the privilege and pleasure of working with him and his collection over the past twenty years. He has assembled a spectacular body of work with keen perception and genuine inspiration. An earlier temporary exhibition held in 1991 of his collection of African works of art in gold has since been superseded by a stunning permanent installation, which opened to the public in 1998. His considerable efforts on many fronts in the art world will reach far beyond the communities of Houston in time and space for posterity to appreciate.

*Frances Marzio*
*Doran H. Ross*

The principal author of this volume would like to add a very special appreciation to both the collective and individual personas of Frances and Peter Marzio. I want to thank them for the invitation to write a book on the Glassell Collection and for splendid conversation and indulgent hospitality in the process. Frances has been a remarkably energetic and insightful partner in bringing this book to fruition. As my Ghanaian friends emphasize, "One head does not go into council."

*D. H. R.*

# Alfred C. Glassell Jr.

## "WHEN AN ELDER IS IN THE HOUSE, IT IS GOOD"

My favorite Akan image is the double crocodile depicting an ancient myth from Ghana [fig. A]. Long ago, along the banks of the Ankobra River, there lived a crocodile with two heads joined to a single body. The heads would argue over which would eat the food they caught until one day they finally realized their need to share. This is an important lesson to us all and the reason I gave my collection of African gold to the Museum of Fine Arts, Houston.

A. Finger ring of two crocodiles with a shared stomach. Gold. L: 2 in. 97.1131.

These are the words of Alfred C. Glassell Jr., who has spent a lifetime pursuing excellence in the petroleum industry, marine biology research, sports, civic affairs, philanthropy, and the collecting of fine art. Born on a cotton plantation near Shreveport, Louisiana, Alfred C. Glassell Jr. distinguished himself at Louisiana State University as president of the student body, member in thirteen honor societies, and ROTC commander. Upon graduation, he became a leader in the energy business, extending and discovering oil and gas fields in the Gulf Coast of Louisiana and Texas. He was a founder of the Transcontinental Gas Pipe Line Corporation, the first gas transmission system from Texas to New York, and has served on the boards of major corporations including Transco, El Paso Natural Gas, and First City Bank Corp.

During the Second World War, Alfred C. Glassell Jr. answered the call to duty and joined the armed forces where he achieved the rank of major. His distinguished war record included active service in the African and European theaters. Upon return to civilian life, he again put his business talents to work, joining efforts to return the United States to prosperity with plentiful, affordable energy.

Alfred C. Glassell Jr. has had a lifelong interest in marine biology and the preservation of sea life. He became a trustee of the International Oceanographic Foundation and an associate of the Woods Hole Institute and the Laboratory for Controlled Environmental Studies of Marine Life at the University of Miami, later named for him in recognition of his contributions. He participated in seafaring expeditions throughout the world, leading the Yale Seychelles Expedition from the Atlantic to the Indian Ocean and the East Coast of Africa. On this trip, scientists identified several hundred new species of ocean life. He also sponsored the University of Miami Marine Institute and the Argosy Expedition to Ecuador, the Bay of Panama, and Colombia. In 1971 he was awarded the International Oceanographic Foundation Marine Science Award for Outstanding Contributions.

**B.** Alfred C. Glassell Jr. with his record-setting marlin, used as the cover image on the March 19, 1956 issue of *Sports Illustrated*. Photograph by Richard Anastasio, Sports Illustrated/Time Inc.

An avid sportsman, Alfred C. Glassell Jr. achieved fame as one of the foremost anglers in the world. In 1953 he set the world record for the largest marlin ever caught on a handheld rod and reel. At 1,560 pounds, this record remains today, and the world's largest game fish resides on view at the Smithsonian Institution. As a tribute to his skills, he was pictured on the cover of *Sports Illustrated* in 1954 and inducted into the International Game Fish Association's Hall of Fame in 2001 (fig. B).

In addition to business, military, scientific, and sports achievements, Alfred C. Glassell Jr. has distinguished himself as a civic leader and philanthropist. Over a lifetime, he has dedicated his time and resources to the Houston Museum of Natural Science, Houston Symphony Society, Society for Performing Arts, Houston Ballet Foundation, Houston Chamber of Commerce, Houston Grand Opera Society, Texas Children's Hospital, American Cancer Society, American Museum of Natural History, Archaeological Institute of America, and the Smithsonian Institution.

Alfred C. Glassell Jr. has fulfilled his greatest role as a leader at the Museum of Fine Arts, Houston. This world famous collector of art was first elected to the Museum's Board of Trustees in 1970. Realizing the fundamental need for hands-on experience in the arts and recognizing the lack of studio opportunities, he established the Glassell School of Art. Since its dedication in 1979, the Glassell School has provided diverse training in the fine arts to children, adults, emerging artists, hospital patients, and older Americans. The school is organized into five specialized areas: the Junior School, the Studio School, the Core Program, Exhibitions, and Community Outreach Programs. A full range of programs in each area is offered during three semesters—fall, spring, and summer—each year. Community Outreach Programs at the Glassell School are part of the Museum's far-reaching educational efforts to serve diverse audiences (fig. C).

Alfred C. Glassell Jr. was elected chairman of the Board of Trustees of the Museum of Fine Arts, Houston, in 1990, a time when the need for physical

c. Alfred C. Glassell Jr. with school children at the Museum of Fine Arts, Houston.

expansion was evident. With characteristic optimism and belief in the generosity of Houston, he led a ten-year effort that resulted in the Audrey Jones Beck Building as home for the Museum's collection of Western Antiquities and European and American art.

In his tenure as chairman, Alfred C. Glassell Jr. also oversaw the establishment of a conservation and storage facility, an administrative center, and extension of the Glassell Junior School; the renovation of Bayou Bend, the center for American decorative arts; the opening of Rienzi, the center for European decorative arts; and the renovation of the Caroline Wiess Law Building for Twentieth-Century, Asian, Pre-Columbian, and African art. To this last endeavor, Alfred Glassell made his most generous gift. As a lover and collector of Asian, Pre-Columbian, and African gold, he donated and loaned the work of a lifetime to the Museum. He has given the Museum of Fine Arts, Houston, one of the most important collections of African gold in the world, making it the only museum in the United States where visitors can view such an extensive collection. Alfred C. Glassell Jr. explains, "I am pleased to be able to offer this collection to the citizens of Houston as a cultural resource, one that enriches our understanding of the art of Africa. I am told that this collection is one of the Museum's most popular among children, and one of the most awe-inspiring among adults."

The Glassell Collection of African Gold comprises more than nine hundred artworks representing African cultures and traditions still flourishing today. It features objects created by the Akan peoples of Côte d'Ivoire and Ghana, as well as works from the cultures of Mali and Kenya. Dating from the nineteenth and twentieth centuries, objects in the collection include crowns, jewelry, sandals, swords, and counselors' staffs used by royalty and court officials in a variety of ceremonies and festivals. As Alfred C. Glassell Jr. has noted, "When I started collecting these masterpieces, very few museums in Europe and the United States had any African gold artworks. And yet, as early as the late 1400s, European adventurers and merchants wrote about the richness of African gold objects, which various kings used for adornment and symbolic beauty. I have loved these inventive designs and wonderful animals for decades. It is not just that they are made of gold, but that the artworks seem so alive and vital. To my eye, they have a life force which I admire. It is this original and sometimes amusing artistry which fires my imagination and inspires me to collect."

Alfred C. Glassell Jr. describes the patience required to collect these works with another favorite folktale from Ghana. "There was once a hornbill that owed a debt to a viper. The bird refused to pay his debt and flew high in the skies and nested in trees. The snake, bound to the ground, waited patiently. Eventually, a drought came, and the hornbill was forced to the last watering hole where the viper hid. The viper seized the hornbill and made him pay the debt. In the end, good things come to him who waits." Not surprisingly, the Glassell Collection of African Gold includes many depictions of the viper and hornbill.

*Frances Marzio*

# Preface

A mystique surrounds the Asante and the related Akan peoples of Ghana, and this accounts for their prominence in most publications dealing with the kingdoms of Africa, as well as for the attention paid to them by scholars and tourists over the past fifty years. Part of the mystique can be attributed to the allure of gold, for the Akan live in what was once known as the Gold Coast of West Africa. The tragic history of the slave trade—originating in part from the large forts established by the Europeans in coastal Akan areas—also serves to explain the areas significance for researchers and visitors. During the nineteenth century detailed accounts by political envoys and missionaries to the Asante and other Akan groups led to their becoming among the best known of African peoples. The numerous published reports by British soldiers and journalists documenting the Anglo-Asante wars of 1874 and 1900 and the imprisonment of the Asantehene (the king of the Asante) in 1896 further contributed to their notoriety. Later, Ghana became something of a pilgrimage site as the first sub-Saharan country to regain its independence from colonial domination in 1957 under the charismatic Kwame Nkrumah.

Historical and political realities aside, some of the most compelling and attractive elements of Akan culture are rooted in its rich artistic traditions. At least three artistic genres have put Akan arts on the world stage. Even if most Akan sculpture in wood has not been widely celebrated, the fertility-inducing figure called Akua'ba (pl. Akua'mma) remains one of the five or six most famous of all African sculptural forms. Similarly, Asante kente cloth is probably the most admired of all African textile traditions. On equal footing are the majestic array of jewelry and other items of regalia made from or adorned with gold. The Asante Kingdom, along with other Akan states, proclaimed its wealth and power and indeed recounted its history through displays of gold regalia at annual festivals and during the installation of new chiefs. This volume examines the arts surrounding Akan chieftancy as represented in the Alfred C. Glassell Jr. Collection in the Museum of Fine Arts, Houston, the largest and finest collection of Akan regalia anywhere in the world.

As the most populous, best-known, and most carefully researched of all the Akan groups, the Asante will form the core of much of the discussion that follows. This is only appropriate as they have the most complex and fully realized body of regalia of all Akan peoples. The Asante, along with the Fante, have been the focus of most of my own research in Ghana since 1974. As will become clear, my emphasis is on the context, meaning, and history of the regalia. For discussions of gold-working techniques I refer the reader to Garrard 1980 and 1989.

Following the introduction, the chapters are basically organized by major object types coupled with related items. This should not obscure the fact that each object is part of a complex whole where items are utilized in differing combinations depending on political and ritual demands. The penultimate chapter shifts from Ghana to address Akan-inspired regalia of the Baule and lagoon peoples of Côte d'Ivoire. The final chapter attempts to suggest the wonderful and kaleidoscopic efficacy of regalia performance by examining key festival events that feature these objects in theatrically and ritually charged contexts. The first of three illustrated appendixes presents a nearly comprehensive list of the Asantehene's regalia as it is presented during a major festival procession. Appendix B discusses nonroyal figurative carvings used as display pieces for traditional popular bands. The last appendix includes several pieces of non-Akan gold jewelry from Senegal, Mali, and Kenya.

### Notes to the Reader

Unless otherwise noted, all objects are from the Alfred C. Glassell Jr. Collection at the Museum of Fine Arts, Houston. All photographs unless otherwise credited were taken by Thomas R. DuBrock. Dimensions cited are the largest for each object or for the largest object within a group. State names coincide with the names of their capitals unless preceded by an additional place name. All chiefs, queen mothers, and other officials appearing in photographs or cited in the text or notes are identified by their titles at the time of the photograph or interview, and these do not necessarily represent their current status. Since this volume is intended for the general reader occasionally the literal translations of recorded proverbs were supplanted by freer translations felt to more clearly convey the intended meanings. The Twi as recorded is presented in the endnotes. Conventions for spelling words in Twi have yet to be fully resolved. Spellings used here attempt to conform to the most recent Asante conventions with the occasional inclusion of other localized Akan variants. The Twi letter "ɔ" is pronounced like the "o" in *dog* and "ɛ" is pronounced like the "e" in *bed*. All materials listed as gold are cast unless otherwise noted. The quality of most Akan gold typically ranges between eight and twelve carats with exceptional works approaching pure gold (twenty-four carats). Dates are only provided for objects when I am confident of the approximate, or very rarely the precise, year(s) of creation.

*Doran H. Ross*

# *1* "Gold Is Sharper than a Sword"

## THE RISE OF THE AKAN STATES

The Twi-speaking Akan peoples occupy most of central and southern Ghana and constitute the largest ethnic group in five of Ghana's ten political divisions (Western, Central, Eastern, Brong-Ahafo, and Ashanti). The estimated population of Ghana is nearly nineteen million, and approximately eight and a half million people identify themselves as Akan. The Asante, who number perhaps three million, are the largest and most famous of the various Akan subgroups, which include the Fante, Brong, Akyem, Akuapem, and Kwahu (in roughly descending order by population). Smaller groups include the Aowin, Nzima, Wassaw, Sefwi, Ahafo, Denkyira, Ahanta, and Akwamu (figs. 1.4, 1.6). Some groups, especially the Brong (Bono or Abron), and Nzima cross over the border into Côte d'Ivoire, and others often identified as Akan, such as the Agni and Baule, live wholly within the borders of Ghana's neighbor to the west. Although the Agni can be confidently associated with the Akan, the situation of the Baule is more problematic, as are the histories and cultures of the various non-Twi-speaking lagoon groups of southeast Côte d'Ivoire, which nevertheless share regalia traditions with most Ghanaian Akan.

The first Akan states probably came to power during the fifteenth and sixteenth centuries—at least two hundred years before the rise of Asante—in what were then relatively sparsely populated and densely forested areas of south central Ghana. At that time a dramatic canopy of trees, one to two hundred feet above the forest floor, sheltered a tangled mix of shrubs, herbaceous plants, magnificent stands of bamboo, and climbing vines that reached the top of the canopy in some places (figs. 1.2, 1.3). The British envoy Joseph Dupuis described the forest in 1824 as

1.1 Fante counselor with a staff depicting an elephant and a palm tree. Photograph by Doran H. Ross, Mankesim, 1975.

1.2 Forest view near Asin Foso. Photograph by Doran H. Ross, 1979.

1.3 Bamboo grove off of Kumase-Offinso road. Photograph by Doran H. Ross, 1979.

1.4 (OPPOSITE) The peoples of Ghana with Akan areas labeled in red type.

Magnificent as it was dense and intricate. Numerous plants and creepers of all dimensions chained tree to tree, and branch to branch, clustering the whole in entanglement.... The opacity of this forest communicated to the atmosphere and the surrounding scenery a semblance of twilight; no ray of sunshine penetrated the cheerless gloom, and we were in idea entombed in foliage of a character novel and fanciful. [Dupuis 1824 (1966), 15–16]

With two rainy seasons, annual rainfall in the area ranges from fifty to seventy inches. Kumase, the Asante capital, averages about fifty-nine inches. Only in the southwest corner of the Akan region is there a true rain forest with precipitation in excess of seventy-five inches a year. Most of the Akan heartland is relatively low-lying and less than one thousand feet above sea level, although occasional peaks may rise above two thousand feet (Dickson and Benneh 1988, 21–25).

The most southerly Akan live on or near the relatively flat Ghanaian coastal plain (roughly five degrees north of the equator), which in many areas is lined with coconut palms or covered with scrub and grasses and periodically

1.5 Coconut palms with shore fishermen between Cape Coast and Elmina. Photograph by Doran H. Ross, 1974.

1.6 (OPPOSITE) Major cities of Ghana.

punctuated by lagoons (figs. 1.5, 1.7, 1.8). These form the termini of southern Ghana's many rivers, the most important of which are the Tano, Ankobra, and Pra. The first of these is especially significant as the source and namesake of the most important deities of the majority of the northern Akan, although it actually flows into a lagoon on the Côte d'Ivoire side of the border. The more than forty major European forts and fortified trading stations, built between 1482 and 1784 were often located near the mouths of rivers (fig. 1.9). The northern Akan areas range from humid deciduous forests to wooded savannas with their characteristic baobab, acacia, and shea nut trees, the latter a frequent trade item to the south for use as a multipurpose vegetable oil (fig. 1.10).

Ivor Wilks, the foremost scholar of Asante history, has convincingly argued that the early development of the Akan states in the fifteenth and sixteenth centuries was stimulated by the demand for gold on the world bullion market. Gold was first traded by the Akan to the Mande states to the north in what is now Mali. With the arrival of the Portuguese on the coast in 1471 gold was traded in both directions. Writing of the founding of the Portuguese fort São Jorge da Mina in 1482 at what is now Elmina, Wilks emphasizes "the impressive fact is that within the space of a few years a fishing village had become transformed into a principal supplier of bullion to the world market and was exporting upwards of half a ton of gold annually" (1993, 5).[1]

Wilks refers to the process of state development as an "agricultural revolution," referring to the "big bang" theory of Akan history, and discussing it under the heading "From Estate to State" (1993, 94, 95). Critical to this

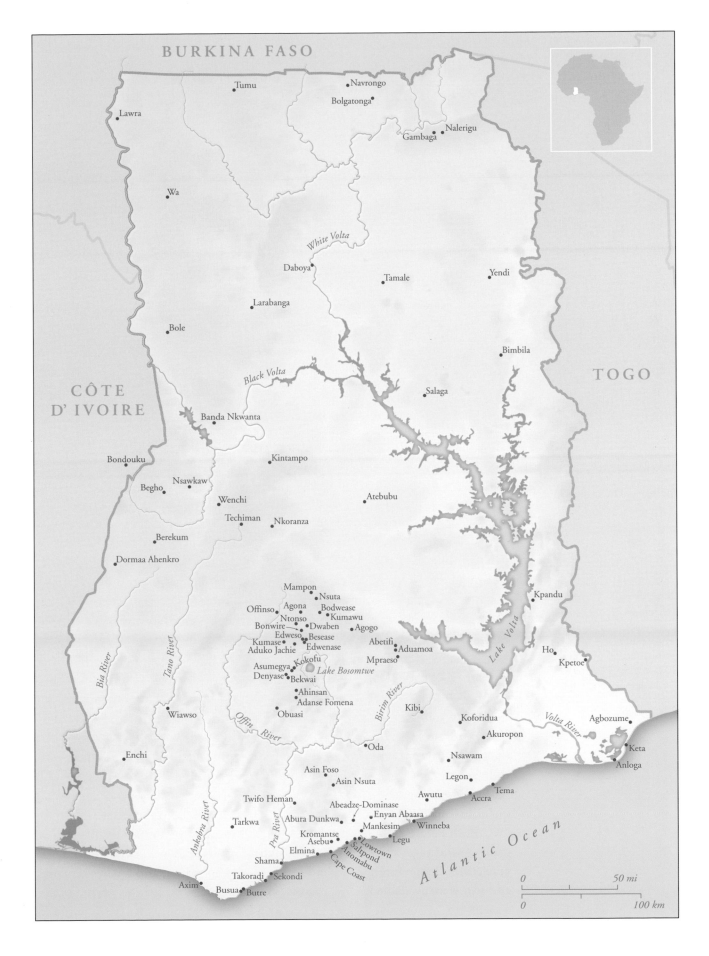

BURKINA FASO

CÔTE D'IVOIRE

TOGO

Tumu
Navrongo
Bolgatonga
Lawra
Nalerigu
Gambaga
Wa
White Volta
Daboya
Tamale
Yendi
Larabanga
Bimbila
Bole
Black Volta
Salaga
Banda Nkwanta
Bondouku
Kintampo
Begho
Nsawkaw
Atebubu
Wenchi
Techiman
Nkoranza
Berekum
Dormaa Ahenkro
Kpandu
Mampon
Nsuta
Offinso
Agona
Bodwease
Ntonso
Kumawu
Bonwire
Dwaben
Agogo
Edweso
Besease
Kumase
Edwenase
Abetifi
Aduamoa
Aduko Jachie
Kokofu
Mpraeso
Ho
Asumegya
Lake Bosomtwe
Kpetoe
Denyase
Bekwai
Ahinsan
Birim River
Adanse Fomena
Kibi
Koforidua
Agbozume
Obuasi
Volta River
Wiawso
Akuropon
Keta
Offin River
Oda
Anloga
Enchi
Nsawam
Legon
Asin Foso
Asin Nsuta
Awutu
Tema
Twifo Heman
Accra
Abeadze-Dominase
Enyan Abaasa
Tarkwa
Abura Dunkwa
Mankesim
Winneba
Kromantse
Legu
Asebu
Lowtown
Elmina
Saltpond
Shama
Anomabu
Takoradi
Cape Coast
Sekondi
Axim
Busua
Butre

Pra River
Ankobra River
Tano River
Bia River

Lake Volta

Atlantic Ocean

0          50 mi
0          100 km

23

1.7 View to the east from Fort Batenstein of the lagoon and beach. Photograph by Doran H. Ross, 2001.

1.8 (OPPOSITE, TOP) View from Fort Batenstein (built by the Dutch beginning in 1656) of the Ahanta fishing village of Butre. Photograph by Doran H. Ross, 2001.

1.9 (OPPOSITE, BOTTOM) Elmina "castle" with foundations originally built by the Portuguese beginning in 1482. Photograph by Doran H. Ross, 1979.

process was the reorganization of the Akan from foraging bands into more sedentary matriclans that led to new political structures and the early Akan states *aman* (sing. *ɔman*). A number of Akan states, including Akwamu, Adanse, and Denkyira, preceded the rise of the Asante Kingdom (circa 1700). In addition to the exchange of gold for slaves to clear the forest and to mine or pan for more gold, the early states traded gold and kola nuts to the north for cotton, metalware, and leather goods, and they traded gold, ivory, and slaves to Europeans on the coast for firearms, cloth, liquor, and an assortment of copper and brassware. Many of the conflicts between Akan states from the fifteenth through the nineteenth century involved the control of trade and trade routes.

Trade and agriculture were partners in state building, but early Akan farmers quickly discovered that the nutrient soils were never very deep in the recently cleared forest, averaging only four to six inches. This required a fairly rigorous system of crop and field rotation that allowed a field to lie fallow for ten or more years. The average farm was only between two and three acres, but the system of shifting agriculture maximized the productivity of the shallow soils. Indigenous yams and plantains were probably the first cultigens but were quickly supplemented by food crops from the Americas introduced by Europeans, including maize, cassava, peanuts, avocados, tomatoes, and pineapples.

Both before and after the shift to agriculture, the forest provided abundant game—wild pigs, antelope, monkeys, and a large succulent rodent called a grasscutter. Large forest snails and tortoises were gathered, and freshwater crabs and fish were available from the rivers, as well as marine species from the ocean. The forest environment was also home to elephants, leopards, porcupines,

1.10 (OPPOSITE, TOP) View of the weaving village of Bonwire north of Kumase. Photograph by Doran H. Ross, 1998.

1.11 (OPPOSITE, BOTTOM) Late nineteenth-century view of the Asante paramountcy of Bekwai. Photograph by Max Otto Schultze. Courtesy Basel Mission Archive. D-30.19.017.

antelopes, crocodiles, and numerous species of snakes and birds. All of these and many more examples of the flora and fauna of the region constitute the imagery of Akan arts, arguably the most varied in all of Africa in terms of subject matter. Even today when many species have largely disappeared from the forest, their images and the collective memories of them persist in the arts including royal regalia.

As Akan towns expanded, Asante architecture in particular developed into much-admired structures with considerable scale and elaborate decoration (fig. 1.11). Near the beginning of the nineteenth century, Kumase had an estimated population of between fifteen thousand and twenty-five thousand with as many as fifty thousand living in and around the capital (Wilks 1975, 93, 94). Thomas Edward Bowdich, another early nineteenth-century British envoy observed that there were four major thoroughfares, each about one-half mile in length and fifty to one hundred yards wide (1819 [1966], 372). Houses of the elite typically had at least one elevated open front room facing the street through which one passed to enter a series of courtyards connected at their corners (fig. 1.12) and flanked by additional open and closed rooms on each of the four sides. Some of the wealthy had residences with a second story. Regardless, most buildings were topped by high-pitched gabled roofs covered with a tightly-pieced palm-leaf thatch.[2]

Construction was basically wattle and daub— a grid of branches and larger timbers with the intervening space filled with and covered by puddled earth. Highly decorative openwork screens or windows often penetrated courtyard walls (fig. 1.13). The more elaborate houses were ornamented with low (two-inch) curvilinear relief covered with a fine clay plaster. The lower reaches of the walls were typically colored with polished red earth, while the upper reaches were whitewashed (figs. 1.14–1.16). Doors were often cut from solid blocks of wood and were secured with either European or Hausa (Muslim) locks.[3]

1.12 Street near the Asantehene's palace, Kumase, 1896. Photograph by Friedrich Ramseyer. Courtesy Basel Mission Archive. D-30.18.065.

1.13 Openwork screen off the courtyard of an Asante shrine at Aduko Jachie. Photograph by Doran H. Ross, 1976.

1.14 Corner of the courtyard of an Asante shrine at Besease with altar to the supreme deity, Nyame. Photograph by Doran H. Ross, 2001.

1.15 Room off the courtyard of an Asante shrine at Bodwease. Photograph by Doran H. Ross, 2001.

Photographs taken during the 1896 occupation of Kumase by the British after years of internal conflict and while the city was in disrepair still suggest some of the grandeur of Asante architecture (figs. 1.12, 1.17, 1.18). The Asantehene's palace was, of course, the largest and most sumptuous—the complex was said to occupy nearly five acres with a Great Court about ninety feet long and forty-five feet wide (Gros 1884, 189; Freeman 1844 [1968], 138). A. A. Y. Kyerematen's plan of the palace as it was organized in 1970 detailed many rooms with very specific functions.[4] Open rooms off the main courtyard housed the palanquins of the Asantehene and queen mother, the state drums, and the large royal umbrellas. The courtyard itself was usually where the Asantehene sat in state,

**1.16** Facade of an Asante shrine at Edwenase (Ajwinasi), 1896. Photograph by Friedrich Ramseyer. Courtesy Basel Mission Archive. D-30-19.028.

**1.17** Great Court of the Asantehene's palace in Kumase, 1896. Photograph by Friedrich Ramseyer. Courtesy Basel Mission Archive. D-30.18.047.

**1.18** Courtyard of an unidentified Asante palace with an altar to the supreme deity Nyame, late nineteenth century. Courtesy Basel Mission Archive. D-30.14.052.

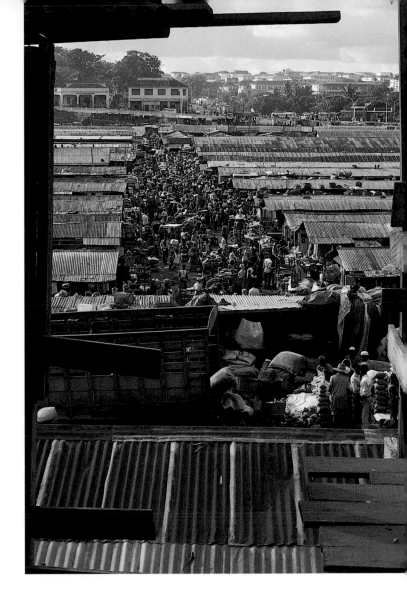

adjudicated disputes, received oaths of allegiance and celebrated minor festivals. A smaller adjacent courtyard served as a dining hall for the Asantehene on special occasions and was the space where a deceased monarch was laid in state upon death. Nearby were bedrooms for select court attendants. One room in the palace is dedicated to purification rites for the Asantehene's soul, another houses the ancestral stools, and a third contains the amulets, talismans, and charms that help sustain the state. Regalia ornamented in gold and the equipment for weighing gold dust were also kept in another dedicated room. In the past specific rooms in the palace served as the Asantehene's bathroom, bedroom, kitchen, and dining area. These are still occasionally employed as ritual demands, but most of these functions have been subsumed by the Asantehene's modern residence where he also typi-cally receives official visitors. Today, Kumase remains the capital of the Asante state with a metropolitan population of well over one million surrounding what is still one of the largest markets in West Africa (fig. 1.19). Ten preserved examples of Asante traditional architecture, some still serving as working shrines, are maintained by the Ghana Museums and Monuments Board and were designated as World Heritage Sites by UNESCO in 1980.

1.19 View of Kejetia market in Kumase. Photograph by Doran H. Ross, 1976.

Ivor Wilks's magisterial study, *Asante in the Nineteenth Century: The Structure and Evolution of a Political Order*, details the complexity and sophis-tication of the Asante court and political hierarchy (1975). At the top of the order is the Asantehene (*hene*, lit., "chief"), or king. He is appointed to office by the Asantehemaa, or queen mother, with the approval of a council of elders. Since descent and inheritance among the Asante are matrilineal, and since a man must marry outside of his lineage, a man's son cannot succeed him. Rather a king or chief must descend from his mother's side of the family, possibly his own brother or his sisters' sons or his sisters' daughters' sons. Obviously the queen mother and the matrilineage exercise considerable power. Since the beginning of the dynasty every Asantehene has come from the Oyoko clan, one of seven recognized by the Asante. The Asantehene originally ruled with the guidance of the Asantemanhyimu, defined by Wilks as the "'Assembly of

1.20 Chief's counselor from the Fante town of Legu shown holding a staff. Photograph by Doran H. Ross, 1975.

1.21 Sword hilt representing the proverb "One head does not go into council." Gold leaf, wood, iron. L (of hilt): 9 ⅞ inches. 97.1378.

the Asante Nation'; the highest legislative council and court" (1975, 729). This consisted of all the Asante paramount chiefs (*amanhene*), senior Kumase chiefs, and select provincial chiefs; it met once a year at the annual Odwira festival (see chapter 9). Meeting more frequently is a group identified by Wilks as the "Council of Kumase," or the "Inner Council," consisting of senior military commanders, other Kumase functionaries, the queen mother, and several counselors (*akyeame*, sing. *ɔkyeame*), who are more often, but misleadingly, called "linguists." A recurring message in Akan proverbial lore and art emphasized the necessity for a chief to consult with these senior members of his court. This message is usually conveyed by a depiction of three or four heads clustered together (figs. 1.20, 1.21). Although, as we shall see, it is also applied to images of a single head. The proverb is typically translated as "One head does not go into council."[5]

Most of the rest of a very large array of court officials have somewhat less power.[6] They serve primarily as custodians and presenters of designated items of regalia during processions preceding official durbars where the Asantehene (or another paramount chief) sits in state to receive and give respect to his subjects and honored guests. The list in appendix A itemizes the extensive variety of royal arts and musical instruments (often works of art in themselves) paraded at major durbars over the past fifty years. These are drawn from A. A. Y. Kyerematen's *Regalia for an Ashanti Durbar* (1961) and Barfuo Boaten I's *Akwasidae Kεsεε, A Festival of the Asante: People with a Culture* (1993). Not included in this summary are the spectacular staffs of the counselors, who are not a part of the procession, and the enormous inventory of personal adornment available to the Asantehene for such occasions, from which he wears a selection, albeit a substantial one. No other chief has such an extensive collection, but most of the items of regalia are found among the chiefs of other Akan states in various combinations.

While kingship traditions have come under increasing criticism in many parts of the world, both from within and outside of their respective cultures, the institution of chieftaincy still seems to have substantial support of the Akan people. Joseph Appiah, brother-in-law of the late Asantehene Otumfuo Opoku Ware II and one of Ghana's most progressive activists and thoughtful statesmen, expressed a profound appreciation for the institution in his autobiography:

> Chieftaincy is one of the noblest and most sacred institutions bequeathed to us by our ancestors. This institution and the stools on which the chiefs are placed during enstoolment or coronation constitute the embodiment of both the spirits of all our departed ancestors and all the living members of the society.
>
> As dispensers of justice and trustees of all the lands belonging to the society or group, the chiefs command the respect and reverence of their subjects; in return, they are expected to live exemplary lives and to act in all things in consultation with their elders or councilors. As an Akan, I have loved this institution since my infancy and prayed for its continued existence." [Appiah 1996, 359]

1.22 Tano River deity Twumpuduo in his shrine room with regalia that includes two state swords, two elephant-tail fly whisks, a counselor's staff, an *asipim* chair, crown, kente cloth, and two "soul discs." Photograph by Raymond Silverman, Tuobodom, 1980.

1.23 Effutu chief's counselor with staff carved by a Baule sculptor. The Effutu are a non-Akan group surrounded and heavily influenced by the Akan. Photograph by Doran H. Ross, Awutu, 1979.

Most Akan today would identify themselves as Christians of a fairly wide variety of denominations, including Presbyterian, Methodist, Anglican, and Catholic with an increasing number embracing various Pentecostal movements. Indigenous religious beliefs, however, often coexist with Christian ones, and it is not unusual to see crucifixes and crosses as part of the aggregate of objects in a traditional shrine. Akan religion recognizes a supreme being and creator of the world called Nyame or Onyame, generally recognized with a simple shrine composed of a basin placed in a forked tree branch that has been erected in the courtyard of a house (figs. 1.14, 1.18). Ritual offerings of food and drink are periodically left in the bowl. Under Nyame are a series of lesser gods or tutelary spirits (*abosom*, sing. *ɔbosom*) frequently referred to as the "servants" or "children" of Nyame. In many Akan areas *abosom* are represented by accumulations of medicinal and spiritual materials in brass pans. Neither Nyame nor the *abosom* are typically depicted in anthropomorphic sculpture, although there are exceptions. Conventionally an Akan town is said to have seventy-seven *abosom*, but only five to ten of them rank among the most important in a given location.

Part of the Akan belief system included the use of *asuman* (sing. *suman*), usually translated as "charms, amulets, and talismans." These are man-made entities that contain various efficacious materials drawn from the natural world, for example, teeth, bones, feathers, and hide. These could be joined with such products as beads, gunpowder, and inscriptions on paper. Most *asuman* were intended to serve very specific purposes, ranging from the benevolent and protective to the malevolent.

It is important to point out that what is typically identified as royal regalia is not necessarily restricted to chiefs. Several Akan deities and their priests possess regalia decorated with gold leaf that is indistinguishable from that found in court treasuries, including such items as stools, "state" swords, counselors' staffs, fly whisks, *asipim* chairs, and kente cloth. Raymond Silverman has documented a number of Tano shrines in the Bono area and has concluded that shrine regalia "function as symbols of success and spiritual efficacy. They also act as indicators of status or rank relative to other deities and in the Bono area, relative to chiefs as well" (Silverman 1998; fig. 1.22). H. Debrunner documented an anti-witchcraft shrine particularly well endowed with regalia and noted that "These emphasize that the *bosomfo* (priest) is indeed the real chief of his village" (1959, 123, pl. 28). While the regalia that function in a royal context vastly outnumber examples found in shrines, it must be kept in mind that some of the pieces discussed in this volume may have come from the latter. Likewise, many neighbors of the Akan have copied or commissioned from the Akan items of regalia for their own use, and in the absence of specific documentation this possibility should also be kept in mind. The reverse is also true with many items of regalia used in south central Ghana being produced by peoples as far away as the Baule of Côte d'Ivoire (fig. 1.23).

### The Role of Regalia in the Akan State

While each item of regalia has its own practical and symbolic functions, the collected royal arts of a given state provide a record of its history, a measure of its wealth, and a statement of its collective identity. In addition, the transference of state regalia to a new chief and its possession help affirm the legitimacy of the hereditary ruler, a theme that is a prevalent subject of the objects themselves. The ostentatious processional displays of regalia serve other functions as well. Kyerematen explains that the displays give the citizens of the state "the opportunity of assuring themselves that he [the king] had kept intact the state treasures he inherited on their behalf.... The regalia were also to disabuse the mind of the ruler of any illusions of his importance by impressing on him the fact that there had been other rulers before him and he was expected to emulate their good deeds." These good deeds include the expectation that a chief will make significant additions to the regalia. Kyerematen affirms that "One of the indices of the success or otherwise of a reign among the Ashanti, and indeed of all Akan speaking peoples, is the extent of the contribution which a ruler makes to the state heirlooms" (1961, 16).

1.24 Treasury bags from the regalia of the Edwesohene. Photograph by Doran H. Ross, Edweso, 1976.

It should be emphasized that these items are traditionally thought to be the collective property of the state and not of the currently reigning chief. As we will see below in some detail, one item of regalia—a stool—may symbolize the whole state. When a chief is officially installed in office, the ritual is called an "enstoolment," and if he should be removed from office, the procedure would be referred to as a "destoolment." Indeed all items of regalia are considered "stool property" and are called *agyapadie*. The anthropologist Robert S. Rattray, who wrote five important books on the Asante, explained the etymology of the word as "'*adie-pe-agya*,' something sought after (by the ancestors) and then put aside (for safekeeping)" (1929, 331). Asante traditional law emphasizes the chief's role as trustee of state regalia:

> There was an immemorial law to the effect that everything which became attached to a Stool became the inalienable property of that Stool. "One does not break off leaves, place them in the mouth of an elephant, and then take them out" and, "something that has fallen into a well does not get taken out again," are two legal maxims bearing on this subject. [Rattray 1929, 331]

Nevertheless issues of property in Asante and elsewhere among the Akan are very complicated, and Rattray's account probably represents something of a nineteenth-century ideal. Sara Berry in her recent study of the complexities of these issues convincingly concluded that

By the early twentieth century, then, the notion that a chief's property was indistinguishable from the stool's was probably anachronistic. It was certainly impractical. If, on succeeding to office, a chief's income and assets became one with the stool's, the reverse was also true: whatever the occupant of a stool decided to do with its resources was, by definition, for the stool's benefit. [Berry 2001, 41]

Although Berry's focus is primarily on land ownership and use, her argument applies equally to more portable assets.

That much of the regalia in the Glassell Collection and in the processional list in appendix A is made of or adorned with gold is obviously significant. Summarizing the work of Timothy F. Garrard (1980) and Malcolm D. McLeod (1981), T. C. McCaskie has noted that "The Asante have always been and continue to be acutely aware that gold (*sika*)—alluvially derived as dust, or mined in the form of nuggets—is located conceptually and materially at the very core of the historical experience of their society and culture" (1983, 26). The noted Asante historian Kwame Arhin is emphatic that gold regalia explicitly form part of the total wealth of the state. "The accumulated hoard of gold was known as *foto* 'treasury bag,' and its contents consisted of a great variety of gold dust and ornaments for the owner, his conjugal family and his retainers, cast in the forms of the artifacts and objects of the Akan social and physical universe" (1983b, 9). Among the Asante, gold dust and gold-weighing apparatus were stored in a pair of brass-ornamented wood treasury boxes (*apemadaka*) or in a pair of large, elaborate leather bags (*kotokua*; fig. 1.24), one with a silver and the other with a gold padlock (cf. Kyerematen 1964, 42, 100). Of course, regalia pertain to those inextricably linked agendas of wealth and power, but they are also about history and identity. Kyerematen views Asante regalia in particular "as chronicles of the total history of Ashanti, the embodiment of her constitution and social organization and the enshrinement of her people's beliefs, attitudes, and sentiments" (1966, 22). Although "total history" may seem something of an exaggeration, Kyerematen's assertion will become more convincing as we discuss specific examples later in this volume.

Implicit in agendas of wealth and power are issues of rank and status. Arhin has noted that "the quantity and quality of regalia were the main index of rank among all grades of rulers" (1983b, 7). But in any given Akan state, the right to own and display select items of regalia was rigorously controlled by the king or paramount chief. The right to ride in a palanquin, the size and number of umbrellas, the use of cast-gold sword ornaments, and the adornment of stools with gold or silver were all strictly regulated. Still these rights could be granted in recognition of distinguished military or political service.

Capturing the regalia of any enemy was often considered a measure of military success, and the loss of regalia a measure of defeat. D. J. E. Maier reports a battle during the Asante-Ewe war of 1869 where the stool, umbrella, and paraphernalia of the Asante general were left behind leading the Asante to mourn through the night over the battle they had lost. The next morning the regalia were recovered, and rather than a defeat, the battle was considered a victory (1990, 126). Measuring victory or defeat in terms of objects rather than personnel lost or ground gained is a telling indicator of the importance of regalia.

### The Verbal/Visual Nexus of Akan Art

The subject matter of Akan art ranges from the flora and fauna of the local environment to most of their material culture and to images of themselves involved in important social, religious, and political interactions, as well as more mundane situations. It can be argued that no other African culture represents more of its worldview in its arts than the Akan. Even more interesting than the range of imagery, the vast majority of depictions represent the "oral literature," or the verbal arts of the Akan, as well. Typically these verbal representations take the form of proverbs, but lengthy folktales, short boasts, insults, praise poems, jokes, riddles, and other verbal forms also appear.[7] Some of these have relatively codified meanings, while others are open to multiple metaphorical interpretations. As a general rule, the more complicated the image, the more conventionalized the message. However, images of a single animal such as an elephant or a leopard may often be associated with different interpretations from place to place or even within the regalia of a single state. Even if the verbal message is the same from place to place, its application and interpretation in various historical, political, or social situations may vary widely. What may be a reference to an enemy in one context may in another refer to one's own chief or family head. Very few motifs, if any, are restricted to a single item of regalia, and many appear on objects as dissimilar as finger rings, sword ornaments, counselors' staffs, and stools, as well as textiles.

Akan gold weights include more of these images than any other object type (fig. 1.25). Despite their name, these are actually brass castings used as counterbalances in the weighing of gold, but they far exceed in creativity what is in most cultures a staggered set of simple forms of slightly varying sizes and

weights. Very little in the Akan universe is lacking from this near encyclopedic corpus.[8] Virtually all items of regalia including stools, chairs, swords, ivory trumpets, elephant-tail fly whisks, and sandals are represented. That so much imagination was invested in such a seemingly ordinary object type is yet another measure of the importance of gold in both the economy and culture of the Akan (see Menzel 1968 and Garrard 1980).

One of the most potent of images found on multiple object types is the elephant. There are many sayings for an isolated image of an elephant that emphasize the animal's size and strength (figs. 1.26, p. 304). Two of the proverbs most frequently cited by Akan elders and those studying their arts are: "The person who walks behind the elephant does not get wet from the dew on the grass" (Christaller 1879 [1990], 22) and "When an elephant is thin, that is not to say that its meat will not fill a hundred baskets" (Rattray 1916, 59).[9]

Other representations of the elephant juxtapose it with a plant, man-made object, or another animal. One of the most common images depicts an elephant and a palm tree. Sometimes the elephant stands next to the tree with its trunk wrapped around the palm. Sometimes the tree appears behind the elephant or looks as if it were projecting out of the animal's back (see fig. 1.1). Although

1.25A–Q  Gold weights, boxes, scale, and blow pan. Brass. L (of longest): 6 in. Gift of Mr. and Mrs. Alvin S. Romansky. (A) Scales. 77.156; (B) Gold-dust box. 77.205; (C) Chair. 77.141; (D) Gold pan. 77.248; (E) Brush. 77.155; (F) Mudfish. 77.89; (G) Sword. 77.149; (H) Geometric gold weight. 77.212; (I) Geometric gold weight. 77.211; (J) Crab claw. 77.75; (K) Spoon. 77.252; (L) Round box. 77.64.1,2; (M) Rectangular box. 77.69.1,2; (N) Stool. 77.181; (O) Man with bird. 77.105; (P) Sandals. 77.151; (Q) Bird. 77.184.

**1.26** Staff finial representing an elephant. Gold leaf, wood. L: 5¾ inches. 97.1020.

there are significant variations in the verbal interpretation of this motif, the most commonly cited maxim is "Only the elephant can pull down the palm tree."[10] The various species of palm in Ghana are seen as among the most resilient of trees, but here the elephant prevails in a contest of strength.

Another image represents an elephant standing on an animal trap: "When elephant steps on trap, no more trap" (fig. 1.27).[11] Other works position a small antelope called a duiker on the back of the pachyderm, illustrating the saying, "The elephant is big for nothing, it is the duiker that rules the forest" (see fig. 3.25).[12] The little antelope is admired for being clever and resourceful. The image asserts that power and strength do not always dominate. While more often than not, the elephant is the quintessential metaphor for the powers of a chief, in some instances, it is subservient to an even more powerful metaphor.

The overriding importance of the verbal message of a work of art in the realm of Akan aesthetics has been emphasized by Dennis Warren, "Items of a chief's or a shrine's regalia or decoration are linked to oral literature in that each pattern [or work] is assigned a name or a proverb; indeed the aesthetic appeal of the title frequently appears to be more important than the actual ornamentation" (1975, 16). In another place he notes that "Frequently a cloth will be purchased because of its popular name even if the buyer does not find the cloth pattern pleasing" (Warren and Andrews 1977, 14). As an example Peggy Appiah noted a very slow selling pattern whose change of name to "James Brown" resulted in enormously enhanced sales (1979, 67).

It is likely that the convergence of word and image in a single object is in fact part of a communication agenda that informs the Akan about key issues

1.27 Counselor's staff from the treasury of the Asantehene representing an elephant stepping on a trap. Photograph by Doran H. Ross, Kumase, 1980.

dealing with all aspects of their life from religion, politics, and war to farming, marriage, and child rearing. Indeed, I have observed on several occasions an elder Akan explaining the meaning of an image for a younger boy or girl in a process that undoubtedly dates back several centuries. The indigenous social discourse about Akan art has not been studied to my knowledge, but I am convinced it constitutes a curriculum that may not be systematic, but is nevertheless an important, if informal, course of study.

Each item of regalia that will be considered in the remainder of this volume helps to define what it means to be a member of the larger Akan community. To be sure, some of the values proclaimed are elitist and self-promoting. Yet others provide protection against the abuse of power by recognizing the rights and privileges of the ordinary citizen and even the slave. All constitute a program of checks and balances in a public and aesthetic manifestation of a system of government that to this day attempts to define itself as a traditional state and simultaneously accommodate a national government that is frequently at odds with traditional agendas. ●

# 2 Seats of Power

## STOOLS, CHAIRS, AND PALANQUINS

In Africa, the seated person, conscious of the privilege of his position, must show awareness of himself as an object of perception. He must present a fitting image to the world. He must teach by manner of composure. To sit well is to savor life on a plane of deliberation.... The position of the body in Akan sitting is strictly chiseled. The limbs cannot be crossed. The head and torso are maintained erect. Gaze is straightforward; a person does not look down, a sign of sadness, evil, or heavy unwillingness. A person makes of his seated body, in other words, a frontal vision, symmetrically disposed.

Robert Farris Thompson (1974, 68)

*2.1* *Akonkromfi* chair, Asante. Wood, brass, hide. H: 39½ in. 97.755

### Stools

State stools are the most important of all Akan royal regalia (fig. 2.2). Depending on the stool (*asesedwa, dwa*), its role within a given traditional area can range from simple domestic functions, to a variety of ceremonial contexts, to a symbol for and embodiment of the whole state. In addition select stools serve as the locus of Akan ancestor veneration. The stools of respected deceased elders are blackened and preserved in a secure stool room and periodically provided with ritual offerings throughout the year. Alfred Quarcoo evokes the broad significance of stools in Akan society when he notes that the stool

> functions as a powerful symbol of unity in the Ghanaian social organization, represents the collective spirits of the wider communities, stands for the solidarity and continuity of the community, and serves

2.2 State stool of Kokofu, Asante. Photograph by Doran H. Ross, Kokofu, 1976.

2.3 (OPPOSITE, TOP) Woman's stool, Asante, circa 1950. Wood, brass. w: 16 ⅝ in. 97.1357.

2.4 (OPPOSITE, BOTTOM) The late Asantehene Otumfuo Opoku Ware II seated next to the Golden Stool. Photograph by Frank Fournier, Kumase, 1995.

in the process of periodic renewal of the identity, history and mores of the people drawing them into a continuous lifecycle of both the living and the dead. [Quarcoo 1990, 493]

It is tempting to say that designated Akan stools function much like European thrones, but that does not do justice to the sophisticated traditions that envelope this most complex of all Akan art forms.

Akan stools are typically carved from a single block of wood. They have a rectangular base, and a seat that curves upward on both sides supported by four struts and a central column (fig. 2.3). There are numerous variations on this basic form, however, and the diversity of support images and structures found today far exceeds that Rattray described on the thirty-one stools he examined in 1927 (in a list that he admitted was not exhaustive even then [1927, 272–73]). Stool supports include a number of abstract and geometric structures that make reference to such object types as locks, amulets, and draughts boards, as well as more clearly representational images of crocodiles, leopards, and elephants. In the past certain stool designs were the exclusive prerogative of paramount chiefs or even the Asantehene alone, but such restricted use has largely disappeared. The simple but elegant wood stool in the Houston collection (fig. 2.3) is consistently identified as a "woman's stool" (*mma dwa*). Rattray notes that this is the stool type a husband typically presents to his new wife upon marriage (1927, 272).

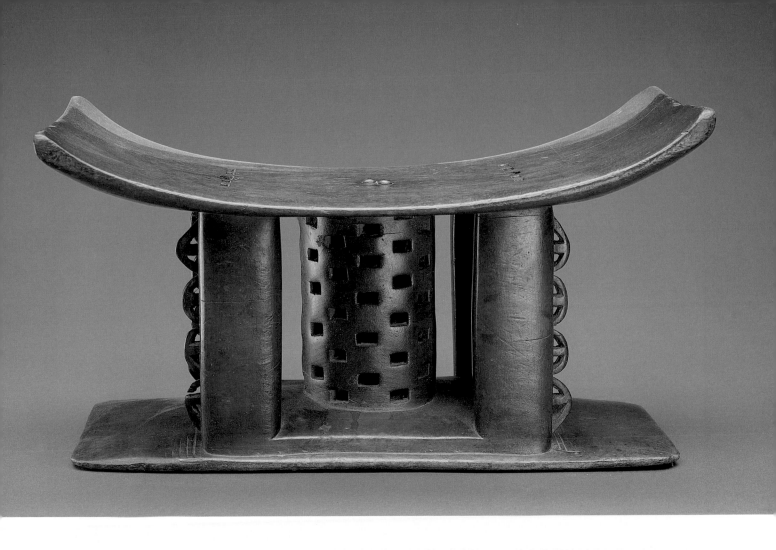

**2.5** The Golden Stool of Asante in procession. Photograph by Frank Fournier, Kumase, 1995.

The most famous of Akan stools is the Asante "Golden Stool Born on Friday" (Sika Dwa Kofi) said to have been miraculously brought down from the sky by the priest/counselor Ɔkɔmfɔ Anokye during the reign of Osei Tutu I (1701–1717) very early in the eighteenth century (figs. 2.4, 2.5). As recorded by Kyerematen in "The Royal Stools of Ashanti,"

> Anokye promised the king that he would conjure from the heavens a stool which would be the symbol of his authority and of the unity of the nation. It would be the repository of the soul of the nation and would have the powers both of bestowing prosperity and of warding off adversity. A condition of its arrival, Anokye insisted, was that all the chiefs in the kingdom, including the king, should surrender all their regalia—their stools, swords, and spears—and thereby avoid reminder of their earlier history and sentiments. A huge cavity was dug in the bed of the River Bantama, and in this all the regalia was buried.... The old regalia having been buried after incantations by Anokye the Golden Stool descended from the sky to the accompaniment of thunder and lightning. It dropped into the lap of the king, to the great joy of the chiefs and people of Ashanti. [Kyerematen 1969, 2, 3]

Although ostensibly a piece of furniture, the Golden Stool is in fact never sat upon. The closest it comes to serving such a function is when the newly selected Asantehene, with a paramount chief on either side, has his buttocks touched three times against the stool as part of his installation rites. For most of its existence the Sika Dwa Kofi resides in its own secluded space, but it is represented in the stool house by a surrogate that receives sacrifices intended for it. Whenever it appears in public, it rests on its side on its own chair (*hwɛdɔm-tea*), which in turn sits on an elephant skin (*banwoma*), the whole ensemble is placed under two designated umbrellas (Kyerematen 1969, 3). Although said to be solid gold, the stool is clearly gold plate over a wood core (Cole and Ross 1977, 137–38). There are a few other Akan state stools that are completely covered in gold. The golden stool of King Adinkra of Gyaman was ostensibly the cause of the war of 1818 won by the Asante (Bowdich 1819 [1966], 244–45). Today the *ɔmanhene* of Akuropon has a gold-covered stool in the shape of an elephant (fig. 2.6) and the king of the Abron in Côte d'Ivoire has a golden stool with a square knot motif said to be a "wisdom knot" by most Akan (Garrard 1989, 11).

In addition to the gold plating, the Sika Dwa Kofi is adorned with a number of other objects that attest to its history and power. Two pair of fetters

2.6 Golden elephant stool of Akuapem. Photograph by Herbert M. Cole, Akuropon, 1972.

or foot-cuffs are references to Ntim Gyakari, the king of Denkyira, who cuffed himself to his wife before playing *ɔware* ( a counting board game called *mancala* in East Africa) while his army fought and was defeated by the Asante at the battle of Feyiase in 1701. Rattray offers an alternative interpretation of the fetters that states that they "chain down the soul to [the stool]" (1923, 298). Ntim Gyakari is also represented on one of four cast-gold "bells" without clappers that symbolize important rulers defeated by the Asante. Another of the four gold bells recalls Sir Charles McCarthy, Governor of Sierra Leone and the Gold Coast, who was beheaded by the Asante in 1824. Two brass bells on the Golden Stool indicate that it also serves as the black stool, or memorial stool, of Osei Tutu I, since the presence of such stools in procession is announced by the ringing of these bells. Like many items of regalia the Golden Stool is also adorned with Islamic talismans (see pp. 159–65, below) and indigenous charms known as *asuman* (Kyerematen 1969, 3–4). Most of the above attachments also appear on other important Akan royal stools.

   The second most powerful stool among the Asante is the silver stool of the Mamponhene (fig. 2.7). Like the Golden Stool, it is never sat upon, and in public it is placed on its side on its own *hwedɔm* chair. Although not completely encased in silver, it is largely covered with bands of silver with the exception of a dramatic silver repoussé disc centered on the seat of the stool. The stools of the queen mothers of Asante and Mampon are also covered with silver strips and central bosses on the seat (figs. 2.8, 2.9). In addition the eight blackened ceremonial stools of previous Asantehenes, illustrated and discussed by

**2.7** (OPPOSITE)  Silver Stool of Mampon, Asante. Photograph by Doran H. Ross, Mampon, 1976.

**2.8** (ABOVE)  Stool of Asantehemaa Nana Afia Kobia Serwaa Ampem II, the queen mother of Asante. Photograph by Doran H. Ross, Kumase, 1980.

2.9 Stool of the queen mother of Mampon. Photograph by Doran H. Ross, Mampon, 1976.

2.10 (OPPOSITE, TOP) Presentation stool. Ewe, Ho (?), 1915. Wood, gold. w: 11¼ in. 97.1358.

2.11 (OPPOSITE, BOTTOM) Presentation stool. Ivory. w: 9¾ in. 97.1360.

Kyerematen (1969), are similarly adorned with either gold or silver repoussé bands and prominent disc forms (see also Davies 1971). It should be noted that the Golden Stool has a subtle but evident circular boss also centered on the seat. We will discuss the importance of these disc forms in some detail in our focus on *akrafokonmu* later in this volume. Suffice it to say for the present that the prerogatives of leadership are further evidenced by the use of silver on privileged stools of the Asante, and the use of gold or silver elsewhere among the Akan is similarly reserved for the elite.

Smaller versions of royal stools were made on occasion as presentation pieces for visiting or retiring dignitaries, just as wooden versions, both full-scale and smaller, were frequent gift items to less-distinguished visitors. During the visit of the Prince of Wales to the Gold Coast Colony in 1925, he was presented with a "Golden Stool" by the chiefs of the Eastern and Central Provinces (anon. 1925, 163, 219). In 1922 a replica of the silver stool of the queen mother of Mampon was presented to Princess Mary of England as a wedding gift (Rattray 1923, 294–99). A small gold-covered Akan-style stool in the Glassell Collection (fig. 2.10) was apparently a presentation piece for some special occasion as suggested by its stamped inscription:

CECRUNDET 26.7.1915
Howusu
Konstantin J. Komla
Ho Dome

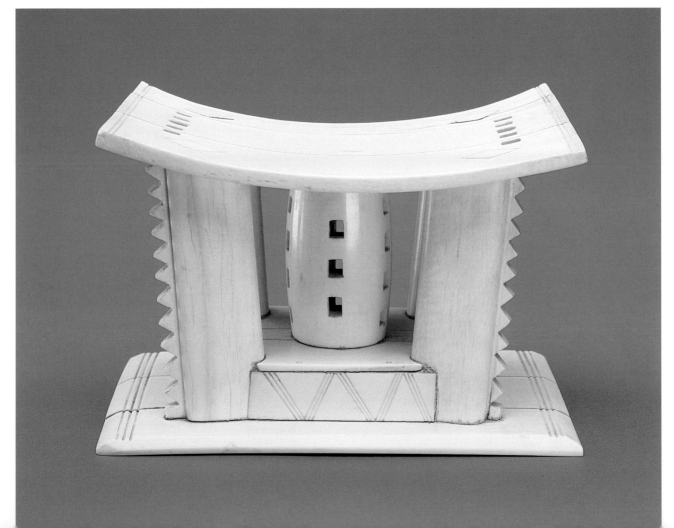

The last line of the inscription locates the stool in Ho, the capital of the current Eastern Region of Ghana; "Dome" is a quarter of Ho. "Howusu" is a northern Ewe family name and "Komla" designates a male born on Tuesday. The date of 1915 and the spelling of Konstantin with an initial "K" temporally places this stool during the German colonial occupation of the eastern edge of Ghana, which was part of German Togoland until 1919. Although I have not been able to identify "CECRUNDET," perhaps it is a reference to a German colonial institution. As noted earlier, the Ewe adopted many Akan traditions concerning material culture, including the use of distinctive stools. The northern Ewe were in closest proximity to the Asante, and Ganyo Fumey has speculated that the family name "Howusu" is a combination of the Ewe word for wealth "*ho*" and the Akan family name "Owusu" (personal communication, 2001). One of the entitlements of wealth among the Ewe is establishment of a family stool, but how this relates to the present piece is not clear.[1] It is possible that this gold-covered stool served as a family stool, but until the inscription is fully deciphered, it will be difficult to say with any certainty.

Although it lacks an inscription, the very rare ivory stool in the Glassell Collection is also most probably a presentation piece (fig. 2.11). To my knowledge there are no ivory stools documented in traditional contexts, but objects made of ivory, like those of gold, were favored as prestigious gifts. On the same visit in 1925 during which the Prince of Wales received a Golden Stool, he was also presented with an "ivory horn with silver clasp" and a "model of the Church of the Holy Trinity [in Accra] carved in ivory" (anon. 1925, 213, 223).[2] This ivory stool may have been a gift to a female dignitary since it is of the type identified as a woman's stool (see fig. 2.3).

### Chairs

While stools are the most important, complex and pervasive of royal arts, they are not the only forms of seating found in the court of an Akan chief. There are at least three structurally conventional chair types that serve as support for people and objects in a variety of contexts. All three were inspired by European examples. The most common in any state and most geographically widespread is the *asipim* (fig. 2.12). Kyerematen translates this as "I stand firm," an affirmation of the strength of the chair and the stability and commitment of the chief. Even minor chiefs may own one or two of these chairs, and important Asante chiefs have been documented as possessing fourteen or more. The *asipim* is a low armless chair with a slightly inclined back. Both seat and back are leather

held taut with European-produced brass furniture tacks. Somewhat evenly spaced among the furniture tacks are more prominent slightly tapered short cylinders with a flat bottom called *mpeaboɔ,* "so called because [they were] shaped like the gold-weight used for weighing gold-dust levied as war tax" (Kyerematen 1964, 26). Although I have been unable to confirm Kyerematen's observation, these ornaments do closely resemble European nest weights, which were also used by the Akan to weigh gold. In either case, they are a clear reference to the commodity that sustained the development of many Akan states. Not surprisingly miniature *asipim* chairs frequently appear in collections of Akan gold weights (see fig. 1.25).

Completing the decorative scheme of a typical *asipim* chair are two cast-brass finials (*ntuatire*) on top of the back. The most common of these are called "eagle talons" (*ɔkɔdeɛ mmɔwerɛ*), a consistent symbol of strength among the Akan that is also found on Asante *adinkra* cloths.[3] The motif is also said to be a symbol of the Oyoko lineage from which every Asantehene has been drawn for the past three hundred years. More elaborate *asipim* may have openwork backs and brass repoussé applied to sections of the surface with the "crossed crocodile" design discussed earlier used as a popular motif (see Kyerematen 1964, 14, 20). *Asipim* are most likely the oldest of the three Akan derivatives from European chair types. The first *asipim* may have been produced in the carpenter shops of the larger slaving forts that stretched along the Gold Coast.

The second chair type, *hwedɔm* (lit., "to look at the enemy"), is also armless (fig. 2.13). Rattray calls it *fwedom,* which he translates as "drive back the enemy"

**2.12** *Asipim* chair, Fante. Photograph by Doran H. Ross, Mankesim, 1975.

**2.13** *Hwedɔm* chair, Asante. Photograph by Doran H. Ross, Mampon, 1976.

53

**2.14** Fante chief in palanquin during annual Odambea festival. Photograph by Doran H. Ross, Lowtown, 1980.

(1927, 138). Johann Christaller defines *hwɛdɔm* as the "war chair" (1933, 201). Significantly this chair type serves as the support for both the Golden Stool and the Silver Stool of Mampon. The chairs are usually distinguished by straight backs, spiral-turned stretchers, silver trim, and a black painted surface. European prototypes for the structure are not difficult to find (see Gloag 1972, 79).

In contrast to the *asipim*, *hwɛdɔm* chairs have hemispherical brass, or more often silver, ornaments interspersed among the furniture tacks. Kyerematen calls this form "*ankaahono* because it resembles a sliced orange," although he does not discuss its significance if any (1964, 26). The most common finials on *hwɛdɔm* are also hemispherical, but they are called "calabashes" (*nkoraa*), a possible reference to the gourd vessels that are often decorated with gold and silver and used for ritual offerings to the ancestral stools (see Garrard 1984, fig. 9). The pans of scales used to weigh gold dust are also called *koraa*, so this name may be another reference to the gold trade as well (Christaller 1933, 255).

The third and most elaborate Akan chair type is called *akonkromfi* or *nnamu* (fig. 2.11). The first name may be translated as "praying mantis," and although the chair is rigid, its name probably derives from its articulated structure and its prototype, the folding chairs introduced by Europeans as early as the seventeenth century. Kyerematen notes that the chair is also called *nnamu* because it is "restful" (*nna* is literally "sleep"). Despite this association, he writes that it is used on "joyous ceremonial occasions" (1964, 28), and it is this chair type that the Asantehene typically occupies during major durbars. There seems to be considerable variation in its use, however, since the *nnamu* chair of the Kumawuhene is employed by the chief at times of bereavement for a member of the royal family or an elder of the state.[4] An alternative interpretation of *nnamu* may perhaps be found in Christaller's definition for *nnanmu* as "change, transformation," which could be a possible reference to its origins and the transformative nature of a folding chair (1933, 327).

A piece nearly identical to the Houston chair, with a slightly more open-work back, was photographed at the Asante paramountcy of Agogo in the early 1960s. Kyerematen identifies the central design on its back as "Kontonkurowi with flourishes" (1964, 23). Christaller translated *kontonkurowi* as "the halo or luminous circle round the sun or moon" (1933, 254), but it is more popularly translated as "circular rainbow." The underlying idea is that the chief encircles and shines a beautiful light on his subjects. On either side of this motif a pair of stylized ram's horns may be found. These frequently evoke the proverb "A ram fights with his heart and not with his horns," meaning that strength of character is more important than weapons in any contest.[5] Kyerematen considers the remaining curvilinear imagery on the Agogo chair to consist of further variations on the ram's horns motif. This interpretation not withstanding, many of these motifs are not unlike the baroque flourishes often found on European predecessors of this chair.

The wood structure of the Houston chair is covered by sheet brass, which is attached by over four thousand European-made brass furniture tacks. While brass obviously does not have the value of gold, on this chair it certainly represents a substantial investment and is a statement of wealth in itself. It is also considerably more durable than gold. Dividing the lines of brass tacks and otherwise visually punctuating the structure of the chair are hemispherical brass ornaments in two sizes. These are also called *ankaahono* due to their resemblance to orange halves. The decorative scheme of the chair is completed with two pairs of finials. Those on the top feature the "calabash" motif discussed in relation to the *hwɛdɔm,* and those on the sides the "eagle talons" generally found on the *asipim.* The side finials are a recurring, but curious and unexplained, feature on *akonkromfi* chairs (Kyerematen 1964, 20–28).

Even though chiefs may have several *asipim,* it is rare for a court to have more than one *hwɛdɔm* or *akonkromfi.* The greater importance of the latter two types is reinforced by their larger scale and their more highly visible ceremonial roles. These distinctions aside, all three chair types often had Muslim talismans suspended below the seat to protect the occupant and the court in general.

**2.15** Odow Kwame, chief of Abetifi, and his entourage with two palanquins. Photograph by Friedrich Ramseyer, before 1895. Courtesy Basel Mission Archive. D-30.14.049.

## *Palanquins*

In addition to stools and chairs, chiefs on selected occasions are also supported by palanquins (fig. 2.14). Among the Akan, palanquins (*patakan* or *apakan*) have long been used to elevate the chief physically and symbolically. This elite form of heightened mobility was documented at least as early as 1602 by Pieter de Marees. This publication was also probably the first to illustrate a chief being carried in a palanquin. The depiction of the litter shares a number of traits with certain nineteenth- or twentieth-century Akan examples, although it looks more like a European sedan chair (1602 [1987], 167). It is possible that the use of palanquins by coastal chiefs was a European introduction. European officials rode in sedan chairs carried by Africans when traveling even short distances along the coast. This highly visible form of prestige transportation would logically appeal to status-conscious Akan chiefs. In addition, both words used by the Akan for such litters (*patakan* and *apakan*) appear to be close cognates with the Portuguese *palanquim*, which in turn came from the Javanese *pelanki*, and ultimately the Sanskrit *palyanka,* or *paryanka.*[6] It is plausible that the litter and its name were introduced to the Akan by the Portuguese in the sixteenth century after the latter had opened up an extensive trading network involving the Iberian Peninsula, Africa, and Asia.

Bowdich's famous drawing of an Asante Odwira festival (see chapter 9) illustrates what is more conventionally recognized as an Akan palanquin. Here

chiefs ride in an elongated cloth-covered "basket" suspended between two lateral carrying poles placed on the heads of four retainers. Until recently there were basically two types of Akan palanquins. Both are seen in a late nineteenth-century Basel Mission photograph taken in Abetifi before 1895 (fig. 2.15). The wicker-work version is covered with a Fulani blanket (called *nsaa* by the Akan) from what is now Mali. The second palanquin (*ɔsako*) is carpentered and is of the type represented in the Glassell Collection (fig. 2.16).[7] Embellished with brass furniture tacks this example today is more often than not associated with queen mothers but is not restricted to use by females. In 1874 Frederick Boyle accurately described one of these in the possession of an Asante chief, "Amanquattiah's riding-chair…was just an arm-chair, cane-bottomed, and fitted with a foot board, solidly dovetailed on a pole before and a pole behind. The several cross-bars necessary to hold it fast in such a trying position showed most excellent carpentry" (1874, 97). That a palanquin of the same design and workmanship as the Abetifi and Glassell examples was also in use on the Swahili coast of East Africa reinforces the argument for the European introduction of at least this second version of the litter.[8] Some southern Akan chiefs, influenced by Ga and Ewe practices have recently created palanquins in the shape of an elephant, a rooster, and even a Mercedes Benz. ●

**2.16** Palanquin. Wood, brass, fiber. L: 108 in. 97.1322.

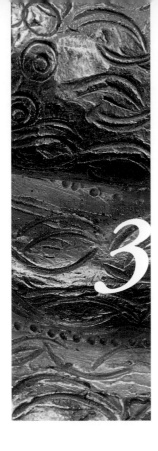

# 3

# Verbal Weapons

## SWORDS OF AUTHORITY

State swords (*afena*; fig. 3.4) are second only to stools in the hierarchy of regalia, playing several critical roles in Akan ritual life even today. They serve their most important political function during the enstoolment of a paramount chief (*ɔmanhene*), when the ruler-elect holds a specific sword while taking his oath of office. Subchiefs hold another sword while affirming loyalty to the new leader. Different swords are used in rituals purifying the chief's soul and the black state stools. Still others are (or were) carried by the chief's official messengers or envoys. This function was the first recorded by Europeans. William Bosman noted that among the coastal Akan "sabre or Sword-bearers" were important court officials: "This…is no mean Post; for the Gentlemen to whom it is entrusted, sometimes become honoured with the Character of Ambassadors to Foreign Courts" (1704 [1967], 194). He also observed that a king going about town was generally accompanied by a sword bearer (1704 [1967], 188). This point underscores another major function of swords, which act as display pieces symbolizing the office of the chief and, of course, his military strength. Whether exhibited at the chief's court (fig. 3.2), carried by bearers in a procession with hilts resting on a palanquin (fig. 3.3), or propped against the bed of a deceased chief as he lies in state, swords emphasize in both number and splendor the power and dignity of the *ɔmanhene*.

The pre-Asante origin of the typical Akan state sword has been demonstrated by Rene Bravmann (1968) based on three swords in European museums that were collected in the middle of the seventeenth century. A Dutch painting of 1641 illustrating what is certainly an Akan state sword corroborates this date (Bravmann 1968, fig. 3; see also van Dantzig 1970), while the visits of de Marees to the Gold Coast before 1602 provide even earlier evidence:

3.1 Sword ornament of a crocodile with a mudfish, Kumawu, Asante, circa 1930. Gold. L: 11½ in. 2002.219.

**3.2** Asante chiefs with counselors and sword bearers. Photograph by Frank Fournier, Kumase, 1995.

They themselves are very clever at making weapons, such as long Poniards, an Ell long, without a cross-bar; they are four fingers broad, double-edged, with a wooden hilt and pommel at the end; they cover the hilt with gold-leaf or the skin of a kind of fish which they catch and which is as much esteemed by them as Gold is by us. They make their scabbards of Dog-or Goat-skin, and at the top of the Scabbard, near the opening, they tie a big red Shell, about a hand broad, which is also held in great esteem amongst them. Others, who are unable to buy such a Shell, make or buy Cleavers in the form of a Ham, broad at the end and narrow near the top, cutting only on the outside. Instead of a red Shell they adorn this weapon with the head of a Monkey or the head of a Tiger. [De Marees 1602 (1987), 92]

De Marees is describing two different sword types that are still found in Akan regalia. The first, with the exception of the second edge, applies to the early swords in the European collections mentioned above and to those swords that are typically sheathed in ray or antelope skin and often adorned with a cast-gold sword ornament (fig. 3.6). The second, by virtue of its wide "tip" could never have a sheath, which would in any event conceal the artistically elaborated openwork blade that often carries substantial symbolic messages (fig. 3.5).

Kyerematen lists at least six categories of swords used in a variety of contexts by the Asantehene, although two of these are better described as knives (1964, 36). The most important of these swords are called *kɛtɛanofena*, "swords of the Bed. The swords are so called because they are laid at the edge of the king's bed when he goes to sleep. It is believed that the spiritual force residing in the swords will protect him while he sleeps" (Kyerematen 1966, 380). The *kɛtɛanofena* are divided into two groups. Those displayed on the Asantehene's right are called *akrafena* (lit., "soul swords"); those on the left *abosomfena* (*abosom* are variously identified as gods, tutelary spirits, or children of Nyame, the supreme being). Each sword is individually named and has its own cast-gold sword ornament (*abɔsodeɛ*), designated headdress, and neckwear (see fig. 2.4). Each new Asantehene is expected to add two new swords to the treasury upon his enstoolment (anon. 1977, 17, 19, 21; Kyerematen 1970, 22).

De Marees's reference to a large red shell or to a monkey or tiger head attached to the sheath is echoed by later authors. Wilhelm Müller referred to ùa lion, leopard, or tiger head (1673 [1983], 195). Since neither writer indicated these were man-made representations, we must assume that a real shell or skull was attached to the sword. These were certainly the predecessors of the cast-gold ornaments found among the inland Akan. Gold shells, lions, and monkey skulls are still found in the regalia of Asante chiefs. Although cast-gold sword ornaments are rarely found among coastal peoples, Godefroy Loyer observed in 1701 in Assin that "The king, Akassini, had gold-hilted swords, each with a

3.3 State swords resting on a palanquin at installation rites for a new chief. Photograph by Doran H. Ross, Kumase, 1976.

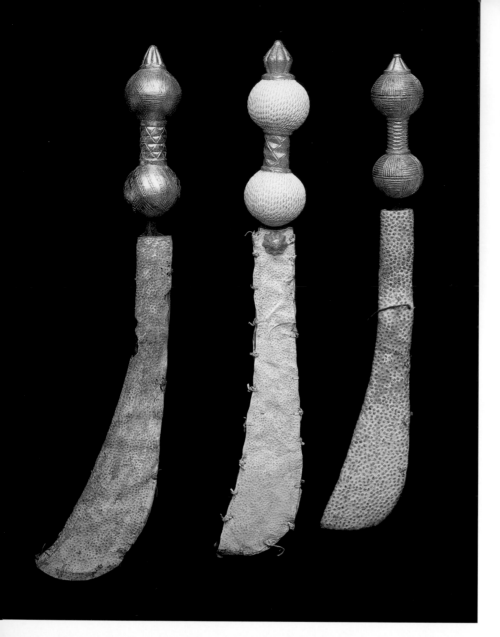

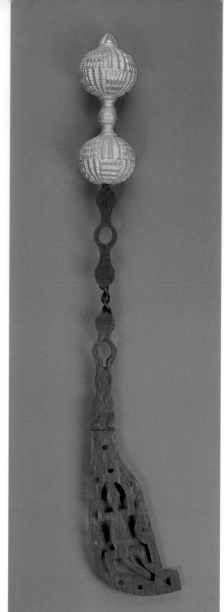

3.4A–C State swords. Iron,
wood, gold leaf, ray skin, fiber.
L (of longest sword): 29 in.
Left to right: (A) 97.1363.A-C;
(B) 97.1393.A-C; (C) 97.1367.A,B.

3.5 State sword. Iron,
gold leaf, wood. L: 42¼ in.
97.1376.A,B.

gold sheep's skull hanging from it" (1714 [1935], 115–16). A gold mangabey skull is still found on what is said to be the oldest sword in the treasury of the Asantehene, the Bosommuru. According to oral traditions recorded by Kyerematen, the skull was "caught from the skies" by Ɔkɔmfɔ Anokye and attached to the Bosommuru sword, which was made for Asantehene Osei Tutu I (1961, 13).

At Kumase in 1817, Bowdich was among the first to document the existence of Asante sword ornaments (abɔsodeɛ): "Wolves and rams heads as large as life, cast in gold, were suspended from their gold handled swords, which were held around them in great numbers" (1819 [1966], 35). Later he mentions a gold snake, which recalls the one still adorning one of the two most important swords of the Asantehene (1819 [1966], 276). The original of this sword was taken from Kumase in 1874 (illustrated in Donne 1977, 102), and the one seen today is a replica (illustrated in Cole and Ross 1977, fig. 309). According to often-quoted Asante sources, the casting depicts a gaboon viper with a hornbill in its mouth, a symbol of chiefly patience that makes reference to a story about a long-standing debt owed by the bird to the snake. After a long drought, the viper eventually triumphed when he caught the hornbill at the only remaining water hole (Kyerematen 1961, 11–12). This story has been repeated many times by various authors despite the fact that both the original ornament and its replacement clearly show a small antelope in the mouth of the snake and not a bird.

At Kumase this ornament adorns the largest principal sword of state, Mponponsuo. The name of the sword means "responsibility," and it stems from the belief that Asantehene Opoku Ware I (r. 1720–1750) used this sword to dedicate his life to his people in war. In addition, other important Asante chiefs use it to swear their allegiance to the Asantehene and to the Asante state. Its hilt and scabbard are covered with leopard skin, alluding to the king's power and bravery. Protective amulets (probably Muslim) also adorn the scabbard. Next to the hilt is a miniature sword that illustrates the proverb, "Some swords are more powerful than others" (Kyerematen 1964, 37). The gold of the abɔsodeɛ represents the chief's wealth.

Two other versions of the abɔsodeɛ adorning Mponponsuo are found in the Houston collection (figs. 3.7, 3.8). The first of these is from Berekum in Brong Ahafo and clearly depicts a gaboon viper holding a hornbill in its mouth. The second is from the Asante paramountcy of Mampon, and according to the elders of that state, it represents the viper with an antelope (duiker) as its prey. This motif on a sword ornament is also found at Kwahu and Offinso with an antelope and a frog respectively. I was able to interview court elders in Mampon

3.6 (OPPOSITE) State swords of the Edwesohene. Photograph by Doran H. Ross, Edweso, 1976.

**3.7** Sword ornament
of a gaboon viper with
a hornbill, Berekum,
Brong Ahafo. Gold.
w: 5 in. 97.1403.

and Offinso about their *abɔsodeɛ*, and at Mampon they told essentially the
same story as cited by Kyerematen substituting the antelope for the hornbill.[1]
At Offinso it was again the familiar tale, but instead of substituting a frog in
the narrative, they insisted on referring to it as a bird.[2] Even when the discrepancy was pointed out, they maintained the avian identification.

Significantly, at Kumase and Offinso the verbal interpretation does not
correspond to the visual image; an antelope and a frog were identified as birds
by the Asante. There is no reason to question the veracity of Kyerematen's
account, undoubtedly received from court elders. The Offinso elders were equally
sincere. In each instance oral traditions clearly take precedence over the visual
so that "word" reigns over "image." The differing "realities" of word and image
point to another important dimension of the verbal/visual nexus of Akan art, its
adaptability. Just as oral histories often change to accommodate new political
situations, so apparently do the identification and interpretation of art forms.

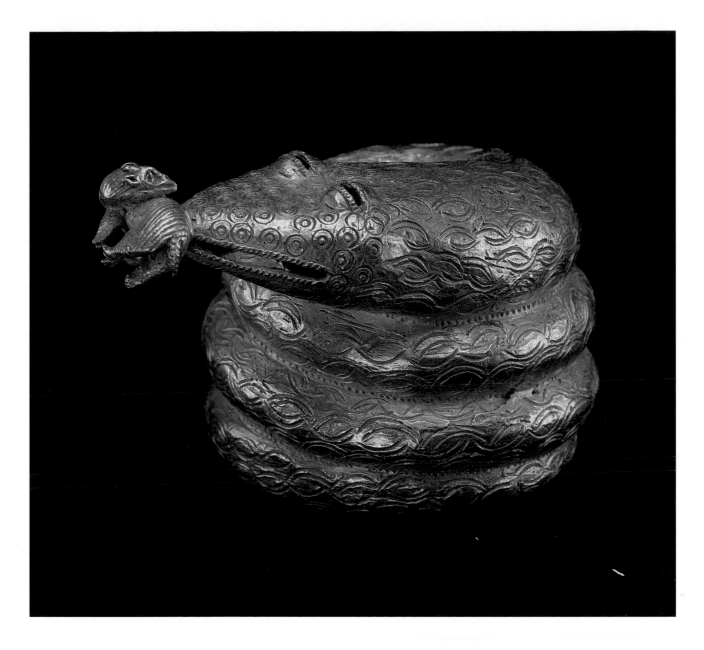

The discrepancies between the image, its identification, and its meaning, while telling are not as serious as they might seem. In all three stories the plot and theme are the same; regardless of its prey, the snake triumphs through patience. Still, the implications to be derived from a viper devouring a frog (a common prey for a snake in Asante minds) differ greatly from those suggested by a snake consuming an antelope (a very quick and intelligent animal) or a hornbill (noted for its treetop noisiness). Perhaps originally the motifs illustrated entirely different stories and ideas. I have not read or recorded any alternate sayings for a snake preying on an antelope, but a snake devouring a frog occurs in a number of Asante art forms and often represents the proverb: "Every part of the frog belongs to the snake." This is based on the observation that snakes swallow their prey whole, and the proverb is used to describe dominant-subservient relationships. Alternate sayings aside, it is equally plausible that the varying prey simply represent different actors in the same role.

3.8 Sword ornament of a gaboon viper with an antelope, Mampon, Asante. Gold. H: 5 in. 97.1399.

3.9 Lion, leopard, and antelope on the finial of a counselor's staff. Photograph by Doran H. Ross, Kokofu, 1981.

Although the hornbill is not physically present in three of the ornaments, a snake capturing a bird is one of the most common images in all Asante art (see figs. 3.23, 3.24). This may account in part for the verbal conventionalizing of related motifs as a snake and a "bird." In the case of the antelope on the Kumase ornament, the head of the animal is turned backward so that it looks in a caudal direction. In this regard, it resembles the *sankɔfa* bird—another extremely common image in Akan art (see cover)—which is regularly portrayed in this backward-looking posture (see p. 81). It is thus possible that the elders misread the image of the antelope on the basis of its orientation. Yet the antelope at Mampon also looks backward and was *not* confused with a bird.

Most sword ornament images are inextricably linked with traditional sayings or proverbs (*ɛpɛ*), but some, such as the lion (*gyata*), are simple metaphors (fig. 3.11). At the Asante states of Dwaben and Nsuta this animal is an emblem for the bravery of the chief. If encouraged, the elders of each state could provide proverbs about lions and chieftaincy, but they insist that the primary meaning of the ornament is the fighting spirit of the chief. Only at Edweso is a proverb given, "If the lion has no intention to attack, it will not show its teeth before you."[3]

3.10 Sword ornament of a lion. Photograph by Doran H. Ross, Edweso, 1976.

At first thought, the lion would seem to be an indigenous image (fig. 3.10). Yet the lion is principally a grassland feline and has always been rare in the heavily forested landscape of most Akan states. On the other hand, the forest-dwelling leopard is relatively common in the environment. This fact is reflected in language. The Akan word for lion, *gyata,* is a loanword from the Mande who live in savanna regions northwest of the Akan; while the word for leopard, *osebo,* is indigenous. Understandably, there are far fewer proverbs about the lion than about the leopard. The ratio is approximately one to four in Christaller's 1879 compendium of 3,600 proverbs.

**3.11** Sword ornament of a lion. Gold. L: 5½ in. 97.1397.

The lion and its relationship to the leopard in Akan art pose an intriguing problem. Lions are rare, if nonexistent, in older art forms such as the cast-brass containers known as *kuduo* and gold weights. The leopard, however, is probably the single most common mammal to appear on these object types. Since the production of *kuduo* and gold weights for indigenous use ceased around 1900, it would seem that the lion was a latecomer to Akan art. Nevertheless, today the lion is seen as superior to its spotted cousin in the only two proverbs that I am acquainted with where they appear together: "Only a lion can drink from the palm wine pot of the leopard" (fig. 3.9) and "A dead lion is greater than a living leopard."[4] Yet if the lion is a more potent symbol of power than the leopard, why doesn't it occur in the older art forms? The answer lies in the nature of its relatively recent introduction.

While the British probably did not introduce the lion to the Akan, they were nevertheless instrumental in popularizing it. The Akan had a pronounced fascination with European heraldry and reproduced heraldic arms and compositional devices on locally made chairs, combs, drums, and other objects. The lion, of course, is by far the most common figure in European heraldry and is found on the royal arms of Great Britain, Denmark, and The Netherlands, the three major European powers on the "Gold Coast" during the eighteenth and nineteenth centuries. These arms were ubiquitous symbols of European authority among the crowns' representatives in West Africa. Lions were found in numerous contexts including the entryways to forts; military and naval banners; ships figureheads; buttons on military uniforms, Victorian chairs, door knockers, and numerous trade items, since lions in various heraldic attitudes were also used as emblems by several West African commercial interests. Without question, the lion was the single most pervasive symbol of European power on the Coast.

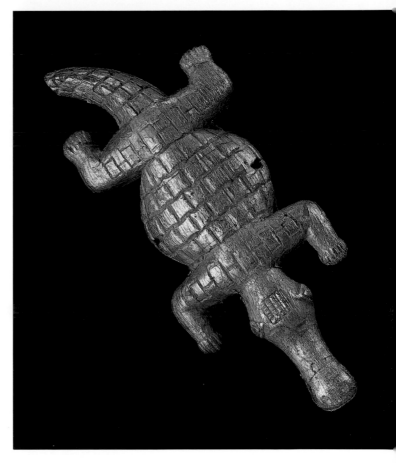

**3.12** Sword ornament of a crocodile. Gold leaf, wood. L: 10⅛ in. 97.1407.

3.13 Sword ornament of a palm fruit, Kumawu, Asante. Gold. L: 7¾ in. 97.2002.218.

The European origins of the lion in Akan Art are emphasized by its distinctive image. The lion is most frequently posed in a highly conventionalized fashion with its head turned to the side, the tail curving over its back in a horizontal S-shape, and occasionally with its tongue protruding (cf. figs. 6.54, 6.56). The recurved tail and especially the head shown in profile recur on Akan lions regardless of object type or medium. All three of these traits are nearly nonexistent in Akan representations of other animals while they are commonplace in European heraldic lions (see Ross 1982a for an extended discussion of this issue).

The meanings of other motifs are more involved. A crocodile alone (fig. 3.12) or with a mudfish in its mouth is found at five Asante paramountcies and is given several interpretations.[5] The crocodile at Mampon represents a praise name for the king, "The great crocodile that swallows a stone every year."[6] "Stone" is a metaphor for "bullet" and refers to the Mamponhene's position as a leader of one of the Asante armies. Kyerematen reports that the crocodile on one of the Asantehene's swords originated with Asantehene Osei Kwadwo (r. 1764–1777) and represents "the totemic" animal of his paternal (*ntɔrɔ*) kin group (1961, 13). At Kumawu the crocodile with a mudfish in its mouth (fig. 3.1), as well as a second mudfish, elicits the proverb, "When the mudfish swallows anything, it does so for its master," meaning that the chief automatically benefits from the success of his subjects. (The predatory nature of the crocodile-mudfish relationship is ignored here.)[7] For the combined motif at Kumawu, Quarcoo records a different meaning, "If that species of fish comes from the river to tell you that the crocodile is dead, there is no need to argue about it," indicating that people who live together know each other's behavior (1975, 16). Yet another interpretation of this image was given at Edweso, "If the crocodile catches the mudfish it does not deal leniently with it," a reference to the supreme power of both chief and state.[8] This multiplicity of meanings attached to one motif is common in *abɔsodeɛ* iconography, as in most Akan symbolism.

Also from Kumawu and echoing the Mampon crocodile ornament in meaning is the *abɔsodeɛ* of a bunch of palm nuts, sometimes referred to as a palm fruit (fig. 3.13). Before the rise of cocoa (see pp. 150–52), palm oil and palm kernels were the major agricultural exports of the Gold Coast through much of the nineteenth century. The by-products of this indigenous palm also provided oil for local cooking, hair and skin care, and medicinal uses. Undoubtedly because of its multifunctionality, the oil palm and its bunches of palm nuts are a recurring feature in Akan royal arts. Sword ornaments with palm nuts are

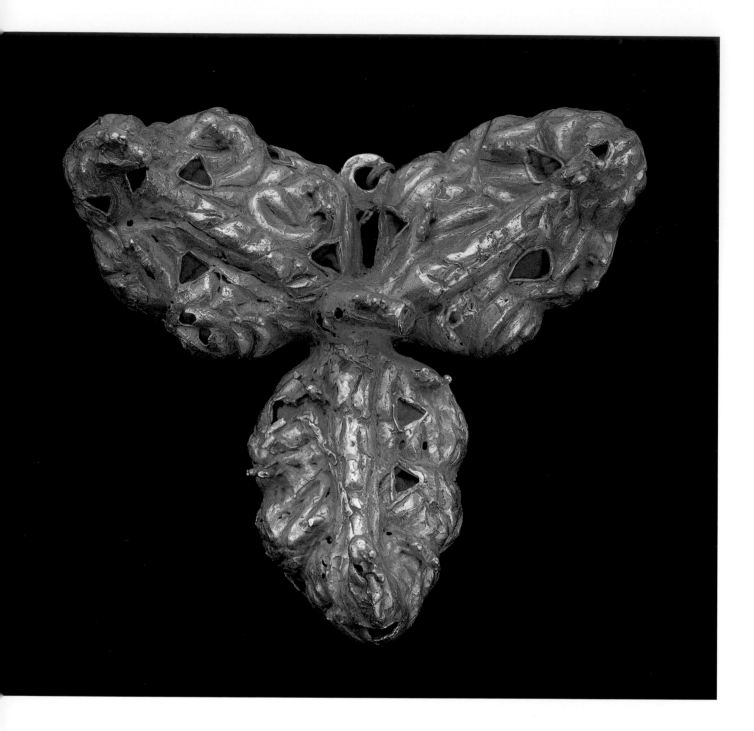

**3.14** Sword ornament of a bunch of cola nuts, Kumawu. Gold. L: 7 ⅞ in. 2002.330.

**3.15** (OPPOSITE) Sword ornament of a baboon eating a grasshopper, Kwahu. Gold. H: 7 ½ in. 97.1402.

found in the treasuries of a number of states including the regalia of the Asantehene and the states of Edweso, Kumawu, and Akim Oda. In the Asantehene's regalia the ornament is found on the *akrafena* of Asantehene Prempeh II (r. 1931–1970), where the kernels refer to his genealogy since they appear on the same stalk and share the same origin (Kyerematen 1961, 12). At Kumawu the motif is a symbol of invincibility, "The chief is like a palm fruit, if you fire your gun into it, you waste your bullets." It was further explained that a euphemism for war is "When hands are pressed on the thorns of the palm fruit."[9] At Edweso the ornament actually depicts a hand on the prickly bunch of palm nuts (see fig. 3.6).

Another plant form represents a bunch of cola (kola) nuts (*bese saka*) and appears to be unique in the corpus of Akan sword ornaments (fig. 3.14). Cola grows naturally in the Akan forest areas and was widely traded to the north. The nut contains caffeine and when chewed serves as a mild stimulant. It was a common ingredient in earlier versions of today's various "cola" beverages. At least two interpretations of this motif were recorded at Kumawu. The elders told this writer that the motif was a sign of respect since "the Kumawuhene takes cola nuts to funerals of other chiefs to show he is mourning."[10] Quarcoo recorded a very different meaning: "The ant clings aimlessly to the cola nut tree; it won't fall down, yet it won't pluck the fruit and chew it" (1975, 18; cf. Rattray 1927, 287). For gold weights of the same image, Brigitte Menzel provides the saying, "To pick cola nuts, one must necessarily climb the cola tree" (1968, 176). The message emphasizes the necessity of hard work to achieve goals.

The *absodeε* of a simian (perhaps a baboon) eating a grasshopper in the Glassell Collection (fig. 3.15) is probably from Kwahu (cf. Kyerematen 1964, 35). The motif is relatively common on finger rings but usually includes a hunter aiming his musket at the monkey, and perhaps the hunter is implied here. According to Garrard the grasshopper is seen as a favored food of the primate, and his attention to his meal in the face of a physical threat is an emblem of fearlessness. He cites the saying "That is the monkey, while we are hunting him he eats grasshoppers" (1989, 232).

A gunpowder keg either alone or with an attached firearm has been documented at the Asante states of Edweso, Kumawu, and Nsuta, and at Nkwanta Ahafo (figs. 3.6, 3.16). The acquisition of muskets in significant numbers by the Akan during the second half of the seventeenth century led to the substantially increased power of Denkyira, Akwamu, and Akyem. Although there were intermittent attempts to control or restrict the trade in guns, powder, and musket balls, commercial incentives coupled with the ephemeral allegiances of European traders with various Akan states generally ensured a steady flow of weapons to the interior from one coastal fort or another. From the beginning of the Asante Confederacy, circa 1700, firearms were instrumental in its successful expansion, and many wars were fought with southern Akan states to maintain access to the coastal trade in powder and muskets. The Asante in turn prohibited their own traders from selling firearms to rival Akan states.

The attachment of a gold powder keg ornament to a ceremonial sword might in itself be seen as a symbol of enhanced armament. In fact, elders at the three Asante states with the motif affirmed that it asserted the military strength

**3.16** Sword ornament of a gunpowder keg and a pistol, Kumawu. Gold. L: 4 ¾ in. 2002.329.

3.17 Sword ornament of a bird with cannons and gunpowder. Gold. L: 6¾ in. 97.1401.

3.18 Sword ornament of a bird with cannons and gunpowder. Gold. L: 6¼ in. 97.1547.

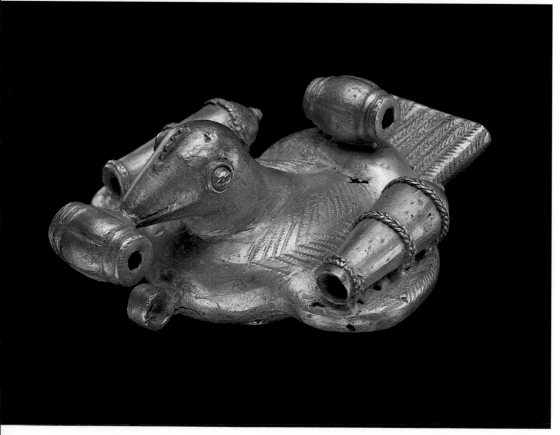

of the state. At Kumawu it also was said to represent a praise name for the chief, "The brave son
Tweneboa who smells of gunpowder."[11]

One of the most explicit, if fanciful, symbols
of power found on Asante sword ornaments is a
bird with cannons on its wings and often a keg of
gunpowder on its back and in its beak (figs. 3.17,
3.18). The body of the bird is typically configured
as a square knot (*nyansapɔ*), a symbol of wisdom
and the ability to solve problems among the Akan
who say "Only a wise man can untie *nyansapɔ*."[12]
This powerful and wise avian ordnance is one of
the most common *abɔsodeɛ* and is also frequently
found in gold weights, counselors' staffs, and
chiefs' finger rings. The expression associated with
this image is primarily descriptive, "The bird that flies with cannons and gunpowder." Nevertheless, it is an evocative metaphor for the martial capabilities
of chief and state.[13]

**3.19** Sword ornament
of trophy head. Gold.
H: 4 ½ in. 97.1405.
Photograph by Doran
H. Ross, Dwaben, 1976.

The two most common sword ornament motifs provide interesting contrasts
between the traditional and the acculturated. A gold cast of a human head usually
represents a decapitated enemy chief, again recalling a preoccupation with war
(fig. 3.19). Trophy heads are common motifs in Akan art, and indeed, actual
human skulls were traditionally incorporated in royal footrests and attached to
state drums. All Asante paramountcies with this *abɔsodeɛ* call the motif "head
of Worosa" (Worosatire). Worosa was chief of the Banda state (about 190 kilo-
meters northwest of Kumase) and was said to have been killed by Asantehene
Osei Kwadwo in retaliation for murdering Asante traders. Ivor Wilks suggests
a possible date of 1765 for this event (1975, 246, no. 21). Presumably the first
casting of Worosatire was created shortly after, while memory of the victory was
still fresh. Kyerematen identifies the famous gold head in the Wallace Collection
(illustrated in Fagg 1974, 43), taken from Kumase in 1874, as that of Worosa
(1970, 20). This attribution is supported by a second Worosatire, a replacement
of the first, now on one of the Asantehene's courier swords. Considering the
signs of wear on the Wallace piece, it may even date from the beginning of
the tradition in the late 1760s or 1770s.

Despite the uniform naming of the trophy head *abɔsodeɛ* as Worosatire,
the chiefs and elders in the six Asante states that employ the motif do not agree

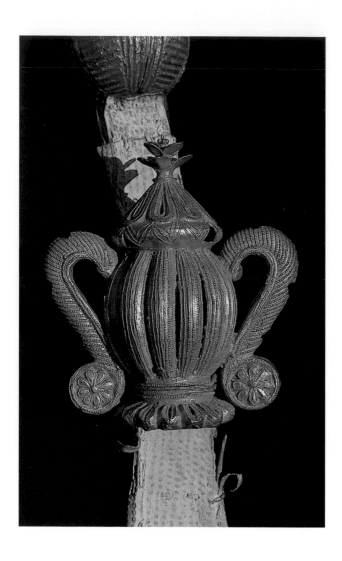

3.20 Asante sword ornament in the shape of a sugar bowl. Photograph by Doran H. Ross, Mampon, 1976.

as to whom it represents. At Kumase and Nsuta the head is identified as Worosa, but at Mampon it is considered to be Adinkra, King of Gyaman, said to have been personally killed by the Mamponhene in 1818. At Dwaben, on the other hand, the head is that of King Ntim Gyakari of Denkyira, killed by a Dwaben warrior in 1701 (see Fynn 1971, 38). The Edwesohene and his elders, however, deny that the head represents a particular person at all and say it stands for the heads of all enemy chiefs taken in battle. A proverb unrelated to the notion of the trophy head was provided at Kumawu, "One head does not go into council,"[14] emphasizing the chief's duty to consult his elders. Clearly the specific attribution of the head is based on local considerations. Still, the consistent naming of it as Worosatire suggests that the origin of trophy head sword ornaments dates from the defeat of the Banda king.

Castings inspired by European vessels provide strong formal, historical, and symbolic contrasts with trophy heads. The "loving cup" owned by the Asantehene is a duplicate of an earlier piece, taken from Kumase in 1900 and now in London (McLeod 1981, 77). The original was probably the same one observed by Thomas Freeman at Kumase in 1839, carried by a messenger from the Asantehene: "In his hand was an immense gold sword, to which was fastened a gold decanter, holding about a pint" (1844 [1968], 53, 122). In Kumase the abɔsodeɛ has been called a kuduo, referring to the use of this cast-brass container as a treasure casket. Kyerematen says the motif "indicated that the King has a responsibility for catering for the material needs of his people" and cites the proverb, "The big pot provides for many" (1961, 13).

Related forms elsewhere in Asante have a significantly different meaning. At Edweso, Offinso, Bekwai, Mampon, and Nsuta, the abɔsodeɛ is called a family or clan pot (abusua kuruwa). This usually takes the form of a terra-cotta funerary vessel used to contain the nail clippings and shaved hair of close relatives of the deceased. It is either placed near the grave or kept in the stool

room. In some states an *abusua kuruwa* is used by bereaved family members
as a drinking vessel at funerals. In either case, the container is a symbol of
royal family unity and lineage continuity. At all but Offinso, the design of the
casting seems to be a free but accurate copy of a European sugar bowl (fig. 3.20),
while at Offinso the prototype is certainly a teapot (fig. 3.21). Silver plate and
tea services were relatively common gifts from European powers to important
paramount chiefs. In many state treasuries these prestigious objects have replaced
traditional *kuduo* and *abusua kuruwa* as ritual vessels.

   Perhaps in keeping with the martial nature of swords, most ornaments
deal with a variety of predatory relationships and exalt the role of the chief as

3.21 Sword ornament
in the shape of a teapot,
Offinso, Asante. Gold.
w: 6¾ in. 97.1404.

**3.22** Fante sword bearers. Photograph by Doran H. Ross, Saltpond, 1976.

a mighty warrior. There are probably fewer than 150 sword ornaments in Ghana today, and over half of these are found in the treasuries of Asante chiefs. Given that Asante was the quintessential conquest state throughout most of the eighteenth and nineteenth centuries, it is rather predictable that the iconography of a handheld weapon embraces the hegemonic ambitions of the empire.

### Sword Handles

The figurative ornamentation of swords is not restricted to cast-gold ornaments. Among the Asante a secondary category of swords are classified as *afenatene*. These have openwork blades and sculpted hilts that feature a variety of representational images. Kyerematen writes that among the Asante they are "used as a complement to or substitute for *kεtεanofena*" (1964, 35). Elsewhere among the Akan this type often serves as the principal sword of state. Only very rarely do these swords have sheaths as these would obscure the proverb-replete images found on the blades. About half of these swords have conventional grips, while the other half have highly sculptural "handles" that seem to discourage actually holding the sword by them. In fact, regardless of the handle configuration, these swords, like the *kεtεanofena* of the Asante, are held by the blade with the gold-leafed handle projecting upward (figs. 3.22). Kyerematen suggests that the gold-leafed, sculptured handles are analogous to the cast-gold sword ornaments discussed earlier (1964, 34). Two sword handles in the Houston collection—both of which are missing their blades—feature the gaboon viper with hornbill motif discussed previously in relation to cast-gold ornaments (figs. 3.23, 3.24); presumably they illustrate the same story.

Two other handles in the Glassell Collection depict a small antelope called a duiker standing on the back of the elephant (fig. 3.25). Even though the elephant is the largest and strongest animal in the forest, the diminutive duiker is admired as clever and wise. The Akan say "Though the elephant is huge, the duiker is the elder" or "The elephant is big for nothing, it is the duiker that rules the forest."[15] This image is just one of many in Akan art where wisdom

and intellect are valued over brute strength. Yet, as we have seen already, it is the powerful and ferocious animal that is more frequently foregrounded.

Wise behavior and the notion that there is an intelligent way to address any problem are implied in another sword handle representing a hand grasping a snake (fig. 3.26). The widely conventionalized maxim associated with this image is "When you hold the head of a snake, the rest is nothing but a rope."[16] While the meaning may seem obvious, the paramount chief at Edweso extended its significance in the context of war. In English he said "If you capture your enemies' weapons, they are defeated; if you capture your enemies' chief they are defeated."[17]

In place of a spherical hilt, one sword handle in the Glassell Collection features a carving of a keg of gunpowder surmounted by a lion preying on a human figure (fig. 3.27). Missing from the lion's mouth is a musket. This image most likely illustrates the expression "When the lion captures the hunter, the gun is useless."[18] In most states the chief identifies with the lion, and the image is a symbol of victory with the implication that it is over superior forces suggested by the musket and gunpowder. This motif may have originated in the struggle with British colonial powers represented by the firearms. An alternate proverb

**3.23** Sword handle of a hornbill and a snake. Gold leaf, wood. L: 13⅜ in. 97.1389.

**3.24** Sword handle of hornbill and snake. Gold leaf, wood. L: 11 in. 97.1392.

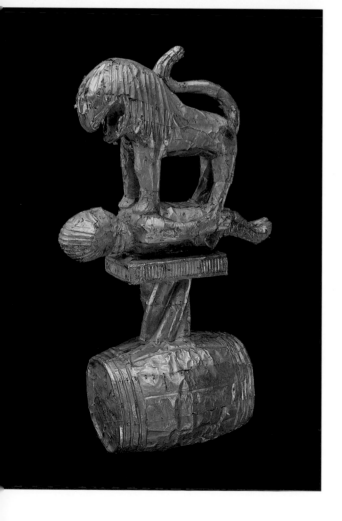

**3.25A,B** (TOP, LEFT)
Sword handles of an elephant with an antelope on its back. Gold leaf, wood. L (of taller handle): 11½ in. Left to right: (A) 97.1395; (B) 97.1387.

**3.26** (TOP, RIGHT)
Sword handle of a hand holding a snake. Gold leaf, wood. L: 13 in. 97.1276.

**3.27** (BOTTOM, LEFT)
Sword handle of a lion standing on a man. Gold leaf, wood. L: 9½ in. 97.1386.

**3.28** (BOTTOM, RIGHT)
Sword handle of a pineapple. Gold leaf, wood. L: 24 in. 97.1391.

for this image argues that "It is better not to have fired at all, than to have fired and missed the lion" (cf. Ross 1982a, fig. 3).[19] Here the message is more about the judicious use of power and exercising it with some care.

The pineapple was introduced from the Americas by the Portuguese (figs. 3.22, 3.28). Its name in Twi *aborɔbɛ* literally means "European palm." The visually compelling fruit of the plant is considered to be beautiful by many Akan, and in some areas it is simply said that "The chief is like the pineapple." A more complex proverb states that "The pineapple is eaten only when it is mature [lit., "red"], or it isn't sweet."[20] One elder in Offinso interpreted this as dealing with patience, but another said it referred to the importance of selecting an accomplished and experienced chief. Significantly a geometric abstraction of a pineapple is the dominant motif on the back of the presidential "Seal of State" of modern Ghana and on one side of the "State Sword" belonging to the president, both of which were designed by Kofi Antubam and said to represent "sovereignty" (Abbey 1997, 50, 51, 57, 58). The connection between this interpretation and the pineapple is not clear.

One of the most familiar and influential images in all of Akan art is the bird with its head turned toward its back—the so-called *sankɔfa* bird (see cover). Its message is most frequently translated as "Pick it up, if it falls behind."[21] The basic idea is that if you have forgotten something, you can return to retrieve it, or that mistakes can be corrected. In part the motif has to do with maintaining and respecting ancestral tradition. The image is so popular that for a time it was the name and logo of two Ghanaian periodicals. In *Sankɔfa Arts and Culture Magazine* the masthead explained that its name "refers to the wise bird who picks for the present what is best in ancient eyes to meet the demands of the future, undeterred" (Bedu-Addo 1981, 3). In the editorial introduction to *Sankɔfa: The Legon Journal of Archaeological and Historical Studies*, the motif was interpreted as "every wise man knows where he is going but only the fool does not know where he is coming from" (Anquandah 1975, 5). The image is so pervasive in Akan art that it appears on stools, swords, staffs, and umbrella finials, as well as stamped, embroidered, and appliqué textiles, among other royal object types.

There is also a rich vocabulary of human gesture in Akan art that carries the meaning of many figurative sculptures. A finger pointing to the eye combined with a finger pointing to the ear illustrates the expression "If you have not seen, have you also not heard?" (fig. 3.29).[22] This is a challenge to be alert, to look, and to listen. It encourages the use of all of one's faculties in assuming the responsibilities of a good citizen.

**3.29** Sword handle of a seated chief with pointed fingers. Gold leaf, wood. L: 15½ in. 97.1388.

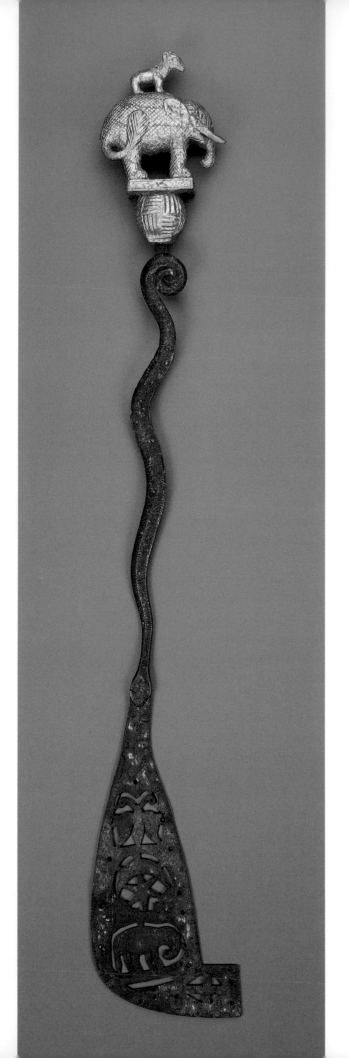

3.30 State sword. Iron.
L: 37⅛ in. 97.1385.

## Sword Blades

The sculpted and gold-leafed handles of swords are more prominent than their often artistically perforated blades. The most elaborate blade in the collection features three openwork images on the tip—an elephant, a star and crescent moon, and a butterfly. A forged snake connects these three images to the handle, which is not original to the blade (fig. 3.30). The variety of proverbs that may be applied to isolated images of elephants has been presented in the introduction. At first thought the star and crescent may seem to be another Islamic borrowing, but the variety of indigenous sayings associated with the image suggests that it has been a long-standing Akan motif. Nevertheless, the Islamic presence in many Akan states probably reinforced the popularity of this image. Two of the most common expressions informing this image were recorded at Kokofu: "Though the moon is brightest the star is most constant" and "The evening star delights in marriage [to the moon]."[23] The former values reliability over the waxing and waning of the moon. Interestingly *nsoromma* (star) is also the name of a certain species of butterfly, a motif that appears just above the star and crescent on this sword (Christaller 1933, 473). The only expression I have recorded for the butterfly is the rhetorical question, "If the butterfly says it does not drink why is it found on the road to the still [or sometimes palm wine bar]?"[24] This is a general comment on a person who says one thing then does another and argues for the integrity of word and action.

An unusual feature of some Akan state swords is the presence of two or three blades and from two to four handles on the same ceremonial weapon (fig. 3.31). The Glassell example has a conventional

**3.31** Fante state swords with tripod blades. Photograph by Doran H. Ross, Anomabu, 1981.

**3.32** Three-bladed sword. Iron, gold leaf, wood. L: 37¼ in. 97.1362.

single handle with three blades, allowing it to stand on its own tripod base (fig. 3.32). The most common version of the sword has either two parallel or two opposing blades and one handle. I have considered these forms in some detail elsewhere and argue that the latter version was ultimately derived from the widespread Islamic symbol of the double-bladed "sword of Ali" or "Dhu-al-Faqar," which was captured by Muhammad at the battle of Badr and subsequently passed on to his son-in-law, Ali, who became the fourth caliph and the impetus for the Shiite sect of Islam (Ross 1983b). The image is found in cultures as far removed as Senegal and the Philippines.

**3.33** Asante sword bearer with *ntakerakye* headdress. Photograph by Doran H. Ross, Kokofu, 1976.

### Sword Bearers' Hats

Some of the most spectacular court headgear is not worn by chiefs but rather by sword bearers. The most flamboyant examples are called *ntakerakye* (figs. 3.33, 3.34) and are distinguished by a spread of eagle feathers, a pair of cast-gold ram's horns, and a series of amulets. These headdresses are relatively rare today with only a single example found in the regalia of those paramount chiefs that do have them. In 1817 Bowdich described and illustrated this form suggesting that it was more common at that time. "The dress of the captains…was a war cap, with gilded rams horns projecting in front, the sides extended beyond all

3.34 Sword bearer's head-dress, Akyem Oda. Feathers, leather, fiber, gold leaf, wood. L: 21½ in. 97.908.

proportion by immense plumes of eagles feathers and fastened under the chin with bands of cowries" (1819 [1966], 32, drawing no. 1; see also Freeman 1844 [1968], 146). Today one of these headdresses is worn by the bearers of the Mponponsuo swords of the Asantehene and Mamponhene and the Bosommuru sword of the Kokofuhene. The ubiquitous ram's horns illustrate the proverb "The ram fights with its heart not its horns," meaning it is strength of character, and not weapons, that leads to success in battle.[25]

A more commonly encountered sword bearer's hat, called *krɔbɔnkye*, is made from hide and is a kind of skullcap adorned with gold ornaments (fig. 3.35).

**3.35** Sword bearer's head-dress with elephants and palm nuts. Leather, gold. w: 8½ in. 97.896.

In some states, such as Kumawu, the ornaments on the hat match those on the bearer's sword (see Ross 1977, figs. 13, 14). This type of hat is also worn by gun carriers (see below) and by chiefs on select ritual and ceremonial occasions, especially funerals. The Glassell example has four elephants with bunches of palm nuts or fruits (*bemu*) in front of and behind each pachyderm. A casting of an oil palm tree that produces the palm nuts is perched on top of the hat. I am unaware of any maxims or stories that bring the elephant and the palm nut together, and the multivalent nature of single elephant imagery has already been discussed in relation to state sword handles.

The palm nut clusters on the Houston hat, however, should probably be interpreted in relation to the tree on top in a composition that also deals with heritage and pedigree. In the Asante state of Dwaben this motif elicited the saying, "At the bottom of a big tree is the best place to find palm nuts."[26] In other words, the heir to an important chief is to be found among his closest matrilineal descendants. The oil palm tree and its fruits are also both recognized for their strength and invincibility. A counselor's staff in the Asantehene's treasury represents the proverb "All trees bend before the storm except the oil palm tree."[27] At Adanse Fomena a related saying is "All trees may shed their leaves except the palm tree."[28] Finally the palm fruit sword ornament at Kumawu is likened to the chief, "If you fire a gun into it, you waste your bullets."[29]

In addition to the gold ornaments on this hat, there are leather cutouts of the fern *aya*. These are also found in gold on *krɔbɔnkye* as seen in one example separated from its hat (fig. 3.36). The highly conventionalized saying associated

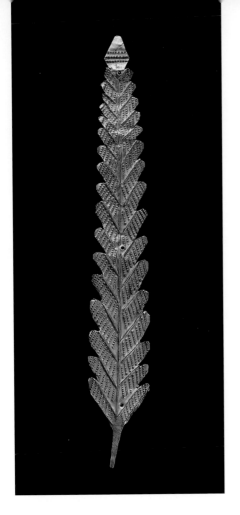

with this image derives from the Akan affection for wordplay and puns, where *ya* or *yaw* means insult or rebuke. Of this image of the fern the Akan say "The chief does not fear insults."[30]

The ram's horns on the third sword bearer's hat in the collection (fig. 3.37) probably share the same meaning as those on the feathered headdress (fig. 3.34). The smaller horns are those of the duiker, a small antelope thought to be very intelligent and whose horns are considered to have medicinal value. Also represented on this elaborate gold-leafed hat are seashells, executioners' knives, and segments of *babadua* (for the latter, see p. 110). ●

**3.36** Fern ornament for headdress. Gold. L: 7¾ in. 97.877.

**3.37** Sword bearer's headdress with horns. Gold leaf, wood. L: 8½ in. 97.907.

# 4 Speaking with Wisdom
## CHIEFS' COUNSELORS AND THEIR STAFFS

While stools and swords are the two most important items of regalia in the courts of most chiefs, their custodians and bearers are not nearly as critical as the *akyeame* (sing. *ɔkyeame*; most commonly translated as "linguist"), or counselors to the chief, who carry carved and gold-leafed wooden staffs (*akyeame poma*). Houston has the largest and most important collection of staffs in museums. The *ɔkyeame* and his staff are quintessential exemplars of the verbal/visual nexus of Akan arts. Among all the regalia the staffs stand out as the most approachable and telling public documents of the Akan ethos (figs. 4.2, 4.4).

The *ɔkyeame's* most visible public role is that of mediator between the chief and those who wish to talk to him. The chief's words and those of his guests are repeated by the counselor—the *ɔkyeame* "makes the chief's words sweet" as the Akan say. While not everyone is satisfied with "linguist" as a translation of *ɔkyeame*, McCaskie notes that "the *ɔkyeame* was a linguist in the sense that his speech was required to be accurate, fluent, conditioned by appropriate rhetorical devices and etiquette, and informed by a knowledge of history, social custom, and legal precedent" (1995, 296). Wilks translates the term as "counselor" and variously describes the role of the office as advisor, judicial advocate, military attaché, foreign minister, prime minister, and political troubleshooter (1975, 270–74). Kwesi Yankah in his important study *Speaking for the Chief: Okyeame and the Politics of Akan Royal Oratory* provides the most comprehensive, and formidable, job description:

> The *okyeame* is the most conspicuous functionary in the chief's exec-utive wing, performing duties in several spheres of activity—social, political, religious, and rhetorical—on the chief's behalf. In addition to being the chief's orator, diplomat, envoy, prosecutor, protocol

4.1 Staff finial of two men at a table. Gold leaf, wood. H: 14 in. 97.1298.

**4.2** Asante counselors' staffs. Photograph by Frank Fournier, Kumase, 1995.

**4.3** Asante counselors invoking ancestors with a libation. Photograph by Doran H. Ross, Asumegya, 1979.

officer, and prayer officiant, the *okyeame* is also the chief's confidant and counselor. Thus his duties require an uncommon familiarity with traditional lore, custom, and history, as well as wisdom, experience, and skills in the forensic arts, oratory, logic, diplomacy, and public relations. To command credibility in his representation of the chief he is also expected to be the quintessence of moral virtues: sincerity, loyalty, probity, and selfless devotion should guide his behavior at all times. [Yankah 1995, 84–85]

The description may be an ideal, but it is also an indicator of the scope of services provided and of the esteem in which this position is held. A frequently cited proverb states, "If a town becomes broken, it is the fault of the *ɔkyeame*, if a town stands [firm] it is the due to the *ɔkyeame*" (Rattray 1927, 277).

Yankah identifies several rationales for mediating face-to-face behavior with an orator. First, in verbal exchanges the counselor can correct or expand upon spontaneous communication and thus protect the chief from misspeaking. The interposition of the *ɔkyeame* also creates a certain physical and communicative distance that reinforces the social status of the chief. In addition, the counselor functions as a witness, although it is perceived that he shares the views of the chief (1995, 12–14).

The position of *ɔkyeame* is generally inherited through designated matri-lineages although on occasion a chief may appoint someone to the position. It is rare for a chief to have only one *ɔkyeame*—two to six are more typical, depending on the size of the state (figs. 4.3, 4.5). According to several sources

the Asantehene officially has positions for twelve, but in 1979 that number had risen to sixteen (fig. 4.6). In most states one ɔkyeame is designated head of the counselors and given the title *akyeamehene,* or chief counselor, and indeed he is recognized as a chief in his own right, undergoing most of the same royal installation rites that his ruler does (Yankah 1995, 85, 89).

The ɔkyeame is traditionally referred to as ɔhene yere, or the "chief's wife." Even in the rare cases where the chief is female and her ɔkyeame male, the counselor is still referred to as a wife and the chief a husband. The ɔkyeame has unlimited access to the chief and has the sole right among court officials to enter the chief's chambers to wake him during a crisis. The appointment of an ɔkyeame follows procedures for the arrangement of a matrimonial engagement. The installation rites for an ɔkyeame parallel those of wedding rites, and when a chief dies the *akyeame* undergo many of the same rituals as his widows (Yankah 1995, 89–91). While Akan queen mothers also have *akyeame,* at least one of whom is usually female, they rarely have staffs.

Critical to the skills of the ɔkyeame is the mastery of the rich proverbial lore of the Akan. The oral presentation of proverbs is a highly developed art in itself, and great orators are respected in large measure for their ability to embellish speech with appropriate maxims. Numerous Akan proverbs emphasize the importance of this ability: "A man dies but his tongue does not rot" (Akrofi n.d., 126); "When you place your tongue in pawn, you cannot redeem it" (Rattray 1916, 180); and "A good mouth blesses itself" (Akrofi n.d., 126). Yankah in particular has emphasized the importance of verbal skills in conflict resolution: "When two mouths meet conflict is averted"; "The sweet tongue

4.4 Fante counselors with staffs. Photograph by Doran H. Ross, Enyan Abaasa, 1974.

**4.5** Fante counselors' staffs. Photograph by Doran H. Ross, Mankesim, 1976.

**4.6** Seven of the Asantehene's counselors. Photograph by Doran H. Ross, Kumase, 1980.

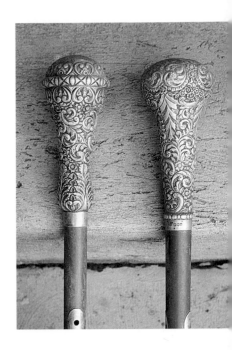

4.7 British-made staffs from the regalia of the Adansehene. Photograph by Doran H. Ross, Adanse Fomena, 1976.

disarms the aggressor"; and "If you do not complain to your barber, you are given an ugly haircut" (1995, 49). Still other proverbs deal with the use of proverbs: "When a poor man makes a proverb, it does not spread abroad" (Rattray 1916, 159); "When the occasion arises, it calls for an appropriate proverb"; and "We speak to a wise man in proverbs, not in plain language" (Akrofi n.d., 142,3).

In 1672 Wilhem Müller became one of the first Europeans to document the position of "Obcjammi" and correctly identify it as "the first royal advisor" (1673 [1983], 108). There is general agreement that the first *akyeame poma* were simple cylindrical staffs covered with gold or silver and sometimes with the skin of a monitor lizard (fig. 4.8). Among the Asante these are inevitably called *asɛmpa yɛ tia* (lit., "truth is brief"). The Mamponhene and his elders explained that these were kept in front of the black stools of past chiefs and used in addressing these royal ancestors at the stool house on occasions when they were presented with ritual offerings.[1] British government anthropologist Robert Rattray observed a number of Brong and Asante Adae ceremonies wherein these rituals were observed and photographed the *asɛmpa yɛ tia* in the presence of the blackened ancestral stools (1923, figs. 31–35). This is probably the most important context for *akyeame poma* and is further evidence for *asɛmpa yɛ tia* as the first of this genre. In some Asante states the *asɛmpa yɛ tia* were also used when judging capital crimes or in appeals to paramount chiefs.

Working independently and citing different combinations of evidence, Cole and Ross (1977) and McLeod (1979; 1981) concluded that the first staffs with figurated finials did not appear until the late nineteenth century, were heavily influenced by European models of "messenger canes" and "government staffs," and originated on the coast (fig. 4.7). There is no evidence of figurated counselors' staffs in the Asantehene's court until after the return of Prempeh I from exile in 1924. Kyerematen confirmed the late arrival of figurated finials at the Asantehene's court in his dissertation.

> Before the reign of Agyeman Prempeh I, the staffs of the Asante-hene's Linguists, although plated with gold, were of simple design without any tops. Other Akan rulers have had elaborate linguist staffs; and it was upon representations made to Agyeman Prempeh I on his repatriation from exile by his linguists that they like linguists in other Akan States, were allowed to have symbolic tops to their staffs. [Kyerematen 1966, caption to pl. VI (ii)]

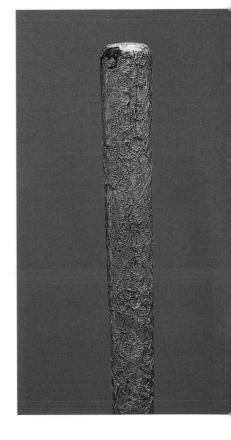

4.8 Staff called *asɛmpa yɛ tia* from the Asantehene's regalia. Photograph by Doran H. Ross, Kumase, 1980.

Two rare and important silver-topped staffs from the last half of the nineteenth century represent the Akan elaboration of the simple gold-covered cylindrical forms (figs. 4.9, 4.10).[2] Both have shafts that are much more elaborately carved than most twentieth-century examples and are monoxylous rather than carved in three parts like most gold-leafed staffs. While the carving on one of these early staffs appears to be purely decorative, the other has clusters of gourd gunpowder containers represented along the shaft. In between one section of these containers are two men with upraised arms with a musket to the side of each, the meaning of this is unclear except to amplify the role of the powder horns.

As noted above, most staffs are carved of wood in three sections and then gold leafed. The sculptured finial, the third section, carries the principal proverbial message, but occasionally the two-piece shaft may have subsidiary motifs. The most popular shaft decoration is a square or reef knot called the "wisdom knot" (*nyansapɔ*), seen earlier on the bird-with-cannons *abɔsodeɛ*. It illustrates the aphorism: "Only the wise man can untie the *nyansapɔ*," meaning that the chief or couselor is a problem solver. This is a particularly appropriate image for a counselor considering his judicial orientation. The only other representational motif found with some regularity on the shaft is a chain (fig. 4.11). Many informants stated that this was "just decoration," but one *akyeamehene* and one prominent carver of staffs argued that the chain represented the strength and power of the chief.[3] Peggy Appiah identifies chain imagery with the Akan family and cites the saying: "If we are linked together like a chain, in life we are linked, in death we are linked. Family links are never broken" (1979, 66). This interpretation is certainly consistent with staff imagery as we understand it. At the Asante paramountcy of Asumegya the chain imagery with padlocks found on two counselors' staffs signified "the unity of Asante" according to the chief.[4]

An occasional staff has human mandibles carved in relief on the shaft (see fig. 4.23). This continues a long-standing Akan practice of decorating drums and ivory horns (both of which speak

**4.9** Detail of staffs in figure 4.10.

**4.10** Counselors' staffs with ornamented finials. Silver, wood. H: 51½ in. 97.1420.1, 2.

in proverbs) with the actual jawbones of defeated enemies, and of adorning the regalia of sword bearers and the jewelry of chiefs with cast-gold replicas. George Preston was the first to note that human mandibles on ivory trumpets represent state enemies singing the praises of their conqueror's chief (1972, 58). Jawbones on counselors' staffs may have originally expressed a related idea. An unusual shaft motif is the human ear (fig. 4.12). Although I have no specific documentation of this motif, it is tempting to speculate that it is a reference to the chief or the *ɔkyeame* being a thoughtful listener. Since this shaft has an elephant as a finial, the human ear may refer to the proverb, "The ears of a chief are as big as those of an elephant" (Christaller 1879 [1990], 109).

The European-influenced globular knoblike tops of early staffs persist as a design element on many *akyeame poma* still in use. One such staff in the Houston collection (fig. 4.13) has two dates on it, "1918" and "1936," and an inscription "KATAVE hd." In addition there are images of a European-style crown and clenched hand with the index finger pointing, a motif discussed earlier in relation to a sword handle. While the dates may refer to the reign of a particular chief, "KATAVE" is neither a proper name nor a place name known to me or my Ghanaian colleagues. As discussed previously the lion perched on top with a horizontal S-shaped tail is also a motif most likely borrowed from the British.

With the development of figurated finials, the expressive potential of the *ɔkyeame poma* expanded. Excepting the enormous corpus of gold weights, there is a greater variety of motifs on counselors' staffs than on any other Akan plastic art.[5] One of the principal themes of staff imagery is the continuity of chieftaincy and the ruling family.

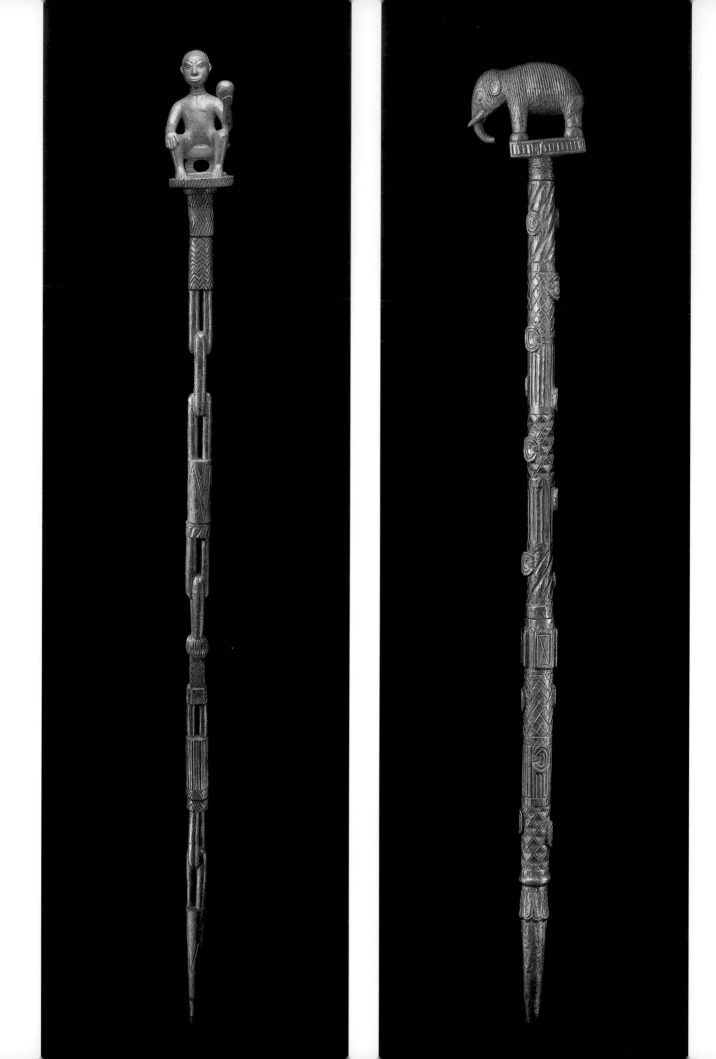

The single most common counselor's staff finial today depicts two men seated at a table with one typically reaching for food and the other grasping his own stomach (fig. 4.1). This illustrates the maxim, "The food is for the man who owns it and not for the man who is hungry."⁶ The food is a metaphor for chieftaincy, which belongs only to the rightful owner or heir to the stool. The popularity of this motif is understandable in view of the large number of chieftaincy disputes that trouble traditional states. The question of succession to the stool is a frequent source of dissension. In Ghana, as elsewhere, many people desire to be king; this motif is designed to discourage such illegitimate pretensions.

Another finial that deals with succession and birthright depicts a crab and a bird (figs. 4.14, 4.15) and represents a readily apparent fact, "A crab does not beget a bird," that is, if the royal family is represented by the crab, there will be no birds in the line of succession.⁷ Although the provenance of the two staffs illustrated here is unknown, the crab is the symbol of the Fante state of Oguaa (Cape Coast). According to the paramount chief Nana Kwasi Attah II, the Fosu River and Lagoon were "congested" with crabs and they were traded inland and became a source of early economic prosperity.⁸ The image of a cluster of birds on a single tree contains a message analogous to that indicated by the bird and the crab, "Birds of the same species roost in the same tree," basically the equivalent of the English proverb "Birds of a feather flock together" (fig. 4.16).⁹ The image argues for unity and solidarity within the state and the royal family.

A fourth motif dealing with who controls the reins of power depicts a monkey, an antelope, and a termite hill, which can be ten or more feet tall in West Africa (fig. 4.17). This same composition is the subject of a sword ornament in the Asante state of Dwaben where the chief and his elders said it represented

4.11 (OPPOSITE, LEFT)
Staff with a finial of a seated man holding an egg. Carved by Osei Bonsu, circa 1940. Gold leaf, wood. H: 62¾ in. 97.1267.A–D.

4.12 (OPPOSITE, RIGHT)
Staff with a finial of an elephant. Gold leaf, wood. H: 60⅞ in. 97.1291.A–C.

4.13 (ABOVE, LEFT)
Staff finial of a lion, 1936. Gold leaf, wood. H: 6½ in. 97.1290.

4.14 (ABOVE, RIGHT)
Staff finial of a man holding a bird and a crab. Gold leaf, wood. H: 12¾ in. 97.1305.A.

**4.15** Staff finial of a bird and a crab. Gold leaf, wood. H: 12 in. 97.1289.A.

**4.16** Staff finial of birds on a tree. Gold leaf, wood. H: 13½ in. 97.1296.

the aphorism "When the monkey rubs its body against the anthill, it doesn't become an antelope."[10] Here the antelope stands for the chief and is actually the little duiker mentioned earlier, which is much admired for its intelligence. Thus the Akan are stating that the imitation of chiefly behavior does not make one a chief (Cole and Ross 1977, fig. 317).

A number of *akyeame poma* represent messages that advocate cooperative behavior within the state and between a chief and his subjects. The cluster of four heads on one staff (fig. 4.18) argues that "one head does not go into counsel," a motif seen earlier on a sword handle. A man pushing a second man up a tree (fig. 4.19) depicts the saying, "If you climb a good tree, you get a push," or if your intentions are good, people will help you.[11] A third image of a man scraping bark from a tree (fig. 4.20) was explained by the artist, the renowned Asante carver Osei Bonsu (1900–1977): "If one man scrapes the bark off a tree, it will fall to the ground." The bark in this case is considered medicinal, and there are proscriptions against it touching the earth. The image stresses the need for a second person working with the first to complete a task successfully.[12]

This staff is one of four in the Glassell Collection by Osei Bonsu. It was probably carved between 1947 and 1956 when the artist was in residence at Adisadel College, Cape Coast. Another staff by Osei Bonsu portrays a man with his leg caught in a trap. He explained the motif in English, "The trap does not know its owner" (fig. 4.21). Bonsu elaborated on this maxim by explaining, "If the person who sets the trap is not careful, he will become a victim of the trap," thus warning that devious intentions may backfire.[13] A third Bonsu staff features

**4.17** Staff finial of an antelope, a monkey, and a termite hill. Gold leaf, wood. H: 10⅝ in. 97.1268.

**4.18** Fante staff finial of four heads, Legu. Gold leaf, wood. H: 11½ in. 97.1301.

**4.19** Staff finial of a man climbing a tree assisted by a second man. Gold leaf, wood. H: 15¼ in. 97.1292.A.

**4.20** Staff finial of a man scraping bark from a tree. Carved by Osei Bonsu, circa 1950. Gold leaf, wood. H: 17½ in. 97.1297.A-C.

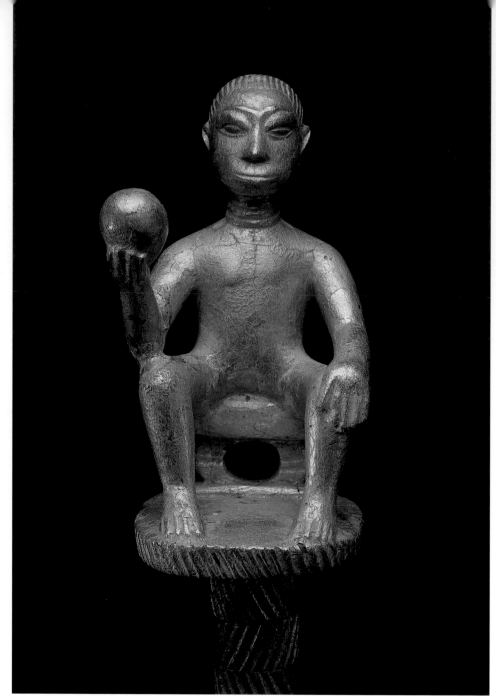

4.21 Staff finial of a man
and a trap. Carved by Osei
Bonsu, circa 1935. Gold leaf,
wood. H: 15½ in. 97.1274.

4.22 Staff finial of a seated
man holding an egg. Carved
by Osei Bonsu, circa 1940.
Gold leaf, wood. H: 7¾ in.
97.1267.A.

a seated man holding an egg in his hand (fig. 4.22), a metaphor for the proper exercise of chiefly power: "To be ruler is like holding an egg in the hand; if it is pressed too hard it breaks; but if not held tightly enough it may slip and smash on the ground" (Kyerematen 1964, 96).

Based on photographs in the Ghana Ministry of Information, it is evident that a fourth staff by Bonsu depicting a whale with a figure in its mouth was originally owned by the state of Ahanta (fig. 4.23).[14] According to the current paramount chief Nana Baidoo Bonsoe XV, the staff recounts the origins of Ahanta when the first chief was ejected from the mouth of a whale to claim the coastal lands between the Ankobra and Pra Rivers.[15] A number of staffs from various paramountcies in different areas represent similar claims of autochthonous origins, which serve in part to dissuade competing demands for property rights (see Ross 1982B, 62, fig. 17). That the current paramount chief is the fifteenth

in a succession of Bonsoes (lit., "whales") reinforces the legitimacy of this particular claim.[16]

The staff with the egg described above speaks of a delicate balance of power, a theme reiterated on many staffs. The popular image of a cock with a hen (figs. 4.24, 4.25) invariably represents the gender-biased proverb, "Though the hen knows when it is dawn, she leaves it for the cock to announce."[17] The Akan are recognizing that a woman and man, or a subject and chief, often share the same knowledge, but the former defers to the latter in decision making and leadership. Another common motif involving a hen has her chicks surrounding her feet and elicits the proverb, "The hen's foot may step on its chicks but it does not kill them" (figs. 4.26, 4.28).[18] Here the hen represents the chief who is providing not aggression but guidance. A third staff depicts a hen sitting on her eggs, another metaphor for the nurturing role of the chief (fig. 4.27). The

4.23  Staff finial of a whale with a man in its mouth, Ahanta. Carved by Osei Bonsu, circa 1950. Gold leaf, wood. H: 18¼ in. 97.1281.A,B.

4.24  Staff finial of a man, a cock, and a hen. Gold leaf, wood. H: 10 in. 97.1304.

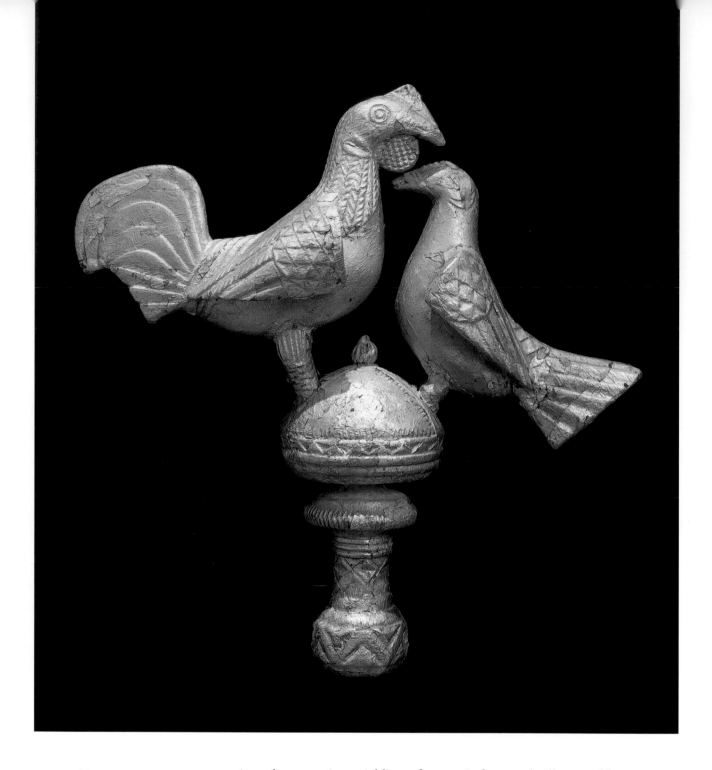

4.25 Staff finial of a cock
and a hen. Gold leaf, wood.
H: 12 5/8 in. 97.1283.

strategic and appropriate wielding of power is frequently illustrated by a man holding a snake by the head (cf. fig. 3.26) or in this case a bird holding a snake: "When caught by the head, the rest of the snake is nothing but a rope" (fig. 4.29).[19]

Some staffs deal with both the expectations and limitations of human behavior. A chameleon standing on a locked box (fig. 4.30) is associated with the saying, "The chameleon can only change the color of the clothes he is wearing, not those in his box," meaning that one can deal only with the immediate environment, only with the problems at hand. This is a warning against trying to exceed one's own abilities.[20]

The relevance of the malevolent forest spirit *sasabonsam* (fig. 4.31) to the imagery on counselors' staffs is unclear, unless it is a metaphor for the chief's

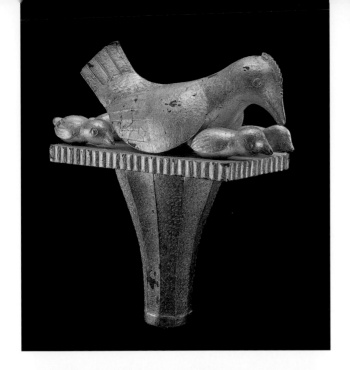

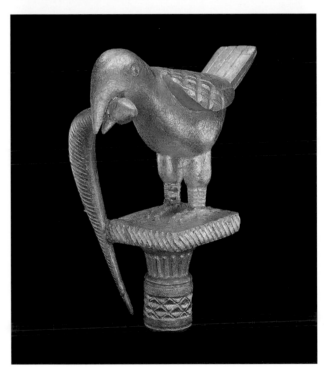

**4.26** Staff finial of a hen and
her chicks. Gold leaf, wood.
H: 8½ in. 97.1306.

**4.28** Staff finial of a hen and
her chicks. Gold leaf, wood.
H: 8 in. 97.1287.

**4.27** Staff finial of hen
with eggs. Gold leaf, wood.
H: 7⅝ in. 97.1497.

**4.29** Staff finial of a bird
with a snake. Gold leaf,
wood. H: 9¼ in. 97.1280.

4.30 Staff finial of a chameleon standing on a box. Gold leaf, wood. H: 6 in. 97.1355.

supernatural powers. *Sasabonsam* is a predatory being described by Rattray as "a monster of human shape, living in the depths of the forest and only occasionally met by hunters. It sits on treetops, and its legs dangle down to the ground and have hooks for feet that pick up anyone who comes within reach. It has iron teeth. There are female, male and little *sasabonsam*" (1916, 18). Elsewhere Rattray adds that "it is covered with long hair, has large blood-shot eyes, long legs, and feet pointing both ways" (1927, 28). Christian missionaries have frequently identified *sasabonsam* with the devil, and the creature is often depicted with stereotypic attributes of the latter, including horns, batlike wings, tail, beard, and cloven hooves (see Ross and Garrard 1983, front and back covers). Christaller notes that *sasabonsam* is seen as "the friend and chief of the sorcerers and witches" (1933, 429). It is possible that this staff served the priest of a shrine rather than a chief since royal regalia is found in both contexts (see fig. 1.22).

An unusual counselor's staff finial depicts a man with an enormous lantern next to what seems to be a four-poster bed (possibly a funeral bed) with a second man next to it (fig. 4.32). One response to a photo of this piece given in English suggested that "The light of the chief continues to shine even after death."[21] Supporting this interpretation is the hand on the stomach of the larger figure, a mourning gesture suggesting hunger for the presence of the deceased (see Ohene 1971, 15–21). An isolated image of a man with a lantern in Sefwi Afere elicited the saying, "It behooves everybody to struggle for money even to the extent of lighting a lamp to search for it at night" (Owusu 1978, 65). In other words, success in life is achieved through extra effort. Perhaps both men on this staff are included in an overtime pursuit of money.

As mentioned earlier in relation to a sword handle, the gesture of a finger pointing to the eye (fig. 4.33) refers to the rhetorical question, "Have you not seen?" This is generally interpreted as an admonition to open one's eyes, to behold. This gesture is also carved on a finial of a man holding a book in his other hand (fig. 4.34). Book imagery in Akan art generally refers to two related subjects, the Bible and literacy. Books are relatively common on counselors' staffs and the related genre of umbrella tops (fig. 4.35 and see below) but are even more frequently found as the carved supports for stools. I have seen stools with book motifs in the parlors or reception rooms of at least twenty different chiefs.

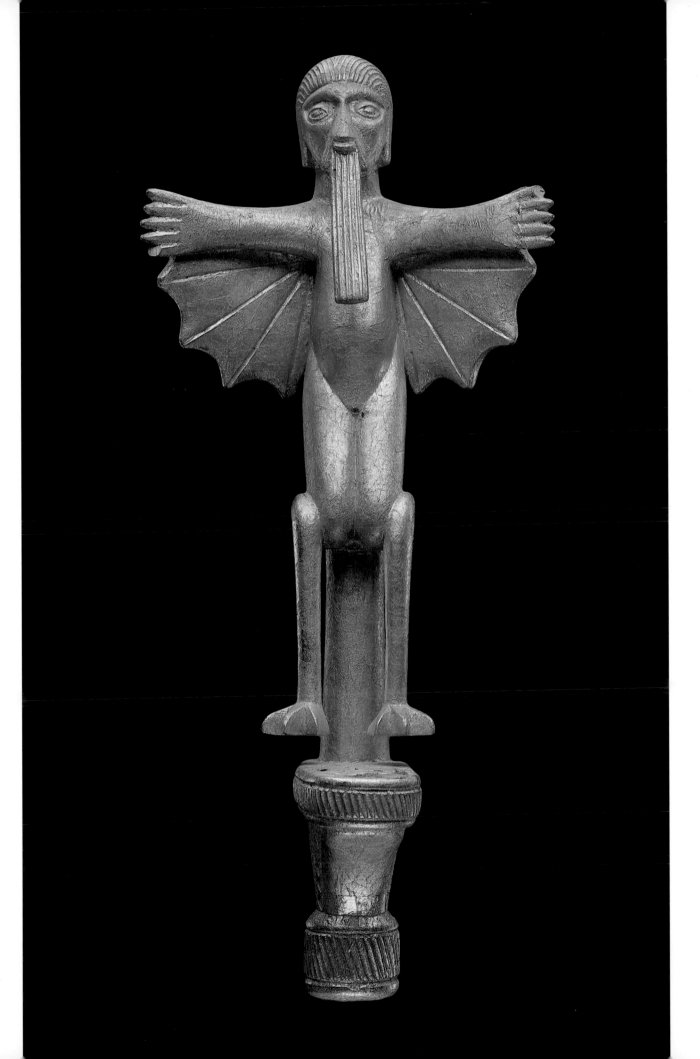

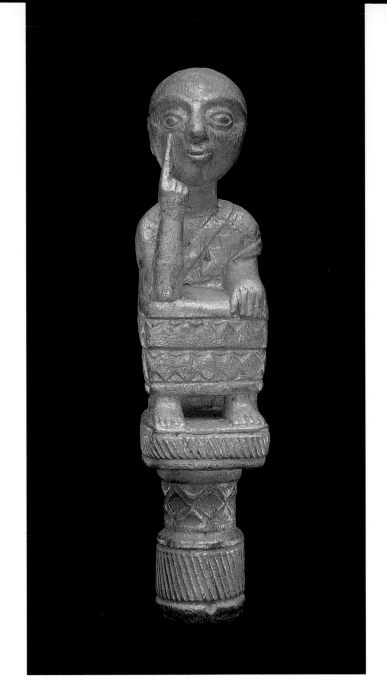

Nana Baidoo Bonsoe XV, the *ɔmanhene* of Ahanta, is a Seventh-Day Adventist and said in English of a book carved on a stool in his living room, "You shouldn't forget your Bible; we pour libations, but we are Christians." He noted that he sat on this stool especially when serving the judicial roles of a chief and when "like King Solomon, I must be fair and firm." He went on to say, "When you read King Solomon, you are a wise man."[22] The paramount chief of Oguaa, Osabarimba Kwesi Attah II (a Methodist) said of the Bible stool in his palace, "We gain our strength from it."[23]

The town chief of Butre has a counselor's staff featuring a canine with a book in its mouth. A dog is the emblem of the chief's lineage (*abusua*), and while the book was identified as a Bible, it was described as the "book where ancestors' names were kept," a reference to the Christian practice of recording births and deaths in family Bibles.[24] As such the book is an apt addition to the traditional symbol of the matrilineage.

4.32 (OPPOSITE)
Staff finial of a figure with a lantern and a second figure. Gold leaf, wood. H: 14 in. 97.1279.A.

4.33 (ABOVE, LEFT)
Staff finial of a figure pointing at his eye. Gold leaf, wood. H: 10⅝ in. 97.1498.

4.34 (ABOVE, RIGHT)
Umbrella finial of a man holding a book and pointing at his eye. Gold leaf, wood. H: 16 in. 97.1273.A-C.

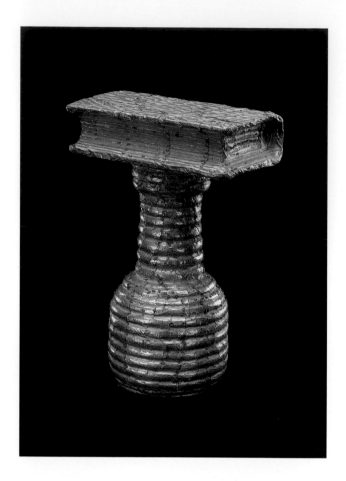

**4.35** Umbrella finial of a book. Gold leaf, wood. H: 7⅜ in. 97.1284.

**4.36** Staff finial of Ananse the spider. Gold leaf, wood. H: 14 in. 97.1269.

Explicit in the above examples is the chief's ability to read and write, which is typically and emphatically stated by a chief's *ɔkyeame* either before or after references to Christianity. Related to book imagery are those Akan works that present all or part of the alphabet. These include warrior flags, drums of popular bands, and *adinkra* cloths. In each case the individual or individuals associated with the object are asserting that they are educated and often implying that their rivals are not. The inclusion of inscriptions in English or Twi on various items of regalia is also a statement of literacy and educational achievement (see, for example, figs. 2.10, 4.12).

The image of one or more spiders on a web represents the trickster-folk hero Ananse who is credited with the origin of many of the proverbs and folktales cited in this volume (fig. 4.36). According to one story Ananse gained his wisdom and knowledge directly from Nyame, the supreme deity, and in turn brought it to the Akan (Rattray 1930, 55–59). Indeed the Akan refer to their folktales as "spider stories," or Anansesem. Several sayings—all associated with wisdom—are applied to the spider motif. Two of the most common are: "No one goes to the house of the spider Ananse to teach it wisdom" and "No one tells a new story to the spider's son Ntikuma."[25] The implication is that the chief and his advisors rule with the collective wisdom of Ananse and by extension his teacher, Nyame.

Taken together these motifs would seem to present a rather evenhanded view of Akan society with the rights and responsibilities of the chief balanced by those of his subjects and with the emphasis placed on model behavior for all. In reality, most paramount chiefs have only three to six staffs, and the prerogatives of the elite clearly outweigh those of the other classes. That the regalia represent obvious disparities in wealth further exaggerates this situation, even though these items are considered the property of the state and not the chief. In the final analysis, it is the chief who rules and holds the reigns of power. As a counselor's staff from the Asantehene's treasury proclaims, "When elephant steps on trap, no more trap."[26]

4.37 Fante chief in procession at the annual Odambea festival. Photograph by Doran H. Ross, Lowtown, 1976.

### Umbrella Tops

Decorated umbrella finials (*ntuatire*) probably have a longer history than the finials on counselors' staffs (figs. 4.37, 4.38). In 1817 Bowdich recorded umbrellas "crowned on the top with crescents, pelicans, elephants, barrels and arms and swords of gold." He also noted finials of "various animals naturally stuffed" (1819 [1966], 34). The latter are no longer found on umbrellas, but all of the former motifs, except perhaps the pelican, can still be seen in various Asante and other Akan states.[27]

The most frequently seen umbrella finial is *babadua*, a segmented bamboolike cane (fig. 4.39, left). This cane is admired for its strength and was commonly used as a traditional building material. At the Asante paramountcy of Offinso, it was reported that a pathway of *babadua* was laid down prior to battle and that the army was deemed large enough when the canes began to break. Quarcoo notes that the plant was thought to have "magical properties capable of neutralizing or counteracting the forces of evil" (1975, 28).

Segments of *babadua* can frequently be seen supporting the primary image on a number of umbrella tops. In one (fig. 4.40), a bird is standing on a stool, which in turn is sitting on *babadua*. A bird on a stool is the emblem of at least ten different Akan states. Akan avian imagery includes the cock, crow, parrot, kite, eagle, and hawk, although the present example does not resemble any of these (see Sutherland 1954). In a second example (fig. 4.41), the wrist of a hand holding a book emerges from the *babadua* segment.

The porcupine (*kotoko*) is one of the preeminent emblems of the Asante kingdom (fig. 4.42). One telling measure of this is the fact that the Kumase soccer team is called Asante Kotoko. A highly codified saying accompanies this image, "If you kill a thousand, a thousand will come."[28] Some say that the Asante believe that a porcupine can shoot its quills and then generate new quills to continue the battle; the quills serve as a metaphor for Asante warriors, who are thought to attack in endless waves.

In sculptural representations the hedgehog (*apese*), which also has spines, is sometimes mistaken for the porcupine and vice versa. In fact, the hedgehog is seen as the little brother to the porcupine and is typically distinguished by

**4.38** Fante chief in procession at the annual Fetu Afahye. Photograph by Doran H. Ross, Cape Coast, 1978.

**4.39** Asante umbrella finials. Left to right: *babadua* (cane), *aya* (fern), *akoben* (war horn), *prekese* (an aromatic plant). Photograph by Doran H. Ross, Dwaben, 1976.

4.40 Umbrella finial of a bird on a stool. Gold leaf, wood. H: 9 ¾ in. 97.1415.

the presence of a log next to it illustrating the saying, "When the hedgehog grows fat, it is to the benefit of the rotten log [in which it lives]."[29] The basic idea here is that the state benefits from the success of the chief. The flat platform base with a hole clear through the center in figure 4.42 suggests that it is an umbrella finial rather than that of a counselor's staff.

In addition to verbal messages, some counselor staffs and umbrella tops represent one of the original seven or eight matrilineages (*abusua*, popularly called "clans") through which the Akan typically trace descent. The names and number of *abusua* actually vary somewhat from state to state.[30] Regardless, the counselor to the head of each matrilineage (*abusuapanyin*) often has a staff with a sculpted and painted emblem of the family group. Depending on the area, these may include images of a lion, leopard, stag, crow, parrot, bat, vulture, buffalo, and dog. Some chiefs also include gold-leafed matrilineage emblems in their regalia. The dog with a burning stick in its jaws is probably such an emblem from the Aduana lineage (fig. 4.43). It is usually explained that this group introduced fire to the Akan, often interpreted as an assertion that they were the first to arrive and clear the forest. At the Asante paramountcy of Asumegya, where the chief is from the Aduana lineage, the dog was said to have climbed out of a hole in the ground with family founders. A counselor's staff with a dog finial refers to the canine's production of fire (cf. Ross 1982b, fig. 18).[31] ●

**4.41** Umbrella finial of a hand holding a book. Gold leaf, wood. H: 11 in. 97.1418.

**4.42** Umbrella finial of a porcupine. Gold leaf, wood. H: 8 in. 97.1417.

**4.43** Umbrella finial of a dog with a stick in its mouth. Gold leaf, wood. H: 9⅜ in. 97.1282.

# 5

# Soul Washers, Praise Singers, and Gun Bearers

## Soul Discs

The Glassell Collection has a number of important examples of the gold disc-shaped chest ornaments called by the Asante *akrafokonmu* and typically translated as "soul discs" or "soul washers' badges." These are conventionally said to be worn by individuals who represent the chief's soul (*ɔkra*, pl. *akra*; fig. 5.1). *Ɔkra* refers not only to the Akan concept of the soul but also to the court official. The plural designation for such officials is *akrafo*, literally "soul people"; *konmu* refers to something worn around the neck.

Akrafokonmu are produced in cast and repoussé gold, as well as gold leaf over wood (figs. 5.2, 5.3, 5.4 B,C). There appears to be no distinction in function or status among the three modes of production, and all are widespread geographically, although gold-leaf versions are more common in the south. Typically all three are suspended from a white pineapple fiber cord, although sometimes gold chains are used. In addition to being worn by *akrafo* the breast plates sometimes adorn chiefs, sword bearers, representatives of royal matrilineages, and even deities (*abosom*). In addition, virtually identical forms appear on stools, swords, ritual containers (*kuduo* and *forowa*), and various other jewelry items. I have argued elsewhere that soul-disc-like imagery originally served generalized apotropaic functions in a variety of contexts (see Ross 2002).

Although general agreement does not exist on the strict translation of *ɔkra* as "soul," Kwame Gyekye in his discussion of the "Akan conceptual scheme" argues strongly for it:

> The *ɔkra* is said to be that which constitutes the innermost self, the essence of the individual person....*ɔkra* is identified with life. The *ɔkra* is the embodiment and transmitter of the individual's destiny

5.1 Fante chief with his niece who wears an *akrafokonmu* representing their matrilineage. Photograph by Doran H. Ross, Abeadze Dominase, 1974.

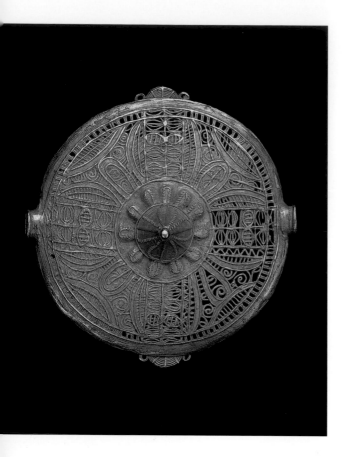

5.2 *Akrafokonmu*. Gold.
DIAM: 4 in. 97.1338.

5.3 *Akrafokonmu*. Gold leaf,
wood. DIAM: 5¾ in. 97.1004.

(fate: *nkrabea*). It is explained as the spark of the Supreme Being (*Onyame*) in man…the *ɔkra* can be considered the equivalent of the concept of the soul in other metaphysical systems. Hence it is correct to translate *ɔkra* into English as soul. [Gyekye 1995, 85; for dissenting opinions see McCaskie 1992, 230, and Wiredu 1983, 113–34]

Despite differences in definition, there is some general consensus that the *ɔkra* comes from Nyame, the supreme being, at birth and returns to Nyame upon death.

In most Akan states today, including those of the Asante, *akrafokonmu* are more often than not worn by sword bearers (fig. 5.5). Nevertheless, the literature on these forms continues to identify them as "soul discs" or "soul washers' badges" worn by individuals charged with the rituals to purify the chief's soul without recognizing that these functionaries are also custodians, or at least bearers, of state swords. While there is some evidence that sword bearers wore these discs in the nineteenth century or even earlier, most accounts from the Asante Kingdom indicate that the persons wearing the gold plates were "slaves" or "servants." They functioned in a variety of roles, and upon the death of their chief were sacrificed as part of the funerary rites (e.g., Ramseyer and Kühne 1875, 105; Christaller 1933, 262, 263). Most nineteenth-century accounts were written by missionaries or government envoys who had a vested interest in using issues of domestic slavery and human sacrifice as justification for their proselytizing and colonizing. Misleading, self-serving, and biased,

those accounts inevitably present a highly prejudicial view of the nineteenth-century Akan. Nevertheless, there is still substantial evidence for considerable degrees of servitude and for funerary slayings.

Perhaps the most accurate and nuanced nineteenth-century account was provided by Bowdich:

> The Ocra's are distinguished by a large circle of gold suspended from the neck; many of them are favorite slaves, many, commoners who have distinguished themselves, and who are glad to stake their lives on the King's, to be kept free from palavers and supported by his bounty, which they are entirely; some few are relatives and men of rank. All of the two former classes, excepting only the two or three individuals known to have been entrusted with the King's state secrets, are sacrificed at his tomb. [Bowdich 1819 [1966], 291]

**5.4A–D** Three *akrafokonmu* and a stool ornament (top). Repoussé gold. DIAM (of largest): 5 ¾ in. Clockwise from top: (A) 97.1327; (B) 97.1335; (C) 97.1337; (D) 97.1336

5.5 Fante sword bearer wearing *akrafokonmu*. Photograph by Doran H. Ross, Anomabu, 1974.

Malcolm McLeod views this position as training for higher office (1981, 84), and the historians Ivor Wilks and Larry Yarak provide convincing evidence for such a advancement from the nineteenth century (1975, 278–79, 332; 1990, 180–83).

According to Kyerematen, the two most important and oldest swords of the Asante, the Bosommuru and the Mponponsuo—identified with Asantehenes Osei Tutu I (r. 1701–1717) and Opoku Ware I (r. 1720–1750) respectively—were involved in the periodic soul washing and purification rituals of the early Asante court. An *akrafokonmu* worn by an *ɔkra* associated with the first of these two swords was said to have been "caught from the heavens by Anokye," and given the name "Bosommuru Aman-nkoto," that is, "through the power of the Bosommuru all nations shall kneel before the Asantehene" (Kyerematen 1966, 169, 193, 252). The current bearer of the Bosommuru sword wears a pair of small *akrafokonmu*, side-by-side, on the familiar pineapple fiber cord. This pectoral is called "*dwenee osi animu*," another phrase dealing with supplication (Kyerematen 1966, caption to pl. vi). These double-disc forms are more commonly called *ewisiado* (orphan's necklace) today and are worn at funerals by the spouses of the deceased (see Gott forthcoming).

At some point in time the Bosompra sword, currently identified with Asantehene Kwaku Dua I (r. 1834–1867), apparently replaced the Mponponsuo as one of the two state swords used in purification rituals. The choice of sword used depended upon which of two patrifilial subdivisions (*ntɔrɔ*) the Asantehene descended from. Like the bearer of the Bosommuru sword, the bearer of the Bosompra wears a distinctive *akrafokonmu* with two semicircular concavities on each side of what would otherwise be a rectangular ornament (anon. 1977, 19; cf. Garrard 1989, 67).[1] Asante elders said the design was that of a stool, and it is found as a prominent bead on a fine old necklace in the Glassell Collection (fig. 6.21, fourth bead to the right of the mudfish). Although McCaskie notes that the two swords are "central to the rite of purification," neither he nor other scholars have published any of the details (1995, 26, 277). Today the bearers of all the Asantehene's *keteanofena* swords wear *akrafokonmu,* and senior officials at the court confirm that the sword bearers indeed serve in soul-washing rituals.

Regardless of Akan state, it is clear that the *ɔkra* (soul) of the paramount chief requires considerable ritual attention and must be "purified" or "washed" in monthly or annual rites. Not every *ɔkra* (the official) is a soul washer (*ɔkradware*), and the responsibilities of the soul washer vary from state to state. In Wenchi the soul washers actually bathe the chief and key items of regalia, especially stools (Busia 1951, 54). In Techiman one *ɔkra* serves as a surrogate for the chief in the cleansing process (Warren and Brempong 1971, 31). Bowdich recorded the "annual ablutions" in 1817 and wrote that the Asantehene "washes in the marsh.... He is attended by his suite, but he laves the water with his own hands over himself, his chairs, stools, gold and silver plate, and the various articles of furnitures used especially by him" (1819 [1966], 279–80).

The annual washing of the Asantehene's *ɔkra* takes place during the Odwira (lit., "purification") festival (see chapter 9). Even taking into account that observers were witnessing the festival in different years, there is substantial discrepancy in the recorded number of *akrafo* wearing breastplates. W. Huydecoper visited Kumase in 1816–1817 and "counted...more than 60 golden plates suspended from the necks of various slaves" (1816–1817 [1962], 21). The missionaries Friedrich Ramseyer and Johannes Kühne wrote in 1870 that "Each of the king's *kra,* about a thousand in number, carries a gold plate upon his breast" (1875, 105). Two years later the French trader J. Bonnat observed hundreds of soul washers wearing *akrafokonmu* (cited in McCaskie 1995, 237). Even if the numbers fell in the low range between sixty and one hundred, *akrafokonmu* would be the most numerous of all regalia and would in themselves represent a substantial exhibition of the Asantehene's wealth.

There appears to be little correlation between the roles of the *akrafo* and the design of *akrafokonmu.* The radiating and concentric compositions of many *akrafokonmu* are typically identified as *tadeɛ,* or a pool of water, with one court official adding that the design is like what happens when a stone is thrown into the water (fig. 5.4c). Within these compositions, especially on the repoussé discs, individual design elements have been identified as cowrie shells, leaves, insects, edible grubs, and moon and star motifs. One disc was simply called both star (*nsoromma*) and crocodile (*denkyem*) based on its two most obvious features (fig. 5.6).[2] This latter example was photographed in 1974 when worn by a young chief in the Fante state of Anomabu, and it is one of the largest known examples (fig. 5.7).[3]

**5.6** *Akrafokonmu.* Gold. DIAM: 7 ¾ in. 97.1326.

**5.7** Fante divisional chief wearing an *akrafokonmu.* Photograph by Doran H. Ross, Anomabu, 1974.

A distinctive but common "soul disc" is shaped like a multipetaled flower called *fofoo* (fig. 5.8A,B). Three versions of this type of *akrafokonmu* were photographed in the Edwesohene's treasury in 1976, and one is worn by the bearer of the *akrafena* of Asantehene Prempeh I (r. 1888–1931; anon. 1977, 16, 17). The motif is also frequently found on stamped funerary cloths called *adinkra,* and the late Asantehene Otumfuo Opoku Ware II (r. 1970–1999) wore three finger rings with this motif on each hand during the celebration of the twenty-fifth anniversary of his reign (fig. 9.4, 9.5). The highly conventionalized maxim associated with this form is said to deal with issues of envy and jealousy, "What the *fofoo* plant wants is for the *gyinatwi* seeds to turn black."[4] The image actually represents the bud of the plant before it opens to reveal yellow florets and subsequently black star-headed seeds used for medicinal purposes. In other parts of the world, the seeds along with other parts of the plant are also recognized as a remedy for a variety of ailments. The proverb is another example of the Akan penchant for the close observation of natural phenomena. The connection with jealousy, however, is not entirely clear. Do the seeds envy the flowers for their beauty? Do the flowers envy the seeds for their curative properties? Or perhaps the name of the plant is another example of Akan wordplay where *fofɔ* is the Akan verb for "to cherish" (Christaller 1933, 131).

The basic composition of a quartered circle found on two discs (figs. 5.2, 5.4B) was identified by Asante court officials as *nkwantaanan* (lit., *nkwan,* "paths" or "roads," and *anan,* "four").[5] In general, crossroads were considered as "nodes of great spiritual power, at which protective 'medicine' was often buried, and

where rituals to defend and affirm cultural space were enacted" (McCaskie 1995, 296). In particular Nkwantaanan was the name of a ward in Kumase and an intersection where according to oral tradition the great priest Anokye buried "medicine" at the beginning of the Asante Kingdom. Shifting the locus of power from medicine to chieftaincy, Garrard recorded the proverb "the chief is like a crossroads, all paths lead to him" (1995, 440). As I have argued elsewhere, this is a motif with considerable antiquity among the Akan. This is also true for most variations of the soul disc genre, which are found attached to stools, swords, jewelry, crowns, sandals, and so forth, and appear to serve as a generalized amulet or talisman in these other contexts (see figs. 6.35, 6.36). Other likely variations of the form are the crescent-shaped pendants (fig. 5.9) that, according to Rattray, were worn by priests committed to serving the supreme deity Nyame (1923, 143).

5.8A–D Four *akrafokonmu*. Gold. DIAM (of largest): 4½ in. Clockwise from top: (A) 97.1541.2; (B) 97.1324; (C) 97.1541.1; (D) 97.1332

**5.9** Priest's ornament. Gold. DIAM: 3 ½ in. 97.1341.

**5.10** Herald's headdress. Gold leaf, monkey fur, leather. W: 11 in. 97.897.

Virtually identical in size and design to the *akrafokonmu* are the repoussé bosses centered on the seat of select royal stools (fig. 5.4A). The present example is distinguished from the former by the absence of conduits on each side to carry the pineapple fiber cord and by the series of over one hundred fifty small holes encircling the perimeter of the piece. These were used to attach it to the stool and to additional repoussé strips that once radiated from it (cf. figs. 2.7–2.9). As mentioned earlier, stools are thought to be the repository of their owner's *ɔkra*, especially those decorated ceremonial stools that are the primary seat for a chief during his lifetime and are destined for the stool room after his demise. It seems likely that the discs found on stools serve as the same kind of signifier as those worn by *akrafo*, designating a locus of protection for the chief that they serve.

### Other Regalia

In addition to those hats worn by sword bearers, another distinctive headdress (*adomasa*) is worn by the court criers or heralds (*nseniefoɔ*, sing. *nsenie*; figs. 5.10, 5.11). Heralds were and still are charged with maintaining silence and order at the Asante court and with imploring the audience to pay attention, punctuating speeches by chiefs and counselors with exclamations such as "Tie! Tie! Kom! Fwe! Fwe! (Listen! Listen! Silence! Behold! Behold!)" (Rattray 1923, 184). They were also couriers of royal decrees, such as the imposition of a new tax or conscription for the army, to outlying towns and villages. In addition, they often accompanied and assisted counselors or sword bearers on official diplomatic missions. In the nineteenth century they were said to number one thousand and were concentrated in a single ward in Kumase (Wilks 1975, 401, 439; McCaskie 1995, 308–9). Distinguished by a large rectangular plaque covered

5.11 Heralds of the Asantehene at the twenty-fifth anniversary of the reign of Otumfuo Opoku Ware II. Photograph by Frank Fournier, Kumase, 1995.

with gold leaf on the front, the remainder of the hat is made from the fur of a black colobus monkey.

Whether the plaque began as an amulet, or *suman*, is unclear. The significance of the colobus monkey skin has not been documented, although Rattray records an Asante myth that says when the supreme deity Nyame "created and named all things he went about accompanied by the *efo* (colobus monkey)" (Rattray 1916, 54), and such precedence perhaps relates to the fact the heralds have the "privilege" on ritual occasions of drinking even before the chief or king" (Rattray 1927, 279). Male hunchbacks in particular were once destined to be heralds, which in no way diminished the importance of the position. In the hierarchy of court officials Rattray indicates that the heralds ranked higher than drummers, horn blowers, and executioners (1923, 263). Today lawyers, industrialists, and bankers hold positions as *nseniefoɔ*.

Some of the most abundant and complex regalia of Akan court officials is that worn by the *adumfoɔ* and *atumtufoɔ*. These two positions are not very well distinguished and are variously translated as "constabulary," "bodyguards," and "executioners" (fig. 5.12). They typically carry gold and silver ornamented firearms and wear skullcaps similar to those worn by some of the sword bearers. Despite European efforts to control the trade, Asante and many other Akan armies were relatively well equipped with firearms by the middle of the eighteenth century. These officials also wear a bandolier (*ntoa*) composed of a ration pouch, cartridge containers, powder horn, and a series of knives called *sɛpɔ* (figs. 5.13, 5.14). *Sɛpɔ* are typically referred to as "executioners' knives" and were once thrust through the cheeks of a criminal to prevent oaths against the chief before another *sɛpɔ* was used to decapitate the victim. Rattray noted that many of the old *sɛpɔ* he saw appeared to have been "bread or carving knives imported from

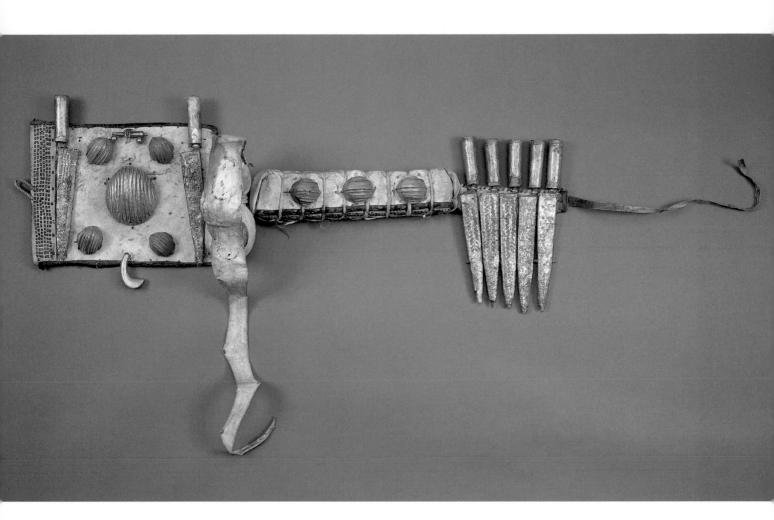

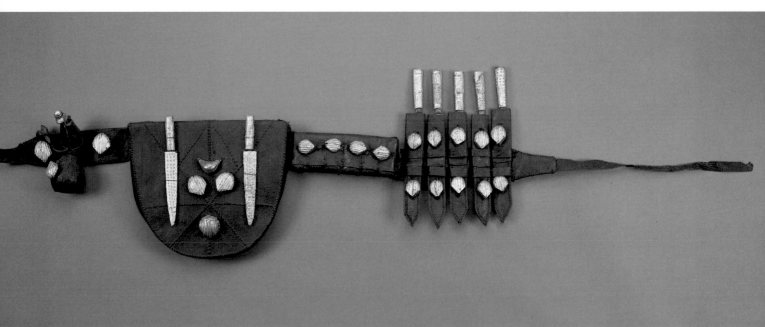

5.12  Asante musket bearer.
Photograph by Doran H.
Ross, Mampon, 1976.

5.13  Gunbearer's regalia.
Gold leaf, metal, leather,
fiber. L: 39 in. 97.743.

5.14  Gunbearer's regalia.
Gold leaf, leather, fiber.
L: 59 in. 97.749.

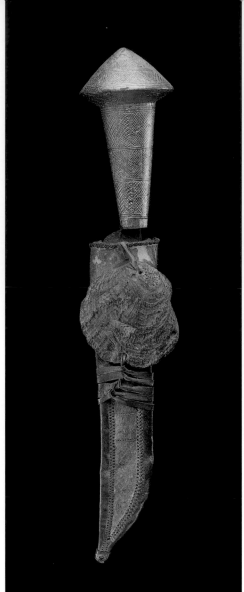

**5.15** Necklace representing gunbearer's regalia. Gold, leather, fiber. L: 19¼ in. 97.1001.

**5.16** Executioner's knife. Gold, iron, shell, leather. L: 13 in. 97.1260.A,B.

Europe" (1929, 375). Some of the Houston examples have the pig's head hall-mark of Joseph Beals and Sons and come from Sheffield, England.

*Sɛpɔ* often have gold-leaf handles and sheaths, and various parts of the rest of the *ntoa* are typically adorned with cast-gold ornaments (fig. 5.17). Some of these represent the red seashells that once adorned some state swords, as noted earlier, and are still are found on an occasional *sɛpɔ* (fig. 5.16). These shells were apparently traded from the Canary Islands at a very early date, at least before 1474, when the Portuguese noted their presence on the coast (Blake 1942, 206). They were considered very valuable and according to Garrard "were worth their weight in gold" (1989, 235). Also found on the *ntoa* are small elbow-shaped bells (fig. 5.17A). Iron versions of these bells are worn by Akan priests, and Garrard speculates that they were intended to "'summon the spirits' around the wearer, so that he would be protected from any misfortune" (1989, 234). A miniature *ntoa*, cast in gold with all of the above components represented forms an unusual, if not unique, necklace (fig. 5.15). The wearer is unknown.

Another anomalous object is the gold-covered gourd with amulets and a strap that suggests it was intended to be handheld (fig. 5.18). The only comparable

form known to me is a cloth-covered gourd with amulets in the Mamponhene's treasury. It was described by the chief as a rattle once used to "sound the alarm for war."[6] Gourds cut into hemispheres are more commonly found in Asante regalia as ritual drinking vessels. They usually occur in pairs, one decorated with silver, the other gold (see Garrard 1984, fig. 9).

Side-blown elephant-tusk trumpets (fig. 5.19) are found in varying numbers in all Akan states. The Asantehene has seven distinct horn ensembles, most with at least seven ivory trumpets. Like the royal drums, trumpets can replicate in part the tonal language of the Akan in conventionalized and idiomatic phrases. These may include announcements of initiations at festivals, praise names for chiefs, historical events, and even reminders to the chief of responsibilities to his subjects (Sarpong 1990; Carter 1971). In the past the jawbones of defeated enemies were attached to the open ends of the tusks so that the horn language was spoken through their "mouths." That the sound of the horn also resembles the "voice" of the elephant itself has the ironic effect of both the defeated enemy and the vanquished elephant singing the praises of the chief and his ancestors. One refrain of the *ntahera* horns of the Asantehene echoes some of the messages on counselors' staffs discouraging pretenders to

5.17A–D Ornaments for gunbearers' regalia. Gold. DIAM: 3½ in. Clockwise from top: (A) 97.1029; (B) 97.1038; (C) 97.1309; (D) 97.1545

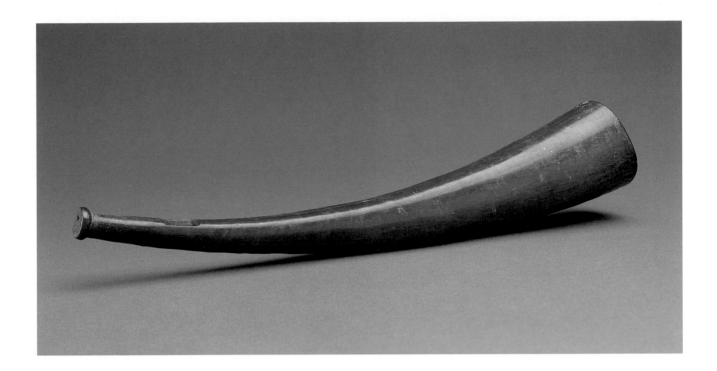

the stool: "The bush dog will like to be a leopard but he could not. Somebody will like to be the King but he could not" (Boaten I 1993, 39).

In the court of the Asantehene the royal gong players fall under the head of the heralds (*nseniehene*). Like the heralds, whom they sometimes accompanied, gong beaters also announced government decrees. Although gongs are not singled out in the regalia lists mentioned previously, they are a standard component of the *fɔntɔmfrɔm* orchestra, the most important of the state drum ensembles, and are part of a number of other drum groups. Figurative handles on gongs are not uncommon, but gold-leaf examples are extremely rare (fig. 5.20). The beautifully carved grip of this gong is configured as if it were a sword handle, and it may have begun as one, being added to the gong at some later date. The end of the handle features one of the most popular of all Akan images— the *sankɔfa* bird discussed in some detail on p. 81.

At one time elephant-tail fly whisks (*mena*) were ubiquitous in the courts of many Akan chiefs (fig. 5.21). At the Asante Odwira festival of 1817, Bowdich observed "elephant tails, waving like a small cloud" (1819 [1966], 39). A photograph from the early 1960s taken as a part of Kyerematen's study for *The Panoply of Ghana* documents twenty-three elephant-tail fly whisks in the regalia at Nkoranza.[7] Traditionally the whisk was a symbol of entitlement, the "heraldic badge" earned by the *ɔbirempɔn* (lit., "big man") and conferred by the Asantehene. This title was given to the most successful accumulators of wealth and was held by the heads of hereditary chiefdoms (McCaskie 1995, 275). In the Asante Kingdom, only the Asantehene is allowed to possess a gold-handled elephant tail (see Ross 1992b, 143–45).

There has been substantial speculation on the relationship between wealth and the elephant tail. Wilks considers it in relation to the proverb, "The elephant's tail is short, but it is able to sweep flies away." He goes on to explain:

5.18 (OPPOSITE)
Gourd with amulets. Gold leaf, gourd, leather, fiber.
L: 10 ½ in. 97.1344.

5.19 (ABOVE)
Trumpet. Ivory.
L: 15 ½ in. 97.1410.

**5.20** Gong with *sankɔfa* bird. Gold leaf, iron, wood. L: 23 in. 97.874.

**5.21** Fly whisk. Gold leaf, elephant tail, leather, fiber. L: 24 in. 97.864.

The sense is that the elephant did not allow the handicap of a short tail to prevent him from achieving preeminence…thus should the citizen sweep away all obstacles in his or her pursuit of riches. The elephant tail or *mena* is the symbol in other words, not so much of wealth as such, but rather of the accomplishment and achievement which characterize the acquisitive process. [Wilks 1975, 15]

A more convoluted, but nevertheless intriguing, analysis by McCaskie sees a connection between "both wealth and excrement [and] their capacity to transgress and to rupture categorical boundaries" (1983, 31).

In 1817 W. Hutchison observed a display for an *ɔbirɛmpɔn*:

This week past Apokoo and several of the captains have been making an exhibition of their riches; this is generally done once in life, by those who are in favour with the King, and think themselves free from palavers. It is done by making their gold into various articles of dress for show. Apokoo, who sent for me before his uproar began, showed me his varieties, weighing upwards of 800 bendas of the finest gold; among the articles, was [a] girdle two inches broad. Gold chains for the neck, arms, legs, &c. ornaments for the ankles of all descriptions, consisting of manacles, with keys, bells, chairs [stools?], and padlocks. For his numerous family of wives, children, and captains, were armlets and various ornaments. A superb cap of eagle's feathers, fetishes, Moorish charms &c. Moorish caps, silk dresses, purses, bags, &c. made of monkey skin. Fans with ivory handles made of tiger [leopard] skin, and decorated with silk. New umbrellas made in fantastical shapes, gold swords and figures of animals, birds, beasts, and fishes of the same metal; his drums, and various instruments of music, were covered with tiger [leopard] skin, with red belts for hanging them. Ivory arrows and bows, covered with silk and skins, and many other weapons of war or fancy, such as the mind in a like situation would devise. [Hutchison 1819 (1966), 395]

Obviously this display includes many of the object types discussed in the present volume, and emphasizes the importance of the position of *ɔbirɛmpɔn*. ●

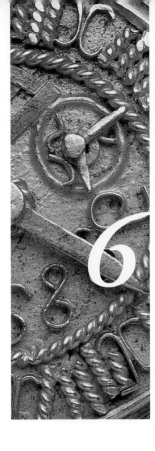

# 6 Clothed in Gold

## THE ADORNMENT OF CHIEFS

The adornment of chiefs may include twenty or more cast-gold or gold-leafed ornaments and other accessories, and queen mothers are only slightly less well-adorned (figs. 6.1–6.3). In wealthier states these are selected from a much larger wardrobe that offers multiple examples of sandals, crowns, cloths, and various jewelry types. Akan royal adornment is among the most ostentatious in all of Africa. It is also among the most conceptually complicated with a rich mosaic of messages proclaimed in the visually stunning ensembles.

### Sandals

A good argument can be made that of all the items worn or held by an Akan chief, the most significant are sandals (*mpaboa*) of which an important chief may have half a dozen pairs or more. In the early 1960s the Asantehene had at least ten pairs. While in European traditions the crown is the defining adornment of a monarch, in most Akan states it is gold-ornamented sandals that identify a ruler (fig. 6.4). The selection of ornaments and their composition on sandal straps are indeed shared by one style of Akan crown (*abotire*), and it seems highly probable that the influence was from sandal to crown rather than the reverse. The Asantehene has a special court official whose sole responsibility is the security and care of the chief's sandals (*mpaboahene*). In other Akan states responsibility for the sandals is grouped with the rest of the regalia, but there would be designated sandal bearers to carry selected pairs in procession in front of the chief during major festivals (fig. 6.5).

During the rite of enstoolment for a new Asantehene, at the climactic moment when he is placed three times upon the Golden Stool, the Asantehene-elect wears the Mpaboakɛseɛ, or Great Sandals, thought to have been originally worn by Osei Tutu I (Kyerematen 1970, 26, 27). These sandals contain special

6.1 Odeneho Oduro Numapau II, paramount chief of the Asante state of Asumegya. Photograph by Doran H. Ross, 1976.

6.2 (PAGE 134) Nana Adoku V, paramount chief of the Fante state of Mankesim. Photograph by Doran H. Ross, 1975.

6.3 (PAGE 135) Queen mother of the Fante state of Abeadze Dominase. Photograph by Doran H. Ross, 1975.

**6.4** Sandals and footrest of Odeneho Oduro Numapau II (see fig. 6.1). Photograph by Doran H. Ross, Asumegya, 1975.

medicines and are worn on only the most important of occasions (Boaten I 1993, 33). As early as 1817 Bowdich noted that the Asantehene's sandals were adorned with amulets, "his sandals, of a soft white leather, were embossed across the instep band with small gold and silver cases of saphies" (1819 [1966], 38–39). Bowdich defined these *asuman,* which he referred to as *saphies,* as "Scraps of Moorish writing [used] as charms against evil" (1819 [1966], 32).

Kyerematen emphasized the importance of sandals in the regalia of a chief: "It is taboo for a chief to walk barefoot; if he does, it is believed that he will precipitate a famine. When the deposition of a chief is declared, one of the first symbolic acts is to remove his sandals and force him to walk away barefoot. At the same time his stool is removed from the public meeting-place where he is declared destooled or deposed" (1964, 85). When coming into the presence of a chief, subordinates are required to remove their sandals (or other footwear) in deference to the ruler; and if they are in traditional dress, they must bare their shoulders or tie their cloths around their waists. The only time a chief would voluntarily take his feet out of his own sandals is when entering the stool room of his ancestors, and even then he would place his feet on top of his sandals.

The German missionaries Friedrich August Ramseyer and Johannes Kühne from the Basel Missionary Society—who were held captive by the Asante from 1869 to 1874 during the reign of Asantehene Kofi Kakari (r. 1867–1874)—seemed to have paid particular attention to the role of sandals in Asante society. Sandals were sufficiently important to be listed among other items as part of the tribute paid by vassal states to the king (1875, 105). They described the palace of the Dwabenhene as "a richly ornamental building, the broad gateway of which was surmounted by some gold sandals" (1875, 53). They also noted that only chiefs

**6.5** Sandal bearers of the Asantehene at the twenty-fifth anniversary of the reign of Otumfuo Opoku Ware II. Photograph by Frank Fournier, Kumase, 1995.

**6.6** Chief's sandals. Gold leaf, leather. L: 14½ in. 97.1349.A,B.

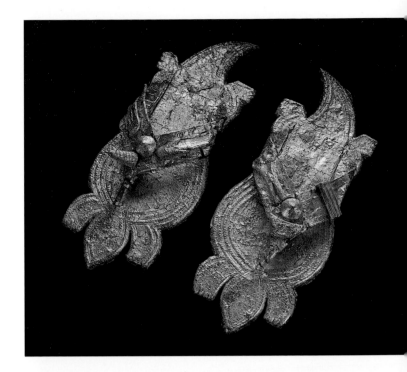

of the highest rank were "allowed to have sandals ornamented with silver and gold, like those of the king" (1875, 307). The missionaries' first meeting with Kofi Kakari was canceled by the king because of the theft of a pair of gold sandals from the palace (1875, 69). Thirty-one months later the missionaries reported a "great disturbance":

> The keeper of the king's sandals had during the last two years sold several cast off pairs. The king found it out, and demanded the name of the buyer, to whom he said, "I do not like any one to dishonour my talisman" (referring to the Arabic writing on the sandals). The affair was brought into court, the man was beheaded, and twenty people imprisoned, six of whom were bound in irons, but at length the king wearied of prosecuting the affair, pardoned the criminals. [Ramseyer and Kühne 1875, 140]

One pair of Arabic-inscribed sandals taken from Kofi Kakari's palace in the Anglo-Asante war of 1874 has been discussed in some detail (Bravmann and Silverman 1987). On the soles of each sandal are several references to Allah and the invocation "in the name of God" along with magic squares incorporating some of the great names of Allah (1987, 106–7; see the discussion of Islamic amulets below).

Two of the five pairs of sandals in the Glassell Collection not only have gold ornaments on the straps but also have the upper surfaces of the soles completely covered in gold leaf ( figs. 6.6, 6.7). As might be imagined, this exceptionally rare feature is reserved for only the highest-ranking paramount chiefs. One of these pairs of sandals has soles made to resemble crocodiles (fig. 6.6), and another pair in the Houston collection is made in the shape of scorpions (fig. 6.8). The focal point of each sandal is located where the straps

**6.7** Chief's sandals. Gold leaf, leather. L: 12 in. 97.1350.A,B.

join the toe piece and is frequently accented with a soul-disc-like rosette. The yellow *fofoo* flower discussed earlier is another motif commonly positioned at this juncture, as are other images drawn from nature, such as the coiled snake in figure 6.9 and the bird in figure 6.10. The latter looks remarkably similar to the *asantrofie,* or night bird, seen as a cast-gold ornament on one of the Edwesohene's state swords. This bird motif addresses the dilemmas inherent in decision making, "If you take *asantrofiie* you bring bad luck, if you leave *asantrofie* you lose good fortune," a kind of "damned if you do, damned if you don't" situation.[1]

In addition to these potent symbolic statements, the straps of the sandals carry additional messages about chieftaincy and governance. The oblong fluted forms on figures 6.7 and 6.9 are actually representations of insect cocoons and are more frequently seen in cast form as gold weights. The form is also found on a sword ornament of the Nkwawie stool (Menzel 1968, 53). The image is meant to suggest a dilemma: "It is a puzzle to know how the caterpillar entered its cocoon; did it build it before entering it or did it build it around itself?" (Menzel 1968, 181). In other words, some things are destined to remain a mystery. The meaning of this proverb in a royal context is unclear. The sandals with scorpion-shaped soles

**6.8** Chief's sandals. Gold leaf, leather. L: 13¼ in. 97.1507.A,B.

**6.9** Chief's sandals. Gold leaf, leather. L: 12 in. 97.1347.A,B.

have four coiled snakes on the straps of each. Although I have not seen this combination before, it is reasonable to imagine the Akan attributing the sting of the insect and the bite of the serpent to the powers of the chief and the military might of the state. Joining the *asantrofie* on the straps of figure 6.10 are a star, moon, and a cock. The round nutlike shapes are tiger nuts said to demonstrate the virility of the chief. The pair of sandals with the crocodile soles (fig. 6.6) has a knife, a fish, and a snail on one set of sandal straps, and a pair of scissors, a moon, and an insect cocoon, like those discussed above, on the other. This complex and important pair of sandals merits more research.

**6.10** Chief's sandals. Gold leaf, leather. L: 11 in. 97.1351.A,B.

The importance of sandals, as well as the related concepts of nobility, mobility, and insulation from harm, is further emphasized by the ankle charms (*abirempon naaseɛ*) that are worn with them on most ceremonial occasions (see fig. 6.4). These amulets are rooted in both indigenous *asuman* and long-standing beliefs in the efficacy of Islam. Most of these anklets feature a series of triangular charms that reflect the much larger triangular amulets suspended from the neck of many chiefs (see below).

### Crowns

Royal crowns do not seem to play the same ritual roles as sandals, nor do they participate in any rigid ceremonial proscriptions. While two or three pairs of a chief's sandals may be present in a festival procession—each with its own bearers—crowns never appear to receive this treatment. The presence of sandals in the gold-weight corpus and the absence of crowns affirm the relative importance of the former and suggest that the latter may be a somewhat late addition to the regalia of the Akan.

While Akan chiefs wear a wide variety of royal headgear—in each case typically referred to as a "crown"—the Asante generally limit themselves to velvet headbands (*abotire*) with two short vertical projections at the back (figs. 6.11, 6.12) called "bongo's horns" after a type of powerful and elusive antelope found in the forest (Rattray 1927, 275). This antelope is also considered the most spiritually dangerous of animals (Rattray 1923, 171). The *abotire* is adorned with wood ornaments covered in gold leaf, which are of the same type and scale as those found on sandals. One of the most common ornaments on both items of regalia is called *musuyideɛ* (lit., "misfortune, remove"), that is, an amulet or charm to protect (fig. 6.13 and see fig. 6.3). This is also a common motif on

**6.11** Nana Boakye Yiadom II, paramount chief of the Asante state of Agona. Photograph by Doran H. Ross, 1980.

**6.12** Barima Asumadu Sakyi II, paramount chief of the Asante state of Kumawu. Photograph by Doran H. Ross, 1976.

Asante stamped cloths called *adinkra*, which was probably originally influenced by Arabic inscribed cloths (pp. 159–67).[2] Nevertheless, its popularity on crowns was probably reinforced by the presence of a virtually identical motif—the Maltese cross—on the crowns of English royalty, which adorned trade goods and royal gifts from Great Britain for over three hundred years. A second crown with *musuyideɛ* also has butterfly imagery and shapes that resemble bowties (fig. 6.14). An *abotire* with much older ornaments actually has a series of leather Koranic amulets covered with delicately embossed gold leaf (fig. 6.15). The intersection of the amulets is punctuated by sheet gold flowers.

Aside from *abotire,* all other hats and head covers, royal and nonroyal, fall under the heading *ɛkye.* Two velvet hats in the collection undoubtedly served as chiefs' crowns, probably among coastal Akan (figs. 6.16, 6.17). Both are covered with simulated amulet forms; and one is topped with a star and crescent, and the other with a standing lion. Given the long-standing and well-documented presence of Muslims at the Asante court in Kumase and in other Akan areas, it would be easy to assume that the star and crescent were Islamic religious symbols. While the associations may exist, the Akan have several proverbs relating to the stars and the moon that deal with the relationship of the chief and his subjects. At the Asante paramountcy of Kumawu elders said simply of this motif that "The star lives longer than the moon," recognizing that the stars are more constant than the moon, which goes through a series of phases. Here the chief is likened to the star and admired for his reliability. A dissenting voice at Kumawu said the image illustrated the saying "The star delights in marriage to the moon,"

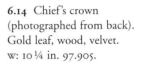

**6.13** Chief's crown. Gold leaf, wood, velvet. W: 10 in. 97.902.

**6.14** Chief's crown (photographed from back). Gold leaf, wood, velvet. W: 10 ¼ in. 97.905.

**6.15** Chief's crown (photographed from back). Gold leaf, wood, velvet. DIAM: 9 in. 97.903.

**6.16** Chief's crown.
Gold leaf, wood, velvet.
DIAM: 9 in. 97.891.

and identified the moon with the chief.[3] Regarding
a series of star and moon motifs on an *abotire* in
Kumase, Garrard recorded the proverb "The evening
star, desirous of being married, always stays close
to the moon." He explained, "In the political
context it would indicate that the people love their
chief and will support him" (1989, 224). The lion
on the hat in figure 6.17 with its recurved S-shaped
("reflexive") tail is part of the complex of heraldic
lion images discussed earlier (see pp. 66–68).

Three crowns in the Glassell Collection clearly
have closer ties with European traditions than with
indigenous practices. The rampant lions flanking
a heart on one are yet another example of the
influence of European heraldry (fig. 6.18). On the same crown the two arches
spanning the sides and front and back, along with the alternating cross and
fleur-de-lis, are historic conventions used by British royalty. The fleur-de-lis is
a popular device on southern Akan crowns and is found on a second Glassell
example (fig. 6.19). Much like the conflation of *musuyidee* and Maltese cross
considered on the *abotire* at the beginning of this section, the Akan identify
an indigenous *adinkra* motif *akokɔ nan* (lit., "hen's foot") with the fleur-de-lis.
The proverb associated with the Akan motif was on two occasions assigned
to the French-inspired design on a crown.[4] It is the same as that elicited with
reference to the counselor's staff of a hen and her chicks (see figs. 4.26, 4.28):
"The hen's foot may step on its chicks, but it does not kill them." This crown
also has three clusters of three zodiac signs each (see the discussion of zodiac
rings below) and is topped by a rampant guardant lion holding a globe.

A final European-inspired crown is perhaps better attributed to the Ewe
peoples east of the Akan (fig. 6.20). Nevertheless, the motif of an elephant and a
small antelope centered on the front represents the familiar Akan maxim "The
elephant is big for nothing, it is the duiker that rules the forest" (see also fig. 3.25).
The leaflike projections surrounding the crown were identified by Kumase
regalia dealers as *aya*, a type of fern, and elicited the assertion "The chief does
not fear insults," an expression apparently prompted by the similarity of the
Akan words for *fern* and *insult*.[5] Stamped, incised, and repoussé crowns such as
this are rare; the closest comparable example is from Akuapem and dates to
1896 (Garrard 1989, 82).

**6.17** Chief's crown.
Gold leaf, wood, velvet.
DIAM: 10½ in. 97. 898.

**6.18** (OPPOSITE)
Chief's crown. Gold leaf,
wood. DIAM: 9 ½ in. 97.787.

**6.19** Chief's crown. Gold,
velvet. DIAM: 9 ½ in. 97.786.

**6.20** Chief's crown.
Repoussé gold.
DIAM: 7 in. 97.788.

**6.21A,B** Bracelet and necklace. Gold, fiber cord. L: 14 ¾ in. (A) bracelet: 97.945; (B) necklace: 97.1012.

*Jewelry*

Among the most frequently encountered royal necklaces are those consisting of a diverse assortment of gold and sometimes glass beads typically strung in an apparently random order. Called *asuman* (charm, amulet, talisman), these are royal versions of more plebian necklaces that are made without gold and might have an assortment of elements made from shell, wood, teeth, bone, and so forth. Both royal and nonroyal variants were worn as a remedy or for protection against malevolent forces. That gold was seen to have certain protective powers in itself enhanced the efficacy of the royal necklaces and bracelets. European recognition of the Akan belief in *asuman* led to the misleading phrase "fetish gold," which unfortunately is still frequently used despite its demeaning implications for Akan religion.

Some of the earliest European accounts of coastal Akan peoples documented the lavish wearing of gold jewelry. In 1482, Caramansa, the ruler of the Fante peoples around the newly constructed Portuguese fort of São Jorge da Mina (Elmina), was described thus: "his arms and legs and neck were covered with chains and trinkets of gold in many shapes, and countless bells and large beads of gold were hanging from the hair of his beard and his head" (Blake 1942, 73). Pieter de Marees's description of the King of Saboe (Asebu) written before 1602 is similar, "He is beautifully adorned in accordance with their fashion and manner, his Beard strung with many gold Beads and other finery; he has gold bangles and other beautifully coloured Beads around his arms and legs, as well as around his neck" (1602 [1987], 96).

Jean Barbot visited the coastal Akan twice in 1678–1679 and 1681–1682 and recorded his impressions in two manuscripts and two published books. He was sufficiently interested in Akan goldwork to execute carefully rendered drawings of gold beads, and he even brought back a small collection, which unfortunately has been lost. Barbot's images of Akan beadwork have been compiled by Garrard (1989, 54, 55), and many are very similar to beads found in the Glassell Collection that were produced between two hundred and two hundred fifty years later. Even more tangible evidence of gold beads from this period has been retrieved from the wreck of the Whydah, a slave ship captured by pirates then lost off of Cape Cod in 1717. A number of cast-gold disc-shaped beads have been recovered from the wreck since 1984, and here again the designs are familiar in much later examples (Ehrlich 1989, 52–57).

One form of chief's bracelet is called *ɔkrakyere* (lit., "soul-binder"), which according to Christaller consists of "gold and precious beads fastened to the

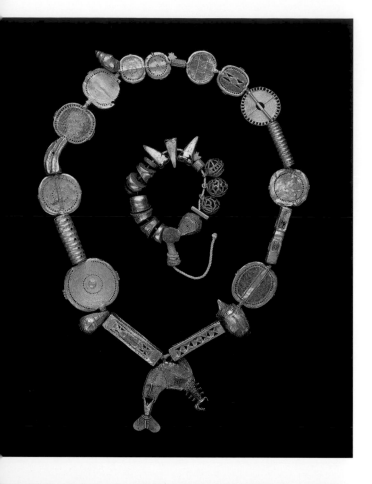

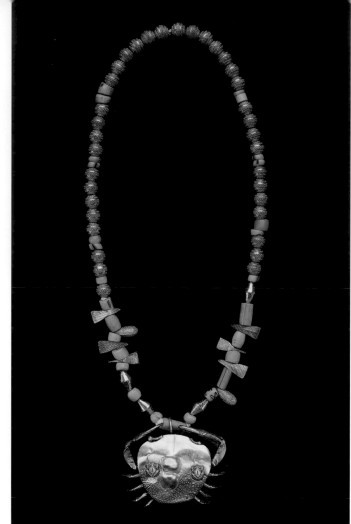

wrist of the right hand in thankful acknowledgment to the '*kra*' for having enriched the person" (1933, 264). I have not encountered this bracelet name myself, but it is tempting to think about this as a partial explanation for the disc-shaped beads often found on bracelets as miniature versions of *akrafokonmu*. At the very least it underscores the various spiritual components that infuse Akan jewelry.

Knowledgeable specialists in the production, selling, and custodianship of royal jewelry are generally careful to indicate with considerable consistency which pieces are appropriate to be worn by a chief versus a queen mother, or which pieces should be worn on the right arm as opposed to the left. These rules, however, appear to be not particularly well known, widespread, or rigid, since they are honored as often in the breach as in the observance.

The inventory of personal adornment of chiefs and queen mothers is enormous and diverse. The variety of chain and bead designs alone has a vocabulary of identification and interpretation that remains someone's future dissertation. The center pieces on the necklaces in the Glassell Collection include several mudfish, a crab, a lock, a stool with lion support, a beetle, and a heart with heraldic lions (figs. 6.21–6.23). Bead elements on these necklaces include a book, tortoise, eagle, teeth, bells, nuggets, and coins.

Jewelry images, due to their small scale and placement, do not offer the same potential for public statement as do sword ornaments or counselors' staffs. Nevertheless, by virtue of its material, jewelry is quite obviously a statement of wealth, a fact made even more explicit by the incorporation of natural nuggets into necklaces and bracelets (figs. 6.24, 6.25). This may have been the first use of gold in personal adornment before techniques for working the precious metal were introduced from the Mande areas in what is now Mali.[6] Paul Isert, resident on the coast for over three years beginning in November 1783, wrote that "Sometimes nuggets are found that weigh one ounce or more but this kind is seldom seen by the European, because the Black drills a hole through such a nugget and wears it as an ornament around his neck or wrist, calling it 'fetish gold'" (1788 [1992], 86). In the absence of natural nuggets, Akan goldsmiths have long produced lost-wax castings of nuggets that convincingly pass for the real thing.

A further extension of jewelry as a self-conscious display of wealth is the inclusion of European coinage as bead elements on jewelry (fig. 6.26). Isert noted this practice during his stay on the Gold Coast in relation to elite female adornment: "These bracelets have pendants of gold pieces, such as louis d'or

**6.22A,B** (OPPOSITE, TOP LEFT) Bracelet and necklace. Gold, fiber cord. L: 30 in. (A) bracelet: 97.925; (B) necklace: 97.1025.

**6.23** (OPPOSITE, TOP RIGHT) Necklace with crab pendant. Gold. L: 15 ¾ in. 97.1008.

**6.24** (OPPOSITE, BOTTOM LEFT) Necklace with ornaments and beads. Gold. L: 15 ½ in. 97.998.

**6.25** (OPPOSITE, BOTTOM RIGHT) Necklace with nuggets. Gold, coral. L: 13 ½ in. 97.999.

**6.26** Necklace with mudfish pendant and coins. Gold, gold coins. L: 12 in. 97.1014.

**6.27** Necklace with beads and ornaments. Gold, glass beads. L: 16 in. 97.1520.

or Johannes." Isert's translator notes that "The Louis d'or is the French gold coin used 1640–1803, and the Johannes is the Portuguese gold coin, the João, minted 1722–1835" (1788 [1992], 116). The Glassell Collection has necklaces featuring cast replicas of European coins, some featuring the image of Queen Victoria as discussed in Frances Marzio's essay in this volume (figs. 6.24, 7.8). Ironically this occasionally involved turning a real silver coin into a faux gold coin where the "replica" is more valuable than its authentic precursor.

The central pendant on figure 6.24 is not, in fact, of Akan workmanship but was produced by the Tukulor peoples (Peul or Fulani) of Senegal (Johnson 1994, 39).[7] Similar Senegalese cruciform pendants were also documented by Garrard in an Akan context (1989, 153, 222). Its small scale and relatively high value make gold jewelry portable wealth, and it is not unusual for jewelry elements to be exchanged over large distances. Just as European jewelry forms found their way as objects and influences into the Akan repertory, so have many African ornaments, still difficult to trace, entered into a rich variety of Akan personal adornment.

Common bead elements on necklaces include cocoa (cacao) pods and tools used in the cultivation, harvesting, and preparation of cocoa, including the distinctive hooked blade used for cutting cocoa from the higher branches of trees (fig. 6.25, 6.28). Cocoa is, of course, the source of chocolate. A plant indigenous to South America, cocoa was unsuccessfully introduced to Ghana

several times in the nineteenth century, and the first prosperous plantation was not established until 1879. By 1911 Ghana was the world's leading producer of cocoa beans (see Dickson and Benneh 1988, 91–96). Today, cocoa is still the leading cash crop in Ghana and significantly most of Ghana's cocoa is produced in Akan areas. One Twi nickname for cocoa is *sika dua*, literally, "gold tree" or "money tree" (Christaller 1933, 456). The importance of cocoa in Ghana's economy was made explicit in a popular highlife song of the 1950s, written in Twi by Fred Sarpong:

> If you want to send your children to school, it is cocoa
> If you want to build your house, it is cocoa
> If you want to marry, it is cocoa
> If you want to buy cloth, it is cocoa
> If you want to buy a lorry, it is cocoa
> Whatever you want to do in this world
> It is with cocoa money that you can do it. [Austin 1964, 275]

Austin notes that "it goes with a much greater swing" in Twi (1964, 275). In jewelry agendas that include such conspicuous displays of wealth as cast beads in the form of gold "nuggets," representations of cocoa are particularly appropriate.

**6.28A–C** Necklaces with cocoa implements. Gold. Length of longest: 37 in. (A) 97.1011; (B) 97.1479; (C) 97.1023.

6.29A,B Chain with lock and key pendants. Gold. Length of longer: 37 ½ in. (A) 97.1019; (B) 97.1255.

In addition to the two cocoa pods and a machete on the left necklace in figure 6.28, there are three representations of keys. The center piece of another necklace has five keys, and a third has a lock and two keys (fig. 6.29). Key and lock imagery is widespread in Akan art and is usually an explicit statement about power and control. As early as 1602 de Marees noted, "Although they may not have many Chests or Trunks, they nevertheless hang many keys around their bodies, because it looks nice" (1602 [1987], 39). One of the treasures of the Akwamu regalia consists of the keys to Christiansborg Castle, the Danish fort captured in 1693 by Akan forces. To this day bunches of keys remain part of the regalia of the Asantehene and are displayed on festival occasions (fig. 6.30). At the 1991 Akwaisidae Kɛseɛ, two officials carried bunches of "steel, silver and gold keys" in procession indicating the "enormity of the size of the palace itself" and the fact that the palace was safely secured when the king was away (Boaten I 1993, 35). While some of these keys may still function, the vast majority serve purely symbolic roles.

The cast-gold watches still found among many southern Akan chiefs also make reference to power and control (figs. 6.31–6.34). The ability to "control time"—to determine when events happen—is frequently asserted on the flags and shrines of the traditional armies (*asafo*) of the Fante. A popular image

shows a warrior holding tethers to the cock and
clock bird, both of which announce the dawn.
The notion is that the warrior group decides when
the day begins. In some examples a third tie leads
to a clock making the concept even more explicit.
Returning to the cast-gold watches of the Akan,
it must be emphasized that these do not have a
time-keeping mechanism. They are solid gold
bracelets in the shape of watches. They are still
worn in conjunction with perfectly functional,
often very expensive, watches with prestigious
logos. The cast-gold watches are obviously less
about keeping the time than with owning it and,
once more, with displaying wealth.

Besides keys and clocks, a third recurring set
of motifs that concern power and control are the
bell-shaped open-worked bead elements seen on
several of the Glassell necklaces (figs. 6.35, 6.36).
Like the keys and clocks, these are European-inspired images rooted in the
routine of slaving forts and their notions of disciplined time keeping, as intervals
were marked with the sounding of a bell. European-style bells adorn some of
the most important Akan state stools, including the Golden Stool of Asante,
where they announce the arrival of the stool while summoning the spirits of
the ancestors. By analogy the bead elements might be seen as symbolically
announcing the arrival of a chief.

Related to power, especially military power, are human teeth—both incisors
and molars—one of the most common motifs on Akan necklaces (fig. 6.36).
While there are a number of proverbs about teeth, these bead elements are
probably best understood as trophies of war. Another one of the miracles of
Ɔkɔmfɔ Anokye involved conjuring a necklace of human teeth from the heavens,
"to be augmented with the teeth of heads of state who were later vanquished
or beheaded" (Kyerematen 1966, 168). Human mandibles (*mmogye*, sing. *abogye*)
from defeated enemies were frequently attached to state drums especially
*fɔntɔmfrɔm* and to the ends of ivory trumpets. Cast-gold or gold-leaf-over-wood
versions of jaw bones are found on the shafts of counselors' staffs, bandolier
bags, sword bearers' hats, and occasionally on the same type of necklaces that
feature teeth. Beyond the trophy aspect, there may be some sense of assuming

6.30 Key bearers of the
Asantehene at the tenth
anniversary of the reign of
Otumfuo Opoku Ware II.
Photograph by Doran H.
Ross, Kumase, 1980.

153

**6.31** (OPPOSITE, TOP) Arm
wear of Nana Adoku V (see
fig. 6.2). Photograph by Doran
H. Ross, Mankesim, 1975.

**6.32A–D** (OPPOSITE, BOTTOM)
Chief's bracelets with watch-
face ornaments. Gold, metal.
L: 7 ¾ in. (A) 97.1423;
(B) 97.1421; (C) 97.1425;
(D) 97.1422.

**6.33** (RIGHT) Chief's watch
and chain. Gold. L: 25 in.
97.1424.

**6.34A,B** (BELOW) Chief's
watch-face ornaments. Gold,
metal. L: 2 ½ in. (A) 97.1426;
(B) 97.1472.

the power of one's enemies as well. This argument also applies to miniature versions of human bones found as cast-gold bead elements.

In addition to beaded forms, there are a number of bracelets and armlets that are not composed of elements strung together. Some are flexible or hinged so they can go around the wrist, and some are designed to slip over the hand (fig. 6.37). The single most common hinged form is called *benfra* and appears in a highly conventionalized form in both cast-gold and gold-leaf-over-wood versions (figs. 6.37, 6.38, 6.39B). It is almost always worn on the left wrist by chiefs, but its complex form remains enigmatic. Another hinged bracelet (fig. 6.40) is more commonly associated with queen mothers and like the umbrella finial mentioned earlier (p. 110), it is named after and represents the segmented cane *babadua* and carries the same attributes of strength and resilience.

Another common bracelet type is worn by both royal men and women. Typically the wrist band is constructed of plaited wirework with a pair of cannons as the commanding motif, evoking the military power of the state (fig. 6.41). Other bracelets worn by both sexes are skeuomorphs of knotted and tasseled cordage—cast-gold or braided-wire versions of ropework designs (figs. 6.42, 6.43).

**6.35** (OPPOSITE) Woman's necklace with ornaments. Gold, cord. L: 13 in. 97.990.

**6.36A,B** (ABOVE) Woman's bracelets with ornaments and beads. Gold, cord. DIAM: 5 ⅝ in. (A) 97.956; (B) 97.949.

**6.37** Bracelet and rings of Nana Diko Pim III (see figs. 6.46, 6.89). Photograph by Doran H. Ross, Edweso, 1976.

**6.38A,B** Chief's bracelets. Largest dimension: 5 ½ in. (A) Gold. 97.936.A,B; (B) Gold leaf and wood. 97.938.

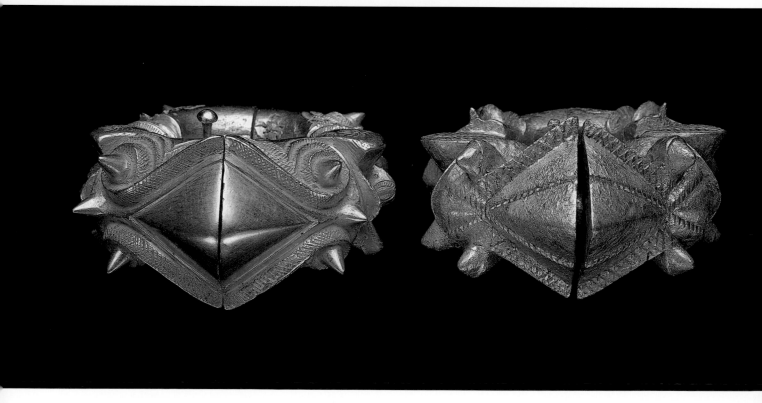

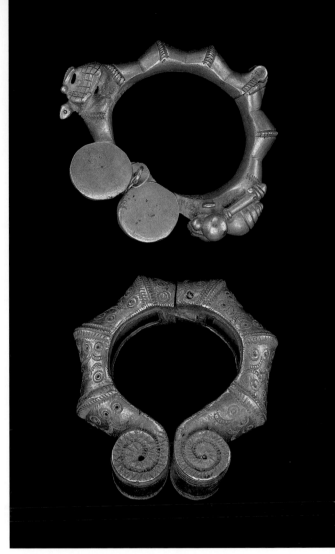

## Muslim-Influenced Adornment

Reference has previously been made to the attachment of Muslim amulets and to their representation on a wide variety of regalia including stools, swords, sandals, and crowns. Asante examples are usually encased in leather and covered with gold foil (figs. 6.31, 6.44). The Asante belief in the efficacy of Muslim charms is well-documented by the nineteenth-century British envoys. Bowdich wrote:

> But the most surprising superstition of the Ashantees, is their confidence in the fetishes or saphies they purchase so extravagantly from the Moors, believing firmly that they make them invulnerable and invincible in war, paralyse the hand of the enemy, shiver their weapons, divert the cause of balls, render both sexes prolific, and avert all evils but sickness, (which they can only assuage,) and natural death. [Bowdich 1819 [1966], 271]

A few years later Joseph Dupuis wrote of the talismans:

> Some are accounted efficacious for the cure of gunshot wounds, others for the thrust or laceration of steel weapons, and the poisoned barbs of javelins or arrows. Some on the other hand, are esteemed to possess

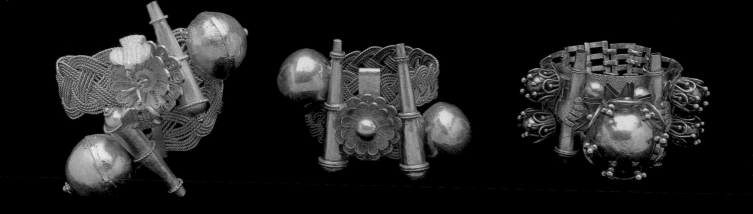

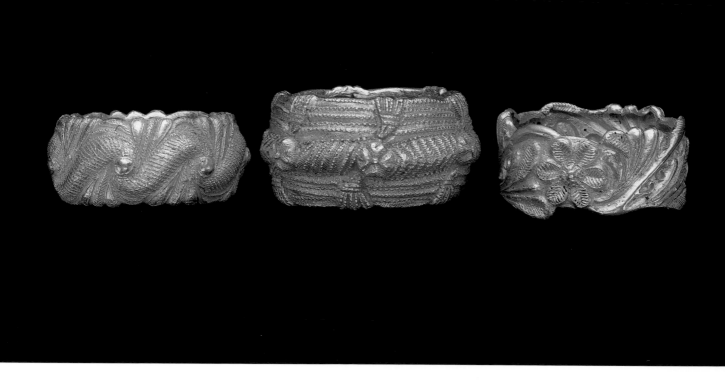

**6.41A–C** (OPPOSITE, TOP)
Chief's bracelets. Gold.
Largest dimension: 4 in.
(A) 97.1463; (B) 97.935;
(C) 97.1462.A,B.

**6.42A–C** (OPPOSITE, BOTTOM)
Chief's bracelets. Gold.
Largest dimension: 4 in.
(A) 97.959; (B) 97.948;
(C) 97.926.

**6.43** (RIGHT)  Chief's bracelet.
Gold. DIAM: 3 ¾ in. 97.1480.

**6.44** (BELOW)  Chief's
armlet. Gold leaf, wood,
fiber. L: 7 ⅞ in. 97.914.

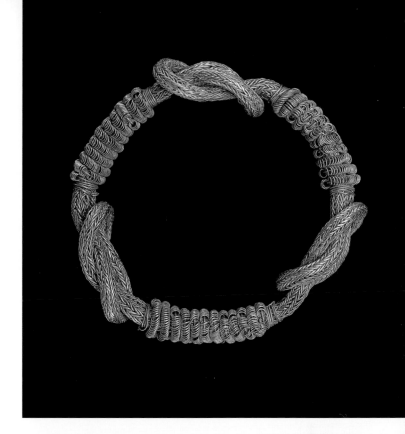

6.45 Fante military leader
in amulet-laden smock.
Photograph by Doran H.
Ross, Legu, 1976.

the virtue of rendering the wearer invulnerable in the field of battle, and
hence are worn as a preservative against the casualties of war. Besides
this class of charms, they have other cabalistic scraps for averting the
evils of natural life: these may also be subdivided into separate classes;
some for instance, are specific nostrums in certain diseases of the
human frame, some for their prevention, and some are calculated
either to ward off any impending stroke of fortune, or to raise the
proprietor to wealth, happiness and distinction. [Dupuis 1824 (1966), xi]

The greatest accumulation of these amulets is found on the war smocks
called *batakari* (figs. 6.45, 6.46), which are still found in many treasuries
and are worn today primarily during enstoolments and funerals. These were
highly valued and costly objects. "The king [Asantehene] gave to the King
of Dagwumba, for the fetish or war coat of Apokoo, the value of thirty slaves;
for Odumata's twenty; for Adoo Quamina's, nine and for Akimpon's twelve"
(Bowdich 1819 [1966], 271).

Bowdich goes on to note that "Several of the Ashantee captains offered
seriously to let us fire at them" as evidence of their confidence in these coats
(1819 [1966], 272). Bowdich actually illustrated one of these amulet-laden jackets
and described them as: "of red cloth, covered with fetishes and saphies in gold
and silver; and embroidered cases of almost every colour, which flapped against
their bodies as they moved, intermixed with small brass bells, the horns and
tails of animals, shells, and knives; long leopard tails hung down their backs,
and a small bow covered with fetishes."

In some instances the Koranic passages are not even encased but are
written on a surface. The sandals of Asantehene Kofi Kakari have already been
mentioned. When Dupuis visited Kumase in 1819, he noted that the king was
wearing "a large white cotton cloth…studded all over with Arabic writing in
various coloured inks, and of a most brilliant well formed character" (1824
[1966], 142). Dupuis also illustrated an Asante war captain riding a horse, the
latter covered with an Arabic-inscribed cloth (1824 [1966], opposite 223). Such
cloths are still in use, and Asantehene Otumfuo Opoku Ware II wore one
during a portion of the proceedings celebrating the twenty-fifth anniversary
of his reign (fig. 6.47).

David Owusu-Ansah has analyzed a corpus of Arabic manuscripts now
housed in the Royal Library, Copenhagen, that most likely originated in Kumase
during the reign of Asantehene Osei Tutu Kwame (r. 1804–1823). He concludes

**6.46** Nana Diko Pim III, Asante paramount chief of Edweso in *batakarikesee*. Photograph by Doran H. Ross, Edweso, 1976.

that they "were written for the king as a result of direct demands he made on the northern imams" and "were probably treasured by the king who saw them as powerful amulets to be consulted in times of crisis" (1991, 15). Most of the nine hundred folios contain prescriptions or formulae for the making of charms and amulets. Owusu-Ansah divides them into six categories:

1. Amulets for military purposes;
2. Amulets for everyday protection;
3. Offensive amulets: to kill one's enemy or bring evil upon him;
4. Amulets to guarantee influence, wealth, respect and peace;
5. Amulets to secure marriages, cure specific diseases, and protect pregnancy; and
6. Multipurpose charms. [Owusu-Ansah 1991, 43]

**6.47** Asantehene Otumfuo Opoku Ware II wearing an Arabic-inscribed cloth at the twenty-fifth anniversary of his reign. Photograph by Frank Fournier, Kumase, 1995.

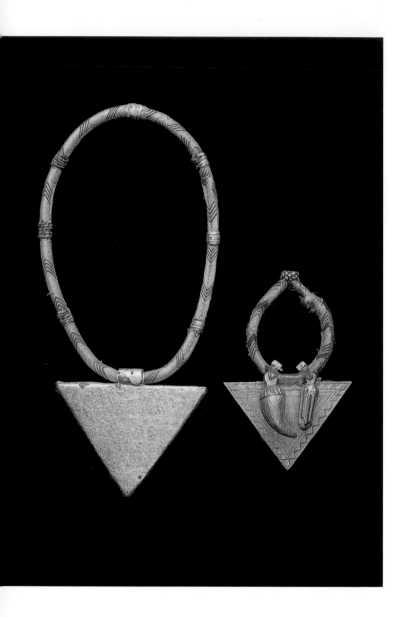

6.48A,B Chief's necklace and armlet. Gold leaf, wood, gold, fiber. Largest dimension: 16 ⅝ in. (A) 97.1006; (B) 97.976.

Many of the texts are passages from the Koran or other Muslim holy books often accompanied by a *khatim* (magical square) or diagrams.

After the inscription is written on paper, it is folded in a prescribed manner and usually wrapped in string according to numerically significant formulae. It is then covered in tanned leather, leopard or lion skin, red felt, gold, or silver and sometimes a combination of the above.[8] Although most amulets are created for specific purposes, they are named by the Akan on the basis of their external shape rather than for any intended function. One of the most distinctive of these forms is the large triangular pendant worn around the neck (fig. 6.48). These charms are found across West Africa and are frequently represented on Yoruba sculpture from southwest Nigeria where they are called *tirah* (cf. Thompson 1974, pls. 55, 94). At the Asantehene's court these talismans are called "hawk's tail" (*asansatɔɔ*) based on a certain visual congruence, but not without allusions to the raptor's predatory skills.[9] The most elaborate ensemble of amulets is worn above the right elbow and called *sɛbɛ dontwon,* the etymology of which is unclear (figs. 6.31, 6.44, 6.49F). Other amulets are named after corncobs, insect cocoons, and guinea fowl beaks based on visual correspondence to their namesakes.

Even though the vast majority of Akan chiefs today are Christian, the shapes of these amulet forms persist (without their efficacious contents) as part of the conventions of personal adornment. As the same time, nineteenth-century examples are maintained in the treasuries of many states.

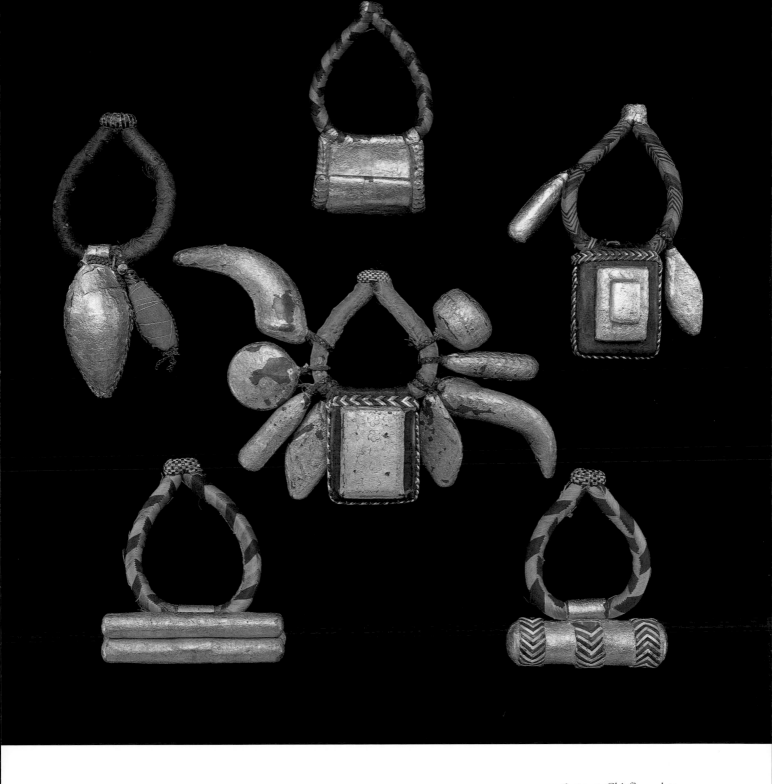

**6.49A–F** Chief's armlets.
Gold leaf, leather, fiber,
wood, and other materials.
Largest dimension: 9 in.
Center and clockwise from
top: (A) 97.978; (B) 97.913;
(C) 97.915; (D) 97.911;
(E) 97.977; (F) 97.912.

167

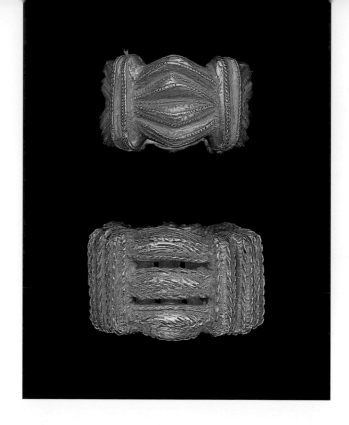

**6.50A,B** Chief's rings. Gold.
Largest dimension: 1½ in.
(A) 97.1200; (B) 97.1238.

## Finger Rings

Gold rings, bracelets, and necklaces were mentioned in some of the earliest European accounts of coastal Akan adornment. James Lok visited the area in 1554 and noted, "Some of their women weare on their bare armes certain foresleeves made of plates of beaten gold. On their fingers also they weare rings, made of golden wires, like a knot or wreathe" (Blake 1942 [1967], 2: 343). Cast skeuomorphs of wirework rings are still found in Akan treasuries (fig. 6.50). Pieter de Marees apparently sailed to the Gold Coast several times before 1602 and wrote that "The people here are very ingenious in making things, especially in working gold; for they make remarkably beautiful gold chains and other ornaments, such as Rings etc." (1602 [1987], 85).

An important Akan chief, on occasion, may wear a cast-gold ring (*mpetea*) on each finger and indeed on each thumb, although slightly more restrained displays are the norm (figs. 6.51–6.53). The hand is one of the most expressive parts of the human body and is integral to the rich Akan arts of gesture and dance. Rings, of course, bring even more attention to the hands and help amplify their expressive potential. Robert Farris Thompson in his celebrated book, *African Art in Motion,* emphasized this point.

> For a Western person to comprehend the moral power of danced art in Africa, he must divest his mind of various prejudicial junk and start from the beginning. Understanding can begin with so simple a phenomenon as the wearing of a ring. On 1 January 1972 the [Asante] king of Agogo, Ghana, during a ceremonial, slowly extended his right arm, and turned his hand slowly, slowly, so that a ring in the form of a fish could be clearly seen. The motif of the fish cited a proverb, "fish out of water dies, king without followers ceases to exist," and the style compared with other forms of classic Akan jewelry and miniaturization.... The ring carried a cutting edge, a warning to the king, a sanction against indifference. [Thompson 1974, 152]

Some chiefs have twenty or more rings from which to select. A number of the most common finger ring motifs are also common sword ornaments and carry the same meaning as their larger counterparts. These include the human

**6.51** Mudfish and scorpion rings of Nana Boakye Yiadom II (see fig. 6.11), paramount chief of the Asante state of Agona. Photograph by Doran H. Ross, 1980.

**6.52** Bracelets and rings of Odeneho Oduro Numapau II (see fig. 6.2). Photograph by Doran H. Ross, Asumegya, 1976.

6.53 Mudfish, frog, and antelope rings of Barima Asumadu Sakyi II (see fig. 6.12). Photograph by Doran H. Ross, Kumawu, 1976.

6.54 (OPPOSITE, TOP LEFT) Chief's ring with lion. Gold. H: 2⅜ in. 97.1128.

6.55 (OPPOSITE, TOP RIGHT) Chief's ring with human head. Gold. H: 2 in. 97.1135.

6.56 (OPPOSITE, BOTTOM LEFT) Chief's ring with lion. Gold. H: 2⅜ in. 97.1141.

6.57 (OPPOSITE, BOTTOM RIGHT) Chief's ring with snake and bird. Gold. W: 2¾ in. 97.1132.

head, lion, snake with bird, bird with cannons, and the porcupine—the latter discussed in this volume under umbrella tops—(figs. 6.54–6.60). The image of two crocodiles sharing the same stomach (fig. A on p. 10) is also found on sword ornaments, as well as counselors' staffs, gold weights, and stamped and embroidered cloths.

The image of a frog might seem to be an unusual royal symbol, but it is a common motif on chiefs' rings as suggested by the multiple examples in the Glassell Collection (figs. 6.61, 6.62). A widely recognized proverb is typically translated as "A frog's length is only apparent after death."[10] The implication is that a chief's accomplishments are often not appreciated during his lifetime and that it is only looking back at his career after his death that his contributions can be fully understood.

Yet another popular ring motif is the mudfish, which often serves as a metaphor for a chief's subjects (figs. 6.63, 6.64). The Akan say of this image: "When the mudfish swallows anything, it does so for its master" (often understood to be the crocodile/chief), that is, what is good for his subjects is good for the chief.[11] Here again the predatory relationship between the two river dwellers seems to be downplayed.

Several rings in the Glassell Collection feature the image of a tortoise and a snail with a firearm (figs. 6.65, 6.66). The highly conventionalized proverb associated with this image is, "If it were only for the snail and the tortoise, the gun would not fire in the forest."[12] Both creatures are valued foods but are collected by hand and not hunted with firearms. Because of this, the snail and the tortoise are seen as peaceful, and in the context of a royal ring the composite image suggests the benevolent intentions of the king. It should be pointed out, however, that even though they are symbols of peace, both the reptile and the snail end up in the soup.

Two other rings with tortoises in the collection are less easily understood. The alternation of a tortoise and a cannon around the ring (fig. 6.67) probably carries the same message as the more familiar tortoise, snail, and musket with some sense of exaggeration. The beautifully cast ring with a pair of sandals topped by a tortoise is very unusual (fig. 6.68), yet as we have seen, sandals are a preeminent symbol of royalty so the tortoise here undoubtedly represents

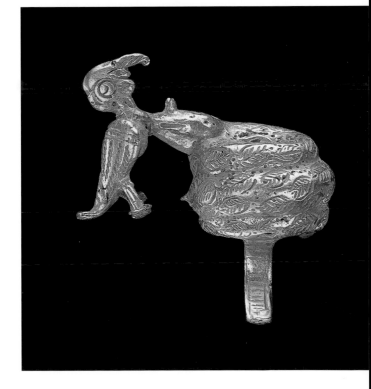

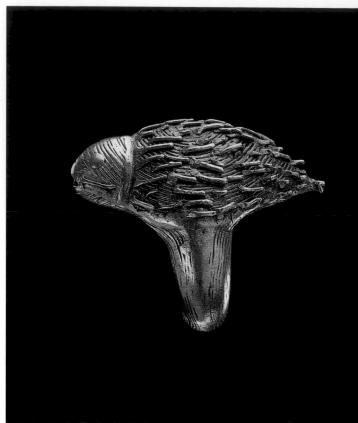

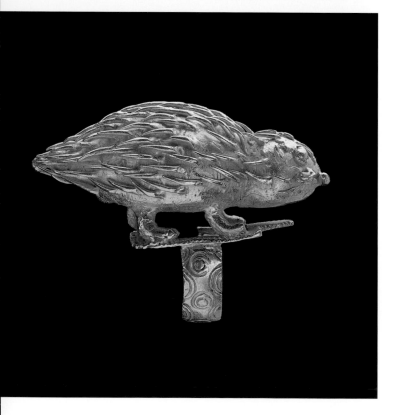

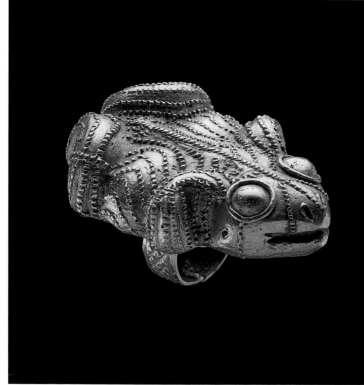

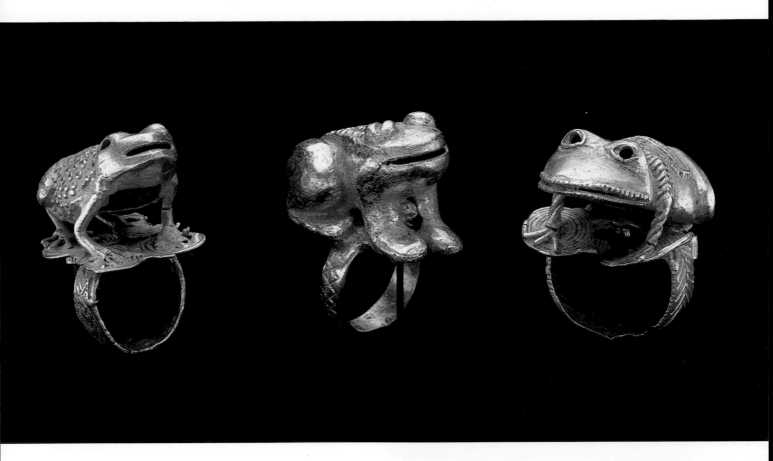

**6.58** (OPPOSITE, TOP LEFT)
Chief's ring with bird
carrying cannons. Gold.
W: 2¼ in. 97.1204.

**6.59** (OPPOSITE, TOP RIGHT)
Chief's ring with porcupine.
Gold. W: 1⅞ in. 97.1096.

**6.60** (OPPOSITE, BOTTOM LEFT)
Chief's ring with porcupine.
Gold. W: 2 in. 97.1537.

**6.61** (OPPOSITE, BOTTOM
RIGHT) Chief's ring with frog.
Gold. W: 2⅝ in. 97.1127.

**6.62A–C** (ABOVE) Chief's
rings with frogs. Gold.
H: 1⅝ in. (A) 97.1201;
(B) 97.1121; (C) 97.1213.

**6.63** (RIGHT) Chief's ring
with mudfish. Gold.
W: 2¾ in. 97.1161.

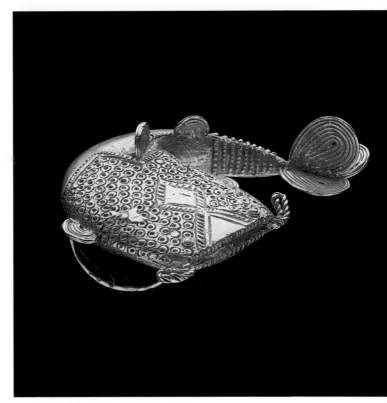

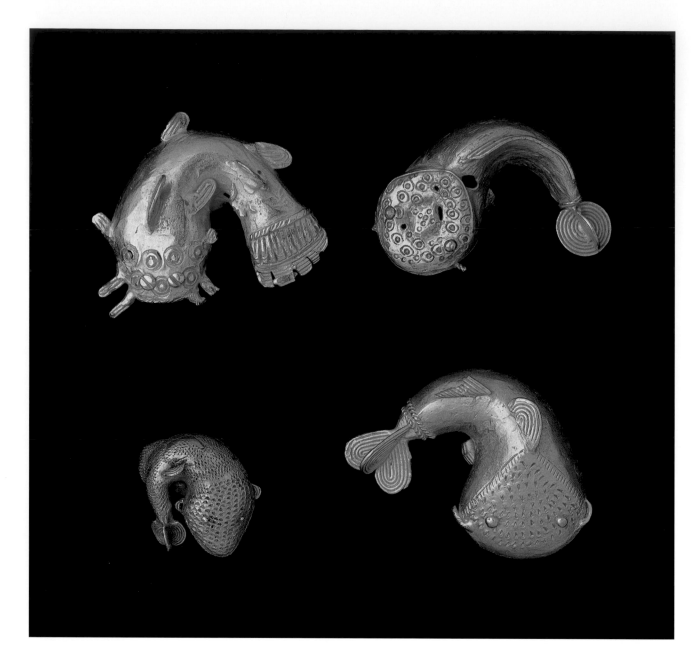

**6.64A–D** Chief's rings with mudfish. Gold. w: 2 ½ in. Left to right, top to bottom: (A) 97.1187; (B) 97.1218; (C) 97.1527; (D) 97.1195.

**6.65A–E** (OPPOSITE, TOP) Chief's rings with tortoises, snails, and muskets. Gold. w: 1 ¾ in. Left to right, top to bottom: (A) 97.1244; (B) 97.1112; (C) 97.1105; (D) 97.1122; (E) 97.1522.

**6.66** (OPPOSITE, BOTTOM LEFT) Chief's ring with tortoise, snail, and musket. Gold. w: 2 ¼ in. 97.1144.

**6.67** (OPPOSITE, BOTTOM RIGHT) Chief's ring with tortoises and cannons. Gold. D: 1 ⅜ in. 97.1145.

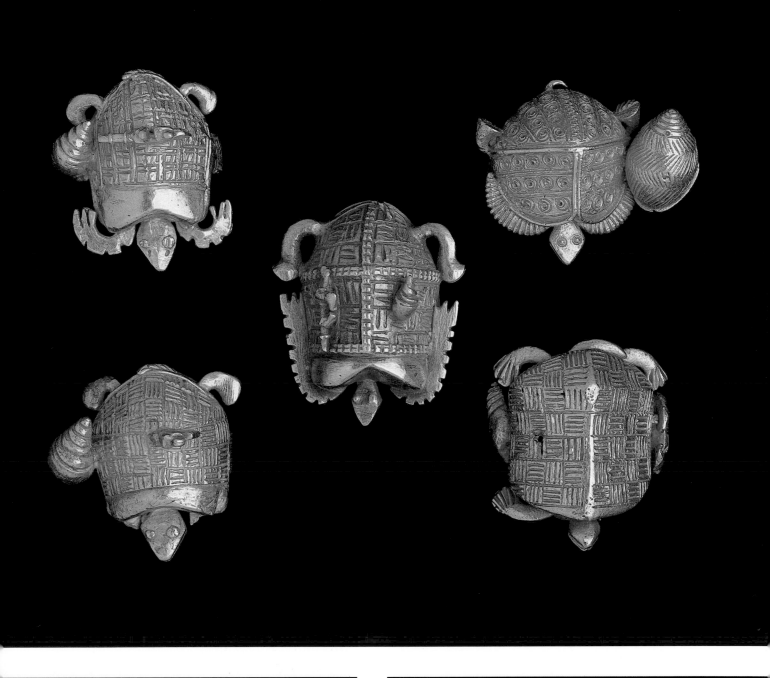

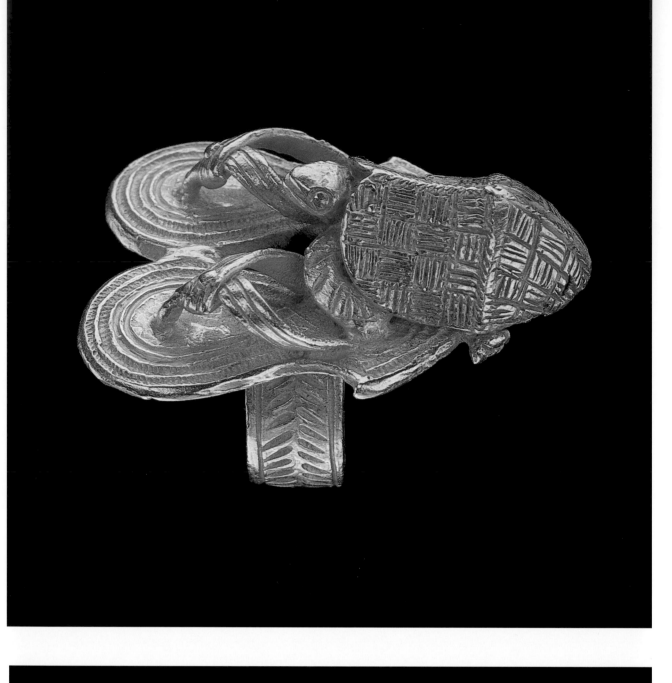

one or more attributes with royal associations. Another group of ring motifs represent other items of regalia including crowns, drums, gongs, swords, and so forth (figs. 6.69–6.73). Most of these motifs are emblematic of royalty and do not typically represent proverbs, although when pushed to provide them most court elders can cite convincing maxims.

Scorpion rings are perhaps the antithesis of those with tortoises (figs. 6.74, 6.75). While many expressions are associated with the scorpion and its painful sting, the most common is probably "The sting of the scorpion is as slow to subside as a fire is to cool," that is, the chief inflicts lasting pain.[13]

Two fowl preying on an oversize cockroach form a motif more familiar in the gold-weight genre than on chiefs' rings (fig. 6.76A). Menzel offers the following proverb in explanation of this scene: "Where is the savior for a cockroach that has fallen among fowls" (1968, 191). Its relevance on a royal ring is unclear, but perhaps the insect represents enemies of the state; and the fowl, its soldiers. The group could then suggest the invincibility of the chief and his

**6.68** (OPPOSITE, TOP) Chief's ring with sandals and tortoise. Gold. w: 1⅝ in. 97.1119.

**6.69A,B** (OPPOSITE, BOTTOM) Chief's rings with crowns. Gold. w: 1⅛ in. (A) 97.1211; (B) 97.1245.

**6.70** (ABOVE) Chief's ring with sword on stool. Gold. w: 1⅜ in. 97.1203.

6.71 Chief's ring with drum.
Gold. H: 2 in. 97.1533.

6.72 Chief's ring with
hand holding sword. Gold.
H: 1½ in. 97.1229.

6.73 Chief's ring with gong.
Gold. W: 1½ in. 97.1247.

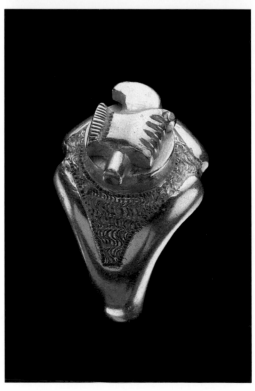

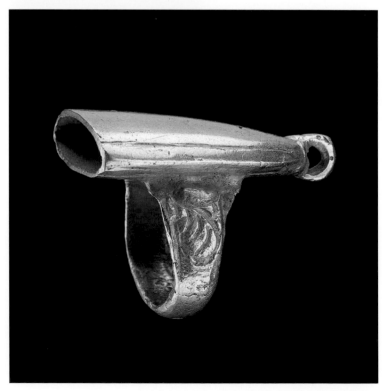

**6.74** Chief's ring with scorpion. Gold. W: 3 in. 97.1534.

**6.75A.B** Chief's rings with scorpions. Gold. W: 2¼ in. (A) 97.1158; (B) 97.1232.

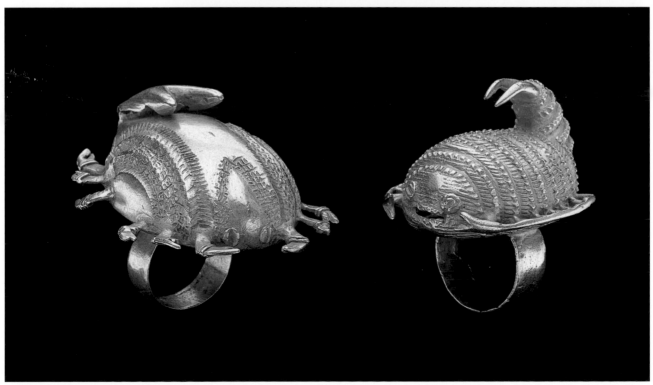

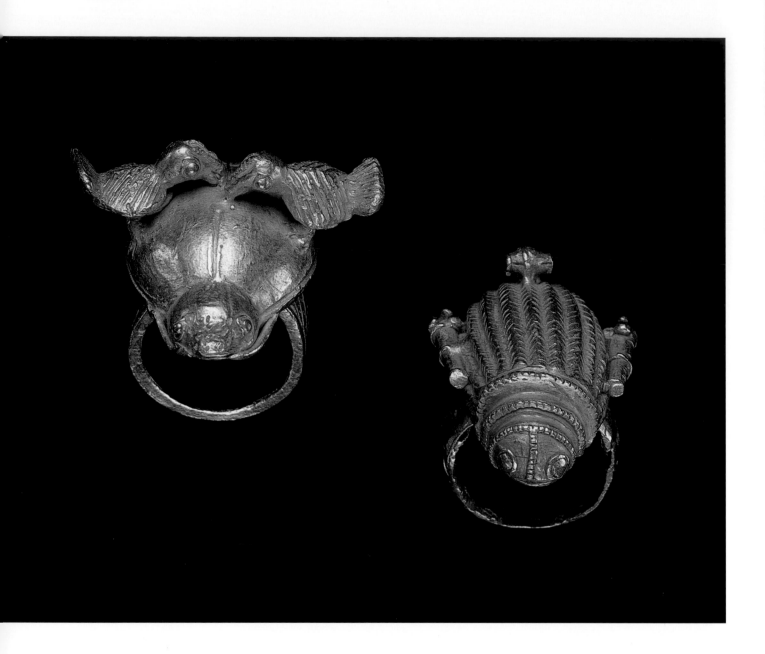

6.76A,B Chief's rings with cockroaches. Gold. H: 1⅞ in. (A) 97.1097; (B) 97.1126.

forces. Another cockroach with cannons and a barrel of gunpowder on its back is even more puzzling (fig. 6.76B).

A very rare, if not unique, ring motif depicts a sailing ship with cannons (fig. 6.77). This motif is represented by a few gold weights dating from the nineteenth century or earlier (Plass 1967, fig. 112; Cole and Ross 1977, fig. 401), and ships still referred to as "Men-of-War," also appear on an occasional *asafo* flag (Ross 1979, fig. 10; Adler and Barnard 1992, figs. 72, 73). Regardless of object type these images are generally emblematic of power and do not seem to represent specific proverbs.

Rings with multiple projections in a kind of starburst pattern are found in the treasuries of most Asante paramount chiefs including those at Bekwai, Kokofu, Asumegya, Edweso, and Nsuta (figs. 6.78, 6.79). The motif actually represents the cocoon of an insect, the shape of which belies its function. The Akan say of this image, "A person's character is not easily deciphered."[14] This

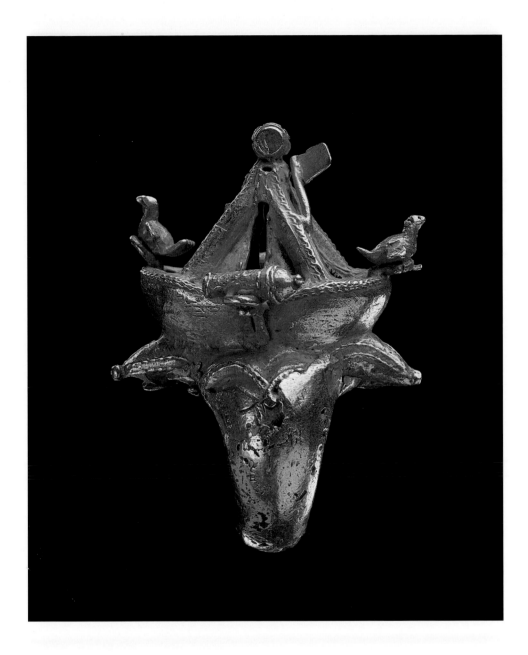

6.77 Chief's ring with ship.
Gold. H: 2¾ in. 97.1202.

approximates the expressions "appearances are deceiving" or "you can't tell
a book by its cover." Although visually related to the other starburst-shaped
rings, the ring illustrated as figure 6.78B is identified as an oil palm with the
fronds indicated by the hatching (see p. 86). Another ring with foliate motifs
(fig. 6.80) represents the kola tree. Garrard, citing the goldsmith Kwasi Agyare,
associates this design with the proverb, "Leaves of two kinds of kola we gather
with wisdom." He further explains that "The leaves of the two kinds of kola
are very similar and it needs skill and experience to separate them. You have
to take care in dealing with problems, and separate them carefully" (1989, 230).

   The representation of Masonic symbols such as compass and square, human
skulls, the capital letter "G," and so forth, on Akan rings is not as surprising
as it may seem (figs. 6.81, 6.82) The late Asantehene Otumfuo Opoku Ware II
was photographed in full Masonic regalia including emblazoned apron and
cuffs with a square and compass suspended from his neck (Braffi 1984, 75). The

6.78A–C Chief's rings with "starbursts." Gold. H: 3 in.
(A) 97.1207; (B) 97.1224;
(C) 97.1109.

program for his funeral reserves a time for Freemasons and Odd Fellows to pay their respects (anon. 1999, 6). Significantly in the above-referenced photograph the Asantehene is wearing a wide three-color ribbon across his chest with the name "Sir Agyeman Prempeh II" displayed on the central band, suggesting that his predecessor may have been a member of the same lodge. Kyerematen in his profile of Prempeh II noted the latter's support of Freemasonry (1970, 6).

Freemasonry had a strong presence in the urban centers of West Africa. Abner Cohen has written about the importance of Freemasonry in providing a "unified authority structure and leadership" among the Creoles of Freetown, Sierra Leone, which had seventeen Masonic lodges in 1970. In neighboring Liberia the ruling elite were all members of local Masonic orders. In what is now Ghana, a lodge was founded at Cape Coast in 1810, and three existed in

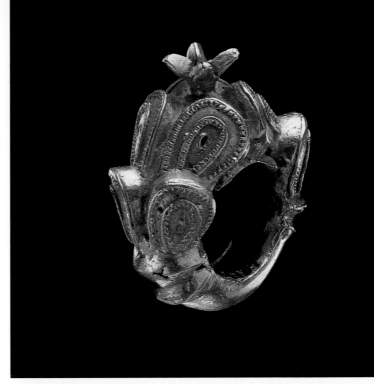

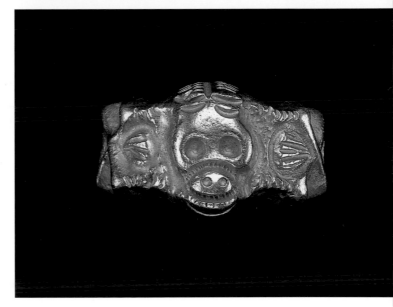

Kumase by 1936 out of a total of thirteen lodges in the Gold Coast Colony at that time (Wright 1936, 230–31).

A number of Masonic symbols—ladders, keys, stars, hands, and so forth—are coincident with long-standing Akan motifs and are often difficult to distinguish from them. This in itself, however, probably reinforced interest in the emblems of Freemasonry. Masonic rites and "charms" were frequently part of Victorian jewelry catalogues, which increased their exposure and availability (Hinks 1991, 230, 294, 302; see Marzio, this volume).

Perhaps equally esoteric are the signs of the zodiac found on the bands of many rings and other jewelry (fig. 6.83). The colonial surgeon Richard Austin Freeman singled out zodiac imagery in his late nineteenth-century account:

**6.79** Chief's ring with "starburst." Gold. H: 2 ¼ in. 97.1240.

**6.80** Chief's ring. Gold. H: 1 ⅝ in. 97.1226.

**6.81** Chief's ring with Masonic symbol. Gold. H: 1 in. 97.1524.

**6.82.** Chief's ring with skull. Gold. W: 1 in. 97.1222.

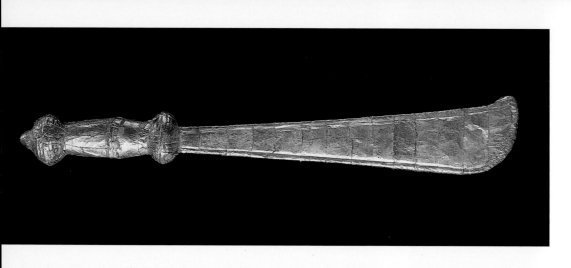

6.83A–E  Chief's rings and a pin with signs of the zodiac. Gold. L (of largest): 3¼ in. Left to right, top to bottom: (A) 97.1225; (B) 97.1189; (C) 97.1185; (D) 97.1165; (E) 97.887.

6.84  Dance sword. Gold leaf, wood. L: 18½ in. 97.815.

6.85  Flintlock handgun acquired with palanquin in figure 2.16. Iron, brass, wood. L: 18 in. 97.1308.

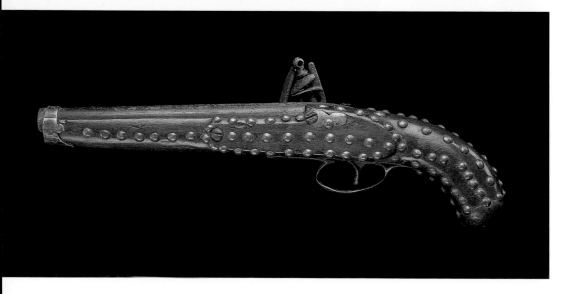

At Cape Coast and Elmina, as well as at Kumasi and some other interior towns, gold rings of very fair design and workmanship are produced. Those of Cape Coast, of course, show very distinct European influence, but nevertheless have a character of their own. Many of them are of filigree work, light and pretty in design; but the most characteristic form is the well-known "Zodiac ring," a specimen of which decorates the finger of nearly every European who visits the Gold Coast, and which has thus become the recognized badge of the "Coaster."

The usual form consists of a flat band of gold with raised edges, which is surrounded by a series of projecting figures more or less resembling the symbols of the signs of the Zodiac. I was unable to discover what had led the Cape Coast goldsmiths to adopt this design, which is a very favourite one of them, for it appears not only on the rings, but also on the broaches, clasps and other ornaments produced by them. [Freeman 1898 [1967], 40]

The Glassell rings reproduce the signs of the zodiac with reasonable accuracy. One can speculate that part of the Akan attraction to this imagery was a combination of astral magic and what was probably perceived as efficacious writing (see the discussion of amulets above). That many of the signs (e.g., lion, ram, crab, scorpion, balance) stand for important and familiar symbols of royalty would certainly reinforce the attraction, although from Freeman's account it would seem that more than just royals were wearing these rings.

The accessories of an important chief also include a small sword held in the right hand and a horsetail fly whisk in the left (fig. 6.84). Occasionally the sword will be replaced by a firearm (fig. 6.85). Although not without symbolic value, these are primarily dance implements that extend and amplify the gestures of the chief as he is carried and performs in a palanquin on festival occasions. The same is true for the nonfunctional, wood and gold leaf, double-barrel shotguns (figs. 6.86, 6.87) that are props in the martial performances of some chiefs.

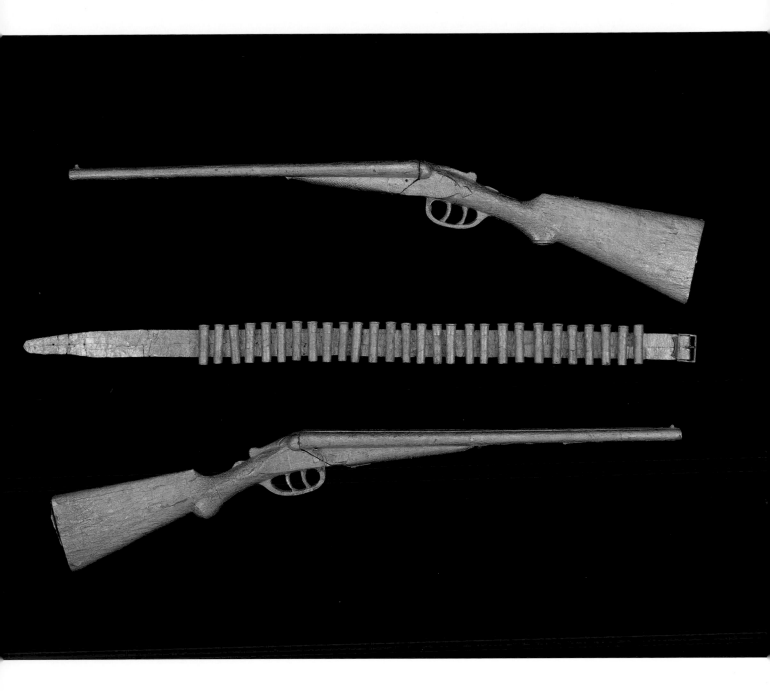

### Kente

Completing the ensemble of elite attire among the Akan are the handwoven cloths called kente produced by the Asante and the non-Akan Ewe peoples of southeastern Ghana and Togo (figs. 6.88, 6.89). These are woven on a horizontal narrow-strip treadle loom generally producing strips three to four inches in width, which are sewn together to produce larger cloths. A man's cloth may have twenty-two to twenty-four strips forming a piece roughly six by twelve feet. A woman will wear two cloths, an upper and lower wrapper of ten or eleven strips each in cloths of approximately four by six feet. (See Ross 1998 for a detailed discussion of kente).

Oral traditions provide two accounts of the introduction of kente to the Asante. One tells of two hunters who encountered the spider Ananse weaving

**6.86** Akuapem chief carrying gold-and-silver-covered wood replicas of shotguns at annual Odwira festival. Photograph by Doran H. Ross, Akuropon, 1976.

**6.87A–C** Shotgun replicas and cartridge belt. Gold leaf, wood. L: 37 in.
(A) 97.812.2.A,B; (B) 97.813; (C) 97. 812.1.A,B.

**6.88** (PAGE 188) Asante paramount chief Nana Akyanfuo Akowuah Dateh II, Akwamuhene of Kumase. Photograph by Eliot Elisofon, 1970. National Museum of African Art. Eliot Elisofon Photographic Archives. Smithsonian Institution. EEPA 1474.

**6.89** (PAGE 189) Nana Diko Pim III (see fig. 6.46). Photograph by Doran H. Ross, Edweso, 1976.

his web. After careful observation they returned to their village and introduced weaving. The second tells of a man named Ota Kraban who visited Gyaman near present-day Bondouku in Côte d'Ivoire and returned with the loom and the knowledge of weaving. There is general agreement among scholars that Asante strip weaving was introduced from the north and that it is basically an extension of weaving practices that date back to at least the eleventh century as evidenced by textile fragments found in burial caves above contemporary Dogon villages in eastern Mali. Originally the wearing of kente was the exclusive prerogative of the Asantehene and those chiefs to whom he designated the privilege. Over the past one hundred years the exclusivity has relaxed, and fine kente may now be worn by anyone who can afford it.

Kente cloths are arguably the best known of all African textiles. Much of the appeal is purely visual, but a significant part of the attraction has to do with the naming of the cloth. Asante kente cloths are named in relation to their warp-stripe patterns, although only rarely is there a visual correspondence between name and pattern. This does not, however, lessen the significance of the names themselves. Cloths may be named after famous men and women in Asante history, historical events, natural phenomena such as rainbows or sunrises, or proverbs, as with many other items of regalia. One popular cloth is Toku Akra Ntoma, or Toku's Soul Cloth (fig. 6.90). Toku was the queen mother of one of the many enemies of the Asante, but she was still much respected for bravery and courage. Nevertheless, she was defeated in battle by Opoku Ware I who gave the vanquished woman's cloth to his own queen mother and had its design perpetuated (Rattray 1927, 239). Another pattern, Frempomaa Bonwire Hemaa, commemorates an early queen mother of Bonwire thought to be the grandmother of Ota Kraban, who, as previously noted, supposedly introduced weaving to Bonwire (fig. 6.91).

One woman's cloth in the collection is called Asante Kotoko (porcupine), which as mentioned earlier, suggests the phrase, "If you kill a thousand, a thousand will come" (fig. 6.92). This quintessential symbol of Asante military power is actually a rather rare warp-stripe pattern and is seldom woven today. Another unusual cloth (fig. 6.93) is a variation of the Ammerɛ Oyokoman pattern but switches the green and red elements (Ross 1998, 113). This pattern in turn is a variation on Oyokoman (see fig. 6.89), named after the matrilineage of all Asantehenes.

Another cloth (fig. 6.94) is named Agyenegyenesu, which is often identified as a water beetle but was considered by Christaller to be a dragonfly. A finger ring with the same name found at the Asante paramountcy of Bekwai is referred to as "The water beetle that makes dirty water clean." This was explained as a metaphor for the chief's ability to solve problems.[15] A proverb cited by Christaller, however, takes the same subject matter in a different direction: "The dragon-fly says he looks closely at the water before he makes it muddy" (Christaller 1879 [1990], 106). Regardless of the identification of

**6.90** (OPPOSITE, LEFT) Detail of man's kente cloth, Asante. Rayon. L: 120 in. 97.767.

**6.91** (OPPOSITE, RIGHT) Detail of woman's broadloom kente cloth, Asante. Rayon. L: 84½ in. 97.765.

**6.92** (ABOVE) Detail of woman's kente cloth, Asante. Rayon. L: 82 in. 97.763.

6.93 Detail of man's kente cloth, Asante. Rayon. L: 124 in. 97.761.

6.94 Detail of man's kente cloth, Asante. Cotton, rayon. L: 132 in. 97.773.

6.95 Detail of man's kente cloth, Asante. Cotton, rayon. L: 125 in. 97.777.

6.96 Detail of man's kente cloth, Asante. Cotton, rayon. L: 125 in. 97.772.

the insect, clearly the chief controls the destiny of the water and thus the sustenance of his state.

A rather dense plaid (fig. 6.95) acquires its name from the proverb "Kindness does not travel far."[16] There is a general notion that if one makes a mistake or behaves poorly everyone hears about it, but exemplary behavior or good deeds are rarely acknowledged. Of the few cloths whose names are not based on warp patterns, two are still among the most popular. Both have compositions that eliminate the alternating blocks of warp and weft face designs and alternate smaller units of weft-faced motifs. One is called "Abusua yɛ Dom" (lit., "The family is strong" or "The extended family is a force" [fig. 6.96; cf Ofori-Ansa 1993, no. 5]). This name, like many of the messages contained in regalia, affirms the strength of the royal matrilineage. At the same time, it reinforces the concepts of family unity and strength throughout Akan communities. This perhaps accounts for its continuing popularity.

The other cloth (figs. 6.97, 6.88) has a slightly more complicated story. Originally it was named "Fathia Fata Nkrumah" and was created in honor

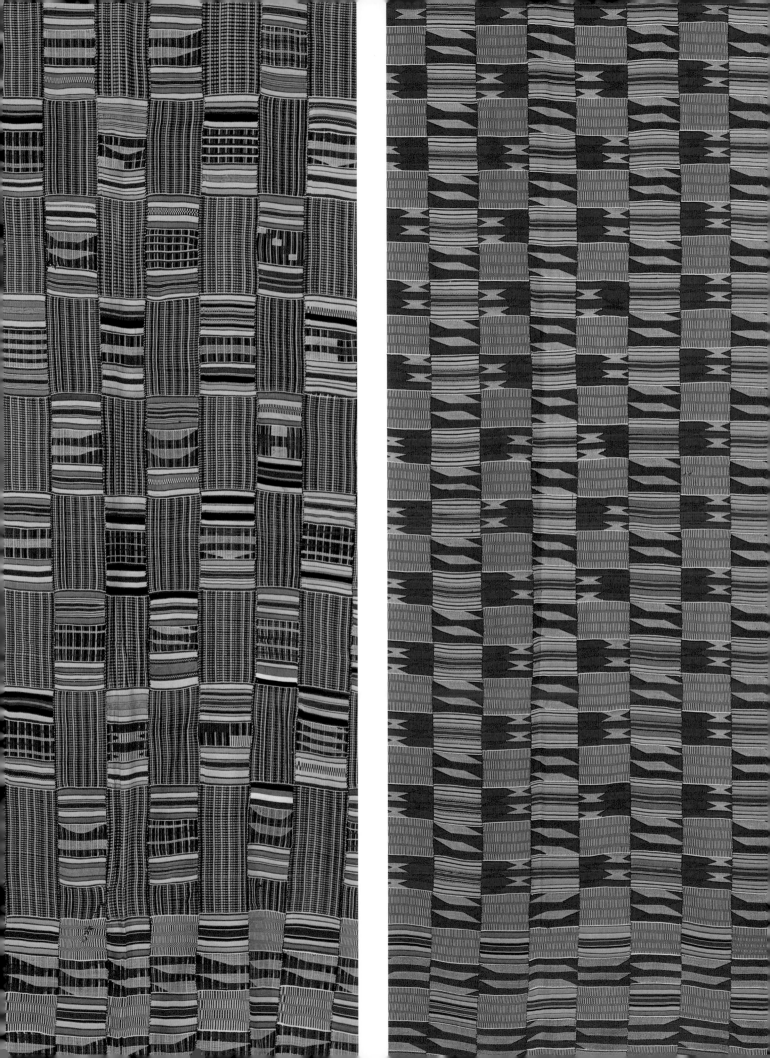

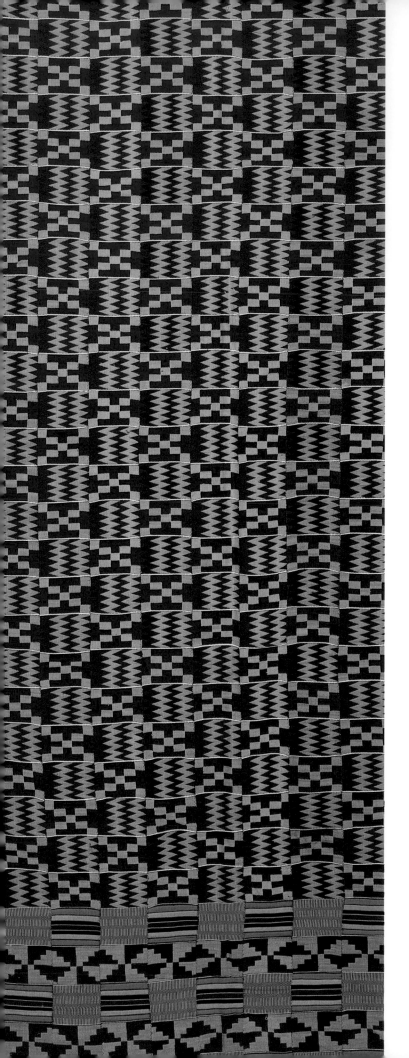

of the marriage of Ghana's first president, Kwame Nkrumah, to his Egyptian wife, Fathia. The name is literally an affirmation of their betrothal, "Fathia Befits Nkrumah." Given Nkrumah's pan-African initiatives, the marriage was considered especially auspicious. When in 1996 the leader was ousted by a coup resulting from the widespread corruption on the part of a number of his senior ministers, the name of the cloth was changed to "Obaakofo Mmu Man," or "One Man Does Not Rule a Nation," a warning against the excesses of Nkrumah's rule. With a reappraisal in the late twentieth century of Nkrumah's enormous contributions to both Ghanaian and pan-African initiatives, the name of the cloth has reverted to the original.

These last two cloths obviously suggest that additional layers of meaning are embedded in the weft-faced designs. In round figures there may be as many as five hundred named cloths (i.e., warp-faced designs), and there are at least that many weft-faced designs as well. While physical evidence of those designs still exists, the names of many extend beyond most memories or experiences. To provide a few examples from the Glassell Collection that suggest the royal origins of those elite textiles, two of the three most important weft-faced designs are called *babadua* and *ɛkyɛm*. The former has already been discussed in terms of umbrella finials and bracelet designs where this segmented cane in its reductionist perspective is a symbol of strength. The second motif, *ɛkyɛm*, is the state shield and it is also found as the subject matter of many other items of regalia, including sword ornaments, counselors' staffs, and gold weights. These two designs are commonly found in various combinations on the borders of Asante cloths and also structure internal blocks of design. The Fathia

Fata Nkrumah cloth already mentioned has two weft patterns repeated within the body of the cloth and three on its borders. The X formed by nine squares represents a hairstyle called *mpuankron* worn by key attendants of the king. The zigzag motif *nkyimkyim* (lit., "to twist or turn") is often related to a person considered to be indecisive or even mentally unstable.

Four other cloths in the collection were produced by Ewe weavers. It is rare to see Ewe cloths worn by Asante chiefs, but it is reasonably common among the southern Akan. Ewe textiles are generally distinguished by the absence of borders on both ends of the cloth, and simpler bordering strips on the sides.

6.98 Detail of man's kente cloth, Ewe. Cotton, silk, and/or rayon. L: 111 in. 97.775.

6.99 Detail of man's kente cloth, Togo, Ewe. Cotton, silk, and/or rayon. L: 121 in. 1868.

**6.100** Detail of man's kente cloth, Ewe. Cotton. L: 115 in. 97.776.

**6.101** Detail of man's kente cloth, Ewe. Cotton. L: 121 in. 1926.

In addition, they often employ a more muted palette, and weft threads occasionally consist of two different colors of thread twisted together, producing a pleasing mottled effect in weft-faced bands (figs. 6.98, 6.99). One of the most distinctive features of Ewe cloths is the presence of explicitly representational inlays. A close examination of figure 6.100 reveals hands, human figures, birds, fish, and a couple of hard-to-identify four-legged creatures. Another cloth alternates a hand and a bird on each strip (fig. 6.101).

The Glassell Collection also has an excellent example of the cloth called Akunitam, or "Cloth of the great." These men's wrappers (I have yet to see them on women) come in two techniques. The first entails appliqué motifs on a background of cotton, rayon, or polyester; the second involves rayon embroidery on a British-made mill-woven wool blanket (fig. 6.102). The cloth is machine embroidered, and the red, green, and gold color scheme of the threads is found on most of these cloths and coincides with the national colors of Ghana. All of the motifs on this cloth have already been discussed in relation to other Akan regalia types. The individual motifs on the cloth are identified as follows.

| crossroads | fish | crossroads | cocoa | crossroads |
| star | tortoise | porcupine | star and moon | cocoa |
| crossroads | heart | stool and swords | heart | crossroads |
| star | lion | crossed crocodiles | bird | Hausa knot |

**6.102** "Cloth of the Great." Machine-embroidered British-made blanket. Wool, rayon thread. L: 129¼ in. 97.769.

All of these images/messages on goldwork, kente, or otherwise beg the question of how well this system of communication is known. Certainly the chief, his counselors (*akyeame*), treasurer (*saanahene*), and keeper of the wardrobe (*abanasehene*), as well as individual custodians and wearers of select items of regalia, have a solid understanding of the objects and the ideas they embody. Likewise the vast majority of artists (casters, carvers, weavers, etc.) have a grasp of the meaning of the objects they are producing. Beyond that it is difficult to measure the reach of these symbolic systems. As with comparable systems, some images like the *sankɔfa* bird permeate the popular culture of the Akan and beyond, and the meanings of other images remain accessible, perhaps even intentionally, only to the knowledgeable elite. ●

# 7

# The Victorian Legacy

## OF BUTTERFLIES, HEARTS, AND TEETHING RATTLES

*Frances Marzio*

In 1819 Mrs. T. Edward Bowdich, a British envoy's wife, described a bride at Cape Coast by cataloging the jewelry she wore from head to toe:

> Her fair hair was combed in the form of a cone to the top of her head, and profusely ornamented with golden butterflies and devices; her shirt was fastened in front with four brooches, and a large golden button at the collar and each wrist; manillas encircled her arms half-way up to the elbow, and the most splendid chains were hung across her shoulders; every finger was covered with rings as far as the first joint; her cloth was girt round her hips, and on this girdle hung golden lions and other ornaments; her ankles were also laden, and every toe was decorated like her fingers.... The workmanship of many of these ornaments is exquisite, and they sometimes represent musical instruments, bells, stools, etc., and many are imitated from European patterns. [Lee 1835, 23]

Nearly eighty years later, the Reverend Dennis Kemp, in his account *Nine Years at the Gold Coast,* made a similar observation: "The power to imitate is most marvelous. A goldsmith will make an exact copy of an elaborately designed piece of European jewellery" (1898 [1982], 56).

Based on earlier contact between Europe and Africa, Mrs. Bowdich was most likely marveling at the work of Akan goldsmiths who were imitating Dutch, Danish, and British models. Unfortunately, little, if any, jewelry of this age remains. Reverend Kemp, remarking on Akan skill in reproducing Western jewelry eighty years later, was undoubtedly referring to many familiar British designs of the Victorian era. For Victorian jewelry was used in a way that was

7.1 Watch face with butterfly. Gold. DIAM: 2 in. 97.1464.A,B.

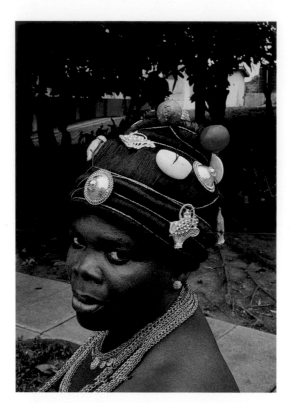

7.2–7.5 Senior women from Fante Asafo companies during Fetu Afahye wearing elaborate wigs with gold hairpins in Victorian styles. Photographs by Doran H. Ross, Cape Coast, 2002.

very "Akan"; and visual symbols expressed verbal meanings immediately recognized by the viewer. This verbal/visual communication made Victorian motifs nearly irresistible to the Akan. Examples of their fascination may be seen today in the Glassell Collection.

It is also of note that the Akan and the British during the Victorian era wore jewelry in quantity. There was no "embarrassment of riches," and jewelry was worn not only for personal adornment but also to indicate social status and wealth. State occasions and court etiquette demanded certain types of ornaments designed to show royal position and relationship to the ruler in both cultures.

Victorians made clear distinctions between primary and secondary jewelry. The former was designed conservatively and reserved solely for state and other very important occasions. The latter, made of less precious materials, incorporated novelty and folk motifs and commemorated personal events and sentiments. Akan peoples seemed to be more flexible than the Victorians, for they wore jewelry with "secondary" characteristics for personal as well as state occasions. Victorians incorporated precious and semiprecious stones, pearls, and multiple types of metal and materials into their jewelry, whereas Akan jewelry was fashioned in the material that was most readily available and preferred — gold. In fact, gold was used ingeniously to imitate stones and pearls. Though both men and women wore jewelry in Victorian England, gender distinctions existed with reference to jewelry types. This seemed to be less the case with the Akan during the nineteenth century, although gender distinctions became much more codified during the twentieth. Victorian styles still persist in Akan jewelry more than a century after the death of Victoria (r. 1837–1901), but they are more dramatically evident in female adornment (figs. 7.2–7.7).

7.6, 7.7 Two views of a senior woman from Fante Asafo company during Fetu Afahye wearing an elaborate wig with gold hairpins in Victorian styles. Photographs by Doran H. Ross, Cape Coast, 2002.

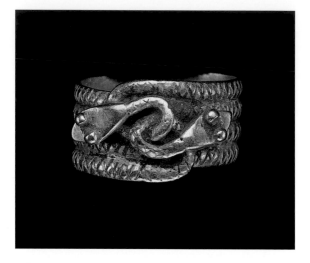

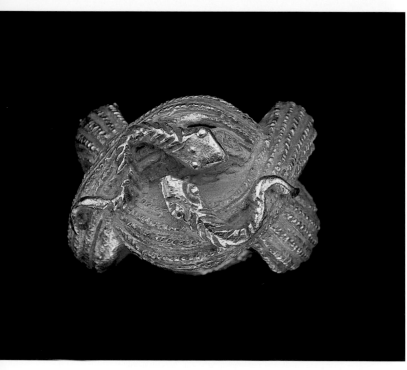

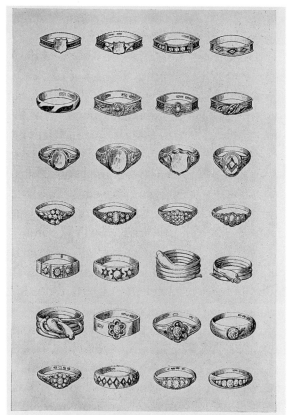

*Fig. 94.* Rings in gold, decorated with enamel and semi-precious stones

From R. Pringle's *Illustrated Catalogue and Price List of Jewellery*, April, 1876.

Queen Victoria, whose taste gave name to the era, was herself a major presence among the Akan. Coins with her image were made locally, sometimes cast in cuttlefish bone from real British sovereigns (fig. 7.8B). Such coins were incorporated into jewelry types such as necklaces and bracelets (see figs. 6.26, 6.27). In 1839, Prince Albert gave Victoria a betrothal ring in the form of a serpent with emerald eyes and its tail in its mouth. She wore this ring, a symbol of eternity, throughout her life, and in 1876 she purchased another serpent ring with a diamond eye from Garrard's (Tooley 1897, 105). These rings, which were popular and reproduced throughout the nineteenth century in Europe, were also made in Africa (figs. 7.9, 7.10). The Glassell Collection contains several such rings, which are identical in form to rings appearing in nineteenth-century English jewelry catalogs (fig. 7.11). The eyes are fashioned in gold, however, rather than set with gemstones. Though indigenous snakes like the python and gaboon viper are popular motifs in Akan regalia—including sword ornaments, sword handles, blades, and linguist staffs—they are quite different in appearance from the serpents decorating these Victorian-inspired rings.

While the intertwined serpents on rings are perhaps the most common Victorian motif/jewelry type, a wide variety of rings, bracelets, necklaces, and other items of jewelry were brought to the Gold Coast by Europeans stationed there and especially by the British after they gained exclusive control of the area in 1872. Some of this jewelry was traded or presented as gifts to Akan dignitaries. These items in turn served as models for Akan goldsmiths. Occasionally British jewelry catalogs may also have been available for inspiration (figs. 7.12–7.17).

Victorian jewelry types were designated for specific parts of the body and bore the influence of contemporary styles and fashions. They included traditional forms, such as necklaces, bracelets, rings, and earrings, as well as hair ornaments, brooches, and decorative watches. Scarf and tiepins were worn by both men and women. Sometimes jewelry adorned the body in particular ways: for example, bracelets were worn two or three per arm, and pairs of bracelets, worn one per wrist, were also popular (Flower 1973, 62). Matching jewelry "sets" also became fashionable. Many of these practices were avidly followed by the Akan (figs. 7.18, 7.19).

Among the Victorians, all types of jewelry were presented as gifts intended to demonstrate affection or gratitude and to mark special occasions such as weddings, funerals, births, and even trips. Queen Victoria, herself a lover of jewelry, led the way, giving gifts of jewelry, including brooches, bracelets, necklaces, and rings, throughout her reign. The British carried on this gift tradition

7.8A,B (OPPOSITE, TOP LEFT) Coins depicting Queen Victoria. Gold. Largest dimension: 1½ in. (A) British. 97.1007; (B) Akan. 97.998.

7.9 (OPPOSITE, TOP RIGHT) Ring with entwined serpents. Gold. DIAM: ⅞ in. 97.1190.

7.10 (OPPOSITE, BOTTOM LEFT) Ring with entwined serpents. Gold. DIAM: 1¼ in. 97.1175.

7.11 (OPPOSITE, BOTTOM RIGHT) "Rings in gold, decorated with enamel and semi-precious stones." From R. Pringle's *Illustrated Catalogue and Price List of Jewellery*, (April 1876): fig. 94.

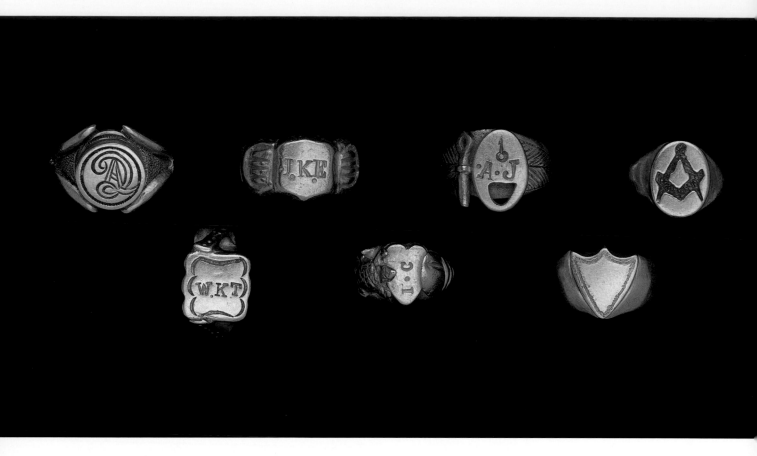

7.12A–G Signet rings. Gold.
Largest dimension: 1⅛ in.
Top to bottom, left to right:
(A) With initials "D A,"
97.1104; (B) With initials
"J K E," 97.1169; (C) With
lock and key, initials "A J,"
97.1242; (D) With Masonic
symbol, 97.1524; (E) With
initials "W K T," 97.1228;
(F) With turtle and shell, initials "I C," 97.1162; (G) 97.1150.

7.13 "22-carat Gold
Wedding Rings." From
Mappin & Webb Ltd.
catalogue (1900).

**7.14A–D** Ball-tip bracelets.
Gold. Largest dimension:
2⅝ in. Top to bottom,
left to right: (A) 97.1458.1,2;
(B) 97.944; (C) 97.1471.2.

**7.15** "Rolled Gold Plate
Bracelets." From S. F. Myers
& Co. catalogue (1894).

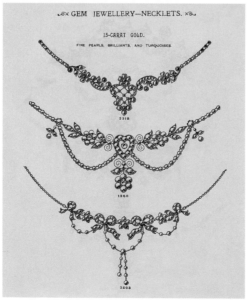

**7.16A,B** Necklaces. Gold. Largest dimension: 17 ¼ in. (A) 97.1021.1; (B) 97.1022.

**7.17** "Gem Jewellery— Necklets." From Saunders and Shepherd Ltd. Catalogue (1903–1904).

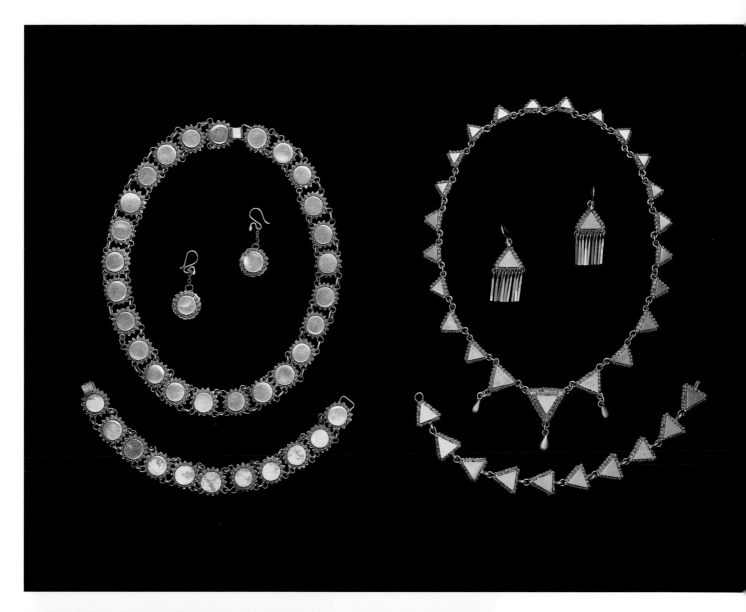

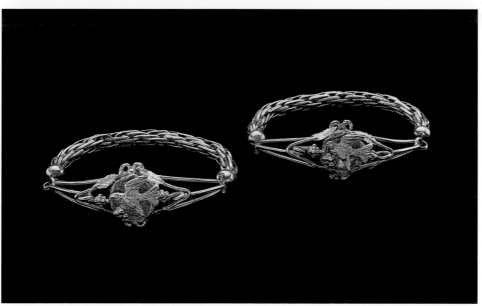

**7.18A,B** Woman's jewelry suites (necklace, bracelet, earrings). Gold. (A) Classical style. L: 17½ in. 97.1250.1-3.A,B; (B) Etruscan style. 97.989.1-3.A,B.

**7.19A,B** Matched pair of bracelets with swallows, nests, and forget-me-nots. Largest dimension: 2⅞ in. 97.1460.1,2.

**7.20A,B** Matched pair of bracelets. Gold. L: 4½ in. 97.1021.1–3.

**7.21** "Gem Bracelets." From Saunders and Shepherd Ltd. Catalogue (1903-1904).

**7.22** Bracelet with heart-shaped padlock. Gold. L: 4 in. 97.943.

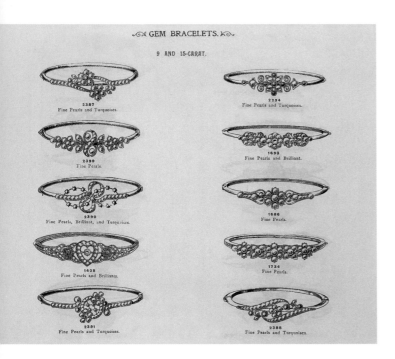

in their relations with the Akan. Nineteenth-century accounts consistently mention gift giving. Trade and contact also brought types of Victorian jewelry to the attention of Akan goldsmiths, who both borrowed the size and shape of forms precisely and also created variations on them. Direct casts in gold from European works were rare and were usually only employed for small ornaments. A very simple casting was sometimes produced by pressing the object into the soft side of the bone of a cuttlefish. Medallions, rings, small ornaments, and faux coins, such as the one illustrated in figure 7.8B, were made.

Akan jewelry forms were sometimes created solely for adornment and show and were not intended to be functional. There are watches that do not tell time (fig. 7.1); lockets that do not open (fig. 7.22); keys that do not fit their ornamental locks and hearts (see fig. 6.29). Sets, which were not part of the Akan tradition, were also made. Old Akan gold jewelry, like that in the Glassell Collection, often looks identical to Victorian jewelry but usually contains a lower-carat gold and bears no hallmarks.

As noted above, Victorian jewelry entailed elaborate verbal/visual associations of its own. Sentiment was clearly expressed through a variety of motifs. Hearts (figs. 7.20, 7.22), flowers, birds (fig. 7.23), padlocks with keys (see fig. 6.29), and knots (fig. 7.24) all spoke the language of love. Heart designs were used for engagement, marriage, and friendship. Forget-me-nots symbolized true love, and roses connoted beauty. Swallows and turtledoves, believed to be constant, were the birds associated with love. Padlocks with keys, carrying the message, "Only you hold the key to my heart," appeared on every type of Victorian jewelry, as did "true-love" knots. Clovers exclaimed, "Be mine." Though these forms were duplicated accurately and embellished with imagination by the Akan, it is unclear if the meaning that informs Victorian jewelry always translated accurately as well.

7.23A,B Matched pair of bracelets with flowers and swallows. Gold. L: 2½ in. 97.933.1,2.

7.24 Bracelet with love knots. Gold. 2⅝ is. 97.1475.

7.25A–D Rings with birds gathering nectar from flowers. Gold. Largest dimension: 1¾ in. (A) 97.1227; (B) 97.1185; (C) 97.1189; (D) 97.1155.

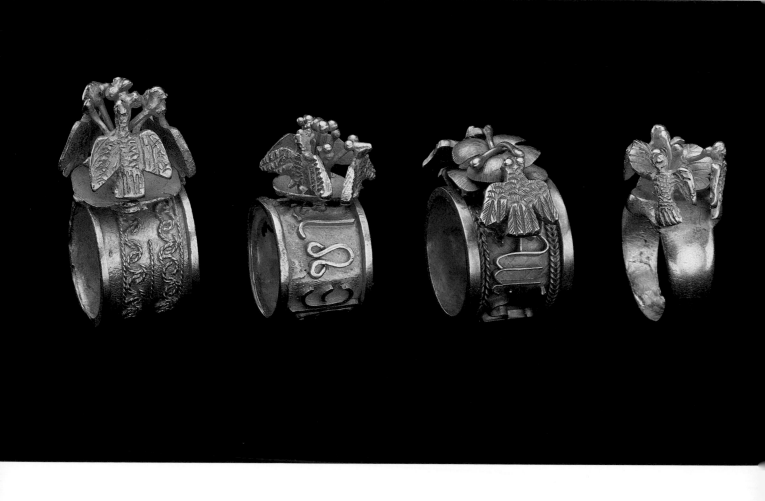

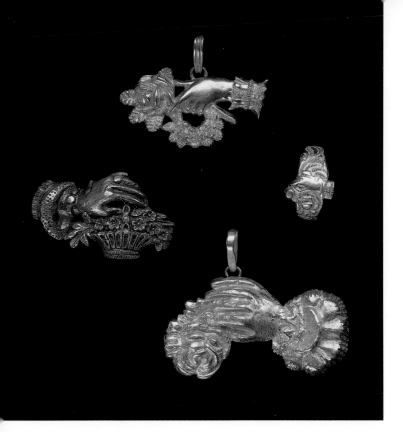

While such visual motifs relayed and conveyed sentiment easily and obviously within the Victorian world, the language of love could also be difficult to decipher. In 1810 Samuel Fletcher, a seal engraver in London, advertised idiosyncratic scripts that he claimed were ancient languages. "These were used for love inscriptions on rings, pendants, and seals which could only be interpreted by those possessing the keys to the alphabets" (Bury 1985, 9). Mysterious letters and numbers appear frequently on Akan rings, brooches, and regalia; they were perhaps inspired by this nineteenth-century fad. The same impulse probably also fostered the popularity of signs of the zodiac among the Akan (fig. 7.25)

An unusual Victorian design for friendship and love was the single extended hand or clasping hands. These disembodied hands often wore lace cuffs, bracelets, and rings and carried flowers, especially forget-me-nots and roses (fig. 7.26). Sheaves of wheat indicated abundance and continuity (fig. 7.27B). The star and crescent, a favorite eighteenth-century motif for constancy, was revived in the nineteenth century (Bury 1991, 695). Among the Akan, it became a symbol for the chief and was associated with a proverb comparing the chief to a star and extolling his constancy (fig. 7.27A).

Notable for its absence in Akan jewelry was the Victorian tradition of "mourning jewelry," made famous by the queen after the death of her beloved consort, Albert, in 1861. Such items would hardly have been popular for trade and would certainly have been inappropriate as diplomatic gifts. However, Akan-made bracelets with gold wire and mesh forms exist, similar in appearance to "hair" jewelry created from the actual woven hair of a loved one. The memento mori motif of skulls with crossbones, meaning "Remember that you must die," which was sometimes apparent on jewelry given as memorials to family and friends after funerals does appear occasionally on Akan rings (fig. 7.28), although also possibly as a Masonic motif.

**7.26A–D** Pendants and rings. Gold. Largest dimension: 2¼ in. Clockwise from top: (A) Pendant of hand with lace cuff holding a rose, 97.1520; (B) Small ring with hand, 97.1108; (C) Pendant of hand with lace cuff holding a rose, 97.1062; (D) Ring with large hand wearing jewelry and holding a basket of forget-me-nots, 97.1142.

**7.27A,B** Pendants. Gold. Largest dimension: 1½ in. (A) Star and crescent. 97.1056; (B) Sheaves of wheat. 97.1092.

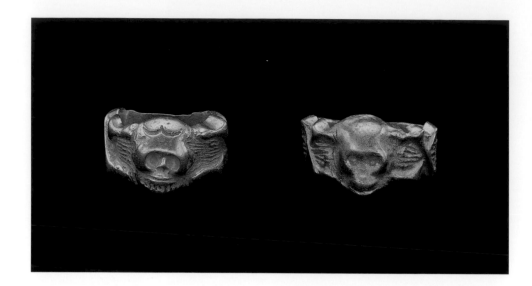

**7.28A,B** Rings with skulls. Gold. DIAM: 1⅝ in. (A) 97.1230; (B) 97.1115.

**7.29** Pendant in shape of a beetle. Gold. L: 1⅜ in. 97.1042.

**7.30** Butterfly pendant. Gold. W: 2½ in. 97.1065.

**7.31** Heart pendant with dragonfly. Gold. H: 3¼ in. 97.1027.

**7.32A–F** Pendants. Gold. Lions, butterflies, birds. Largest dimension: 1½ in. Top to bottom, left to right: (A,B) 97.965.A,B; (C,D) 97.1471.3.A,B; (E,F) 97.975.A,B.

**7.33** Pendant with two-headed eagle. Gold. W: 1⅞ in. 97.1090.

Insects were one of the most novel jewelry motifs to become adopted in stylish circles in Victorian England. This mania seems to have begun with gem-encrusted beetles placed on ladies' bonnets and veils. Soon after, insects appeared on necklaces, bracelets, and pins, and were joined by jeweled versions of butterflies, dragonflies, and other specimens (Bury 1991, n. 4, 34). Though the Akan could doubtless look for inspiration among the multitudes of locally found insects, they adopted the British specimens as well, producing examples like these pendants of a beetle, a butterfly, and a heart with an insect filigree (figs. 7.29–7.31). In 1844 Victorian jewelers created the bracelet watch (Bury 1991, 62). The Akan jewelers responded with their own forms lacking function (see fig. 7.1).

British heraldry also became a rich source for Akan jewelry and regalia. Lions, crowns, eagles, and shields were all adopted as symbols of power by Akan chiefs (figs. 7.32–7.34; see Ross 1982a). The shield shape surmounted by a crown, copied by Victorian jewelers from a brooch given to Princess Alexandra in 1863 (Bury 1991, n. 6, 527), was reproduced in turn and embellished by Akan jewelers (fig. 7.34). On the Glassell shield pendant, the coat of arms was replaced with the owner's initials.

Nineteenth-century archaeological discoveries created a revival of classical jewelry, first in Italy, then throughout Europe. Ancient Greek, Etruscan, and Roman models provided a wealth of sources, and Victorian jewelers imitated them in necklaces, bracelets, and earrings, frequently producing matching suites (see fig. 7.18). Among Victorian ladies, they were indicators of education and refinement. The Akan also mastered these technically difficult works.

Christianity became a presence in the nineteenth century with the establishment of the Basel Mission in 1828 and the Wesleyan Mission in 1835. Missionaries in search of souls brought with them symbols of their faith interpreted in Victorian jewelry. Crosses and the trinity of cross, anchor, and heart, symbolizing the virtues faith, hope, and charity, appeared on Akan adornment (fig. 7.35). In this case, the verbal and cultural messages of Christian symbols translated literally to the Akan peoples, for today the vast majority of Akan chiefs are Christian.

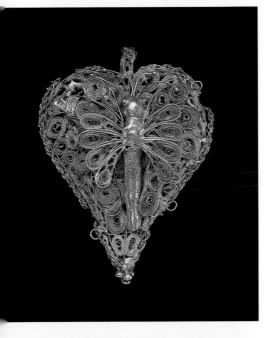

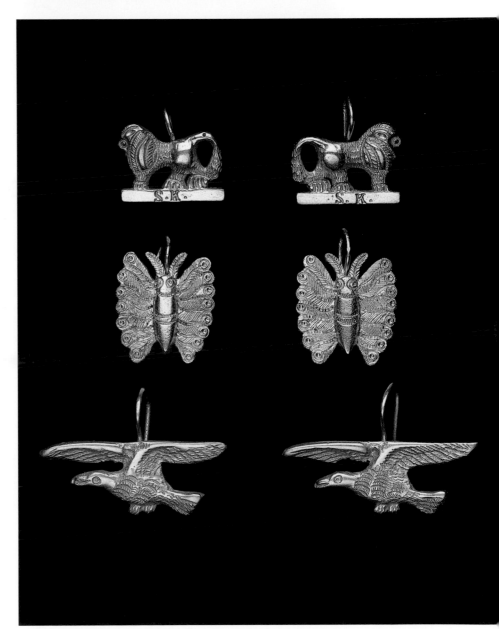

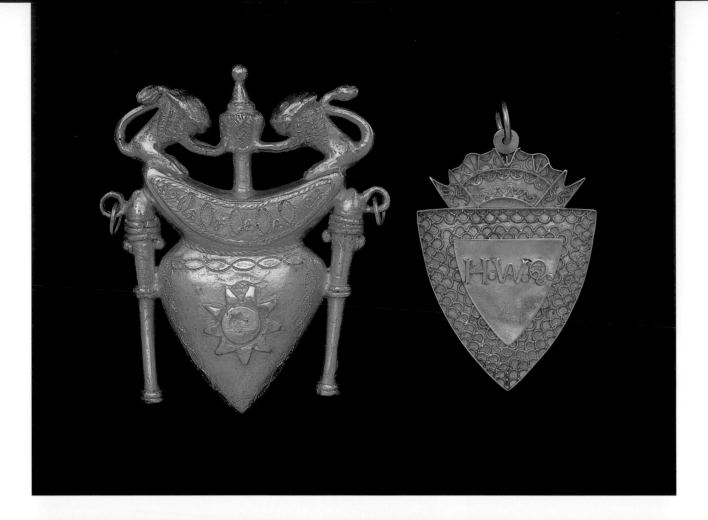

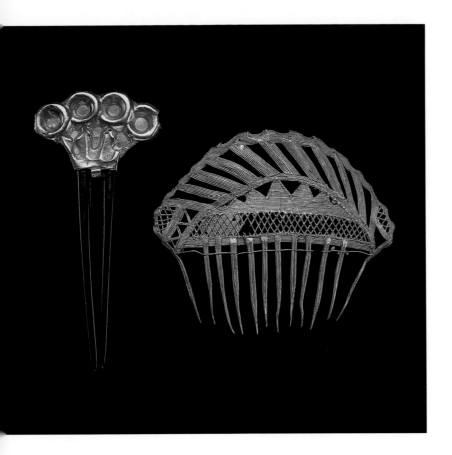

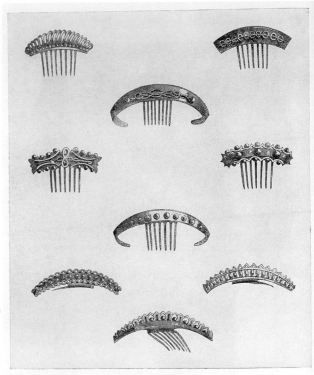

*Fig. 62.* Tortoiseshell combs, from the *Englishwoman's Domestic Magazine,* 1868
The curved combs form bandeaux. The straight ones are worn within
the chignon. (*Mrs James Walker*)

**7.34A,B** (OPPOSITE, TOP)
Jewelry. Gold. Largest
dimension: 4 in. (A) Heart-
shaped pendant with cannons,
British-style lions, and crown,
97.1018.1,2; (B) Shield-shaped
pendant surmounted by
a crown with initials
"H. W. Q.," 97.1009.A,B.

**7.35A,B** (OPPOSITE, BOTTOM)
Jewelry. Gold. Largest
dimension: 3¼ in.
(A) Bracelet with anchor,
heart, and cross, 97.1552.
(B) Crucifix, 97.1080.

**7.36A,B** (ABOVE, LEFT)
Hair combs. Gold.
Largest dimension: 4⅞ in.
(A) 97.884.3; (B) 97.781.

**7.37** (ABOVE, RIGHT)
"Tortoiseshell combs."
From the *Englishwoman's
Domestic Magazine* (1868):
fig 62.

Many Victorian motifs and patterns are still being reproduced in contemporary versions. The continuing interest in this design vocabulary throughout
the twentieth century makes it very difficult to date individual pieces. Victorian
designs are still especially prevalent in hair adornment where multiple versions
of ornamental combs and pins (figs. 7.36–7.41) are embedded in the elaborate
wigs of Fante women (see figs. 7.2–7.7)

When very different cultures meet, it is always interesting to see what
will be adopted and the ways in which crossovers will appear. The Akan, long
famous for lavish personal adornment and profuse use of gold, recorded their
contact with Victorian society in jewelry and regalia, sometimes with precise
and skillful reproduction, sometimes with creative variation. Akan love of
adornment and verbal/visual associations made Victorian jewelry and the messages
it conveyed the perfect medium for crossover. Sarah Bowdich Lee, the formerly
Mrs. T. Edward Bowdich, proved the point with this story: "I once gave the

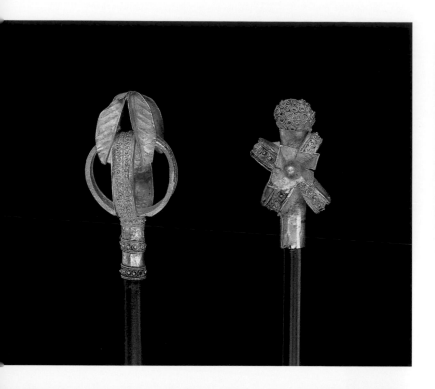

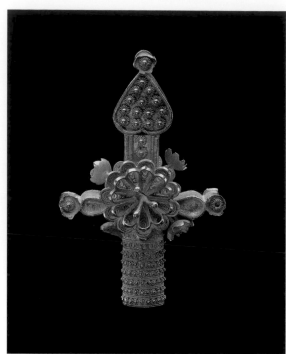

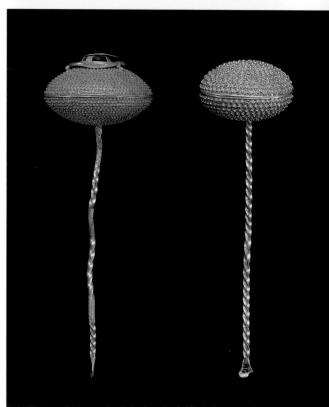

**7.38A,B** (TOP, LEFT)
Hair pins. Gold. Largest
dimension: 6½ in.
(A) 97.884.2; (B) 97.884.1.

**7.39** (TOP, RIGHT)
Ornament. Gold. L: 2¼ in.
97.889.

**7.40A,B** (BOTTOM, LEFT)
Hair ornaments. Gold.
Largest dimension: 4½ in.
(A) Ornament, 97.1091;
(B) Pin with flower and
birds, 97.883.

**7.41A,B** (BOTTOM, RIGHT)
Hair pins. Gold. Largest
dimension: 4¼ in.
(A) 97.1532; (B) 97.1890.

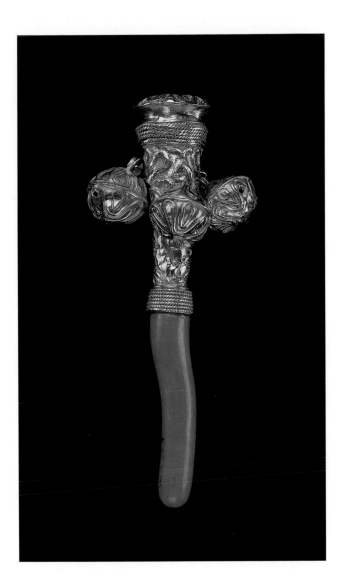

highest pleasure to a native woman, by presenting
her with a pair of Mosaic workmanship (earrings)
they represented the 'Forget me not,' in every stage,
from the bud to the dying petals; and she repeated
my explanation of them, with evident pride at
being the sole possessor of such a treasure'" (1835, 25).
Though Sarah Bowdich Lee returned to London,
her "forget-me-nots" and their message remained
and were reproduced to become part of Akan culture.
There were doubtless many previous varied
influences on the Akan, but it is their nineteenth-
and twentieth-century gold objects that remain
today that show unmistakable Victorian origin.

### Child's Rattle

One of the most interesting and rare works in The
Glassell Collection of African Gold is a child's rattle
made of gold with a coral teether (fig. 7.42). As early
as Roman times, infants received gifts of coral that
were hung around their necks as protective amulets
to ward off illness and promote health. Later, Christianity adopted the tradition,
and even the Christ child is depicted in Renaissance paintings wearing such a
coral amulet. In the seventeenth century, English silversmiths created a charming
object that served as a baby toy, teether, and amulet. It consisted of a cluster
of bells, a rattle, a whistle, and a coral handle that could be used as a teething
stick. These objects were usually made of silver gilded with gold and were so
expensive they were probably used rarely by the infant. Popular in England
as christening gifts from the seventeenth to the nineteenth century, they were
copied by American colonial silversmiths. The Museum of Fine Arts, Houston,
has both an English and an American rattle in its collections. The English rattle,
made by Hester Bateman, a female goldsmith of the eighteenth century, bears
her mark stamped into the mouthpiece (fig. 7.43; Glanville and Goldsborough
1990, 11). The American rattle, fashioned in silver, was made in the shop of
Thauvet Besley, active in New York from 1727 to 1757 (fig. 7.44).

As noted, the Glassell Collection has a third child's rattle, made by the
Akan. The finial of this rattle is decorated with raised motifs, bands of cording,
and three gold bells. Unlike the English and American versions, and typical of

7.42 Teething rattle. Gold.
L: 3 7/8 in. 97.1310.

**7.43** British-made teething rattle. Hester Bateman, eighteenth century. Gilded silver, coral. L: 6½ in. 80.96; Anonymous gift in honor of Ray and Clara Willoughby.

**7.44** American-made teething rattle. Thauvet Besley, 1727–1757. Silver, coral. L: 5½ in. B.87.11; The Bayou Bend Collection, museum purchase with funds provided by William James Hill.

the Akan, the rattle is made of gold rather than silver or gilded silver and bears no hallmarks. A fitted morocco leather case with dark blue velvet and silk lining (fig. 7.45) was created for the rattle and labeled "R & S. Garrard & Co.; Goldsmiths & Jewellers; to the Crown; 25 Haymarket London." The case is typical of those made for Asante gold sold at auction by Garrard's after the Anglo-Asante War of 1874. This lovely and whimsical child's toy is one of the few items of Asante gold in the Glassell Collection that can be traced to Garrard's. ●

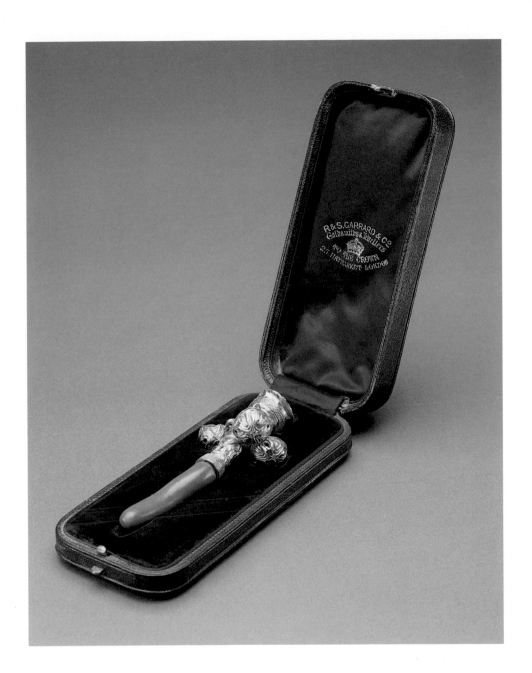

**7.45** Teether, in leather case
with velvet and silk lining,
labeled "R & S. Garrard &
Co.; Goldsmiths & Jewellers;
to the Crown; 25 Haymarket
London," nineteenth century.
Coral. L (of case): 5 ⅝ in.
97.1310 and case.

# 8 Cultural Diversions

### AKAN REGALIA AMONG THE BAULE
### AND THE LAGOON PEOPLES OF CÔTE D'IVOIRE

Baule chiefs of central Côte d'Ivoire share some of the trappings of leadership with the Asante of Ghana but are quite distinct culturally (figs. 8.1–8.3). Nevertheless, a popular legend fosters a connection between the two groups. According to the Baule leaders living in Sakassou, after the death of Asantehene Osei Tutu I (circa 1717), there was a dispute over succession between Opoku Ware I and his rival, Dako, who was killed in the strife that ensued. Fearing further reprisals, Dako's sister Aura Poku (also Abra, Auro, and Alba) escaped to the west with her brother's supporters. When they reached the Comoé River in what is now Côte d'Ivoire, they were unable to cross because of the turbulent currents. A diviner determined that a sacrifice was necessary, and the women threw their gold jewelry into the river without results. It was then determined that a human sacrifice was necessary, and eventually Aura Poku gave her only son to the river. As a result, in some versions of the story, the river parted, and in others it was spanned by a bridge of crocodiles or hippopotamuses. Once on the other side, Aura Poku's followers thanked their "Queen" for her enormous sacrifice and assumed the name *ba au le*, conventionally translated as "the child is dead," to honor her leadership (Weiskel 1987, 262–64; Vogel 1997, 34–35). As the story goes, her supporters founded a number of settlements in what is now the Baule heartland, and her descendants eventually resided at Sakassou where Nana Kouakou Amougble III currently considers himself "the direct descendant of Queen Abra Poku" and "King of the Baules," although most Baule do not recognize him as such.[1] The varying Baule oral traditions temporally locate the conflict leading to the exodus from Asante after the death of Osei Tutu I, but Asante scholars are in agreement that the succession dispute with either one or two brothers, Dako Panin or Dako Kuma, occurred after the death of Opoku Ware I, about 1750 (McCaskie 1995, 175–77). It should be noted that this myth

8.1 Fly whisk and handle with bird with an insect in its mouth, Baule, Côte d'Ivoire. Gold leaf, wood. L: 14 in. 97.860.

8.2 Baule chief N'goran Koffi and his attendants. Kouassiblekro, Côte d'Ivoire. Photograph by Eliot Elisofon, 1972. National Museum of African Art. Eliot Elisofon Photographic Archives, Smithsonian Institution. EEPA 1526.

is not without parallels to that of the founding of the Asante empire wherein a miraculous event leads to the founding of a new state following a conflict and the sacrifice of regalia.

Whether this legend has any basis in fact is widely disputed. The anthropologist Timothy Weiskel finds some credence in the account and concludes:

> What seems to have occurred in the central Ivory Coast, then, was a gradual historical process of incursion, dispute, and resolution between principles of local authority and those based upon derivation from or close association with practices prevailing in the Asante court. Over time in political and judicial realms, Akan cultural metaphors came to dominate the region even though the pure descendants of Akan migrant refugees may never have constituted a majority population. [Weiskel 1987, 269]

Art historian Susan Vogel sees it differently: "The most often published fact about Baule history is also the most problematic: an origin myth of miraculous migration from Asante.... This story...has dominated—and I would say seriously distorted—interpretations of Baule art, history, and political systems for decades" (1997, 34). Vogel recognizes a "root Baule" culture that was firmly in place well prior to any possible Akan migration and that still forms the core of Baule society. In her view, it is an egalitarian culture where the concept of chieftaincy was a superficial overlay in the first place and only sustained through the French colonial occupation and its need for an indigenous puppet leadership.

Regardless of history or myth, it is clear that there is a highly visible veneer of Asante influence in Baule leadership arts especially in the area of elite adornment and buttressing regalia, even if these arts do not share the same depth and complexity of meaning and function as their Asante prototypes. Perhaps closest to Asante practices in form and substance is the veneration of ancestors through the blackening and preservation of stools seen as the repository of the deceased's soul or spirit and the locus of sacrifices and offerings (Garrard 1993b, fig. 305; Loucou 1993, figs. 13, 14). The court at Sakassou also has its own golden stool, which it traces back to Queen Poku (Fischer and Himmelheber 1975, fig. 11).[2]

More publicly visible are the assortment of gold objects and jewelry associated with Baule "chiefs" (figs. 8.2, 8.3). Vogel considers the Baule view of gold to have some supernatural qualities and quotes her colleague Kangah:

8.4 (OPPOSITE, TOP)
Staff finial of leopard with
bush cow, Baule, Côte
d'Ivoire. Gold leaf, wood.
L: 13 in. 97.1277.

8.5 (OPPOSITE, BOTTOM)
Staff finial of figures on
horseback, Baule, Côte
d'Ivoire. Gold leaf, wood.
L: 15½ in. 97.1288.A.

8.6 (OPPOSITE, RIGHT)
Chief's staff, Baule, Côte
d'Ivoire. Wood, gold leaf,
fabric. L: 56 in. 97.1509.

8.3 Detail of the gold jewelry
of Baule chief N'goran Koffi.
Kouassiblekro, Côte d'Ivoire.
Photograph by Eliot Elisofon,
1972. National Museum of
African Art. Eliot Elisofon
Photographic Archives,
Smithsonian Institution.
EEPA 1534.

Gold gives force. If it has no power, it is not real gold. That is why all important things include gold.… When an important person dies, gold honors the deceased; these honors are only for important people. Gold is worn by all Nguessans because they have a hard spirit and the gold softens it. Gold brings strength, but it is also given to [produce] calm. Nguessans are difficult not calm. They cause arguments and are irresponsible. Gold calms evil spirits. [Vogel 1997, 196]

This view is not inconsistent with Asante notions of the spiritual qualities of gold discussed earlier.

Although royal object types—swords, staffs (figs. 8.4–8.6), and personal adornment (fig. 8.7)—and their imagery are borrowed from the Akan, and even though the Baule like the Akan have a profound appreciation of the art of the proverb, the Baule do not consistently seem to interpret their plastic arts with traditional maxims. Hans Himmelheber who made eight research trips to the Baule between 1933 and 1971 wrote, "I have not yet found a Baule who could elucidate any of these animal figures, either those on objects or free standing. But the Akan in Ghana attribute some meaning—or even several meanings—to carvings of single animals on chiefs' staffs" (1972, 200). Despite this, three of the staffs he documents from Sakassou were carved in Kumase by Osei Bonsu, have highly codified proverbs associated with them in an Asante context, and were interpreted by the Baule with meanings very close to the Asante originals (Fischer and Himmelheber 1975, 11, 12, figs. 10, 12, 13). These

**8.7** Chief's headdress with ornaments, Baule, Côte d'Ivoire. Velvet, gold leaf, wood. DIAM: 7⅜ in. 97.892.

examples may be the exceptions, or there may be more meaning imparted to these objects by the Baule than scholars have allowed (see below).

If there is some question of the Baule assigning the same depth of meaning to the motifs on their regalia as the Akan, they do seem to embrace these objects as a statement of wealth in much the same way as their eastern neighbors. As Susan Vogel makes clear these are indeed important and protected heirlooms:

> Solid cast-gold ornaments, carved wooden objects with gold foil, and packets of unworked gold nuggets or gold dust are wrapped in bundles and hidden in pots or suitcases and kept in a sacred family inheritance called the *aja*. The tradition of such an inheritance is said to have come out of the earth with the Mamla, the original Baule. The *aja* is inalienable and indivisible, and includes not only gold but cash, cloth and the family ancestor stools. [Vogel 1997, 195; cf. Rattray quotation cited on p. 36]

It is also of interest that *aja* appears to be a cognate of *agya*, a Twi word translated by Christaller as "progenitor, ancestor" (1933, 153). Vogel goes on to emphasize that the *aja* is considered the "force of the ancestors," "the soul of the family," and "being like a god" (1997, 196). These displays of wealth are somewhat reminiscent of the ɔbirɛmpɔn discussed earlier (see chapter 5). The contents of the *aja* are only displayed on special occasions and most prominently at funerals, where cloth, ornaments, and fly whisks are arrayed

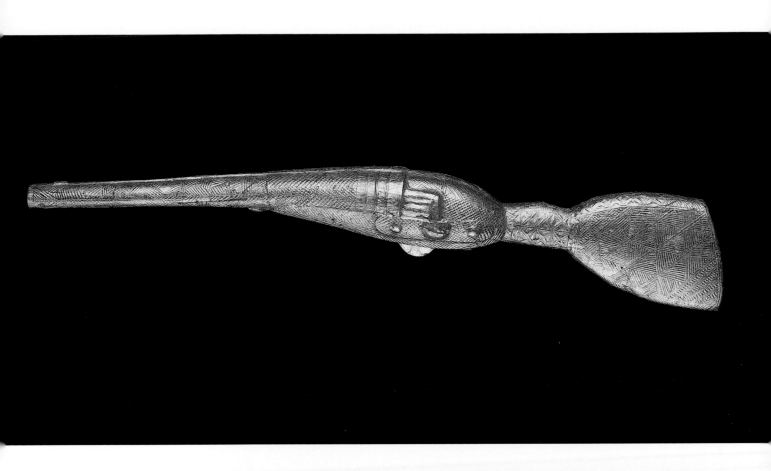

**8.8** Musket, Baule, Côte d'Ivoire. Gold leaf, wood. L: 12 ⅝ in. 97.795.

**8.9A,B** Jug with handle and bird standing on tortoise, Baule, Côte d'Ivoire. Gold leaf, wood. Largest dimension: 5 ¾ in. (A) 97.1419; (B) 97.820.

8.10 "Pith helmet," Baule, Côte d'Ivoire. Gold leaf, wood. L: 12⅜ in. 97.909.

around the deceased as she or he receives final respects. The collective *aja* of the extended family are presented at this time before the items are returned to their individual owners.

Within the *aja* the Baule have an ostentatious assortment of gold-covered wood objects, many of which do not have counterparts in Akan regalia. Most are nonfunctional replicas of elite forms of Baule material culture. Among the European-derived objects are kerosene lanterns, gin bottles, ceramic jugs (fig. 8.9A), firearms (fig. 8.8), pith helmets (fig. 8.10), and bugles (fig. 8.11B). Imitations of indigenous items include sideblown ivory trumpets (fig. 8.11A), combs (figs. 8.12A,B), and cartridge belts (fig. 8.13). The latter often features the distinctive double-knife form that illustrates a Baule proverb, "The blade of a knife cannot carve its own handle," demonstrating the need for cooperation in any endeavor (Garrard 1993c, 155; cf. Fischer and Himmelheber 1975, fig. 17). Perhaps the most unfamiliar item in the *aja* is the gold-leafed replica of the iron gong and wood mallet (*lawre waka*) used by a diviner to enter into a state of trance prior to a divination session (fig. 8.14).[3] In addition to gold-leafed objects, the *aja* might also contain cast-gold animals (fig. 8.15) and also the cast human heads for which the Baule are well known (fig. 8.16). These are thought to be conventionalized portraits of friends or lovers.

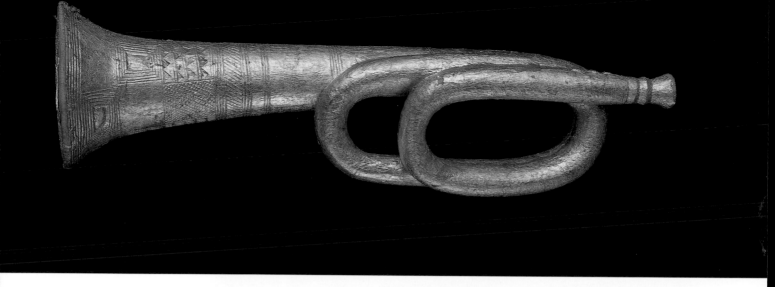

**8.11A,B** Sculptures of horn and trumpet, Baule, Côte d'Ivoire. Gold leaf, wood, fiber cord. Largest dimension: 10½ in. (A) 97.1489; (B) 97.1412.

**8.12A,B** Hair combs, Baule, Côte d'Ivoire. Gold leaf, wood. Largest dimension: 5⅞ in. (A) 97.782; (B) 97.783.

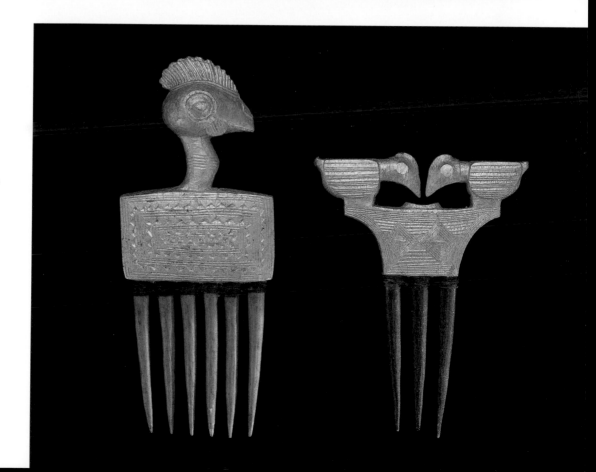

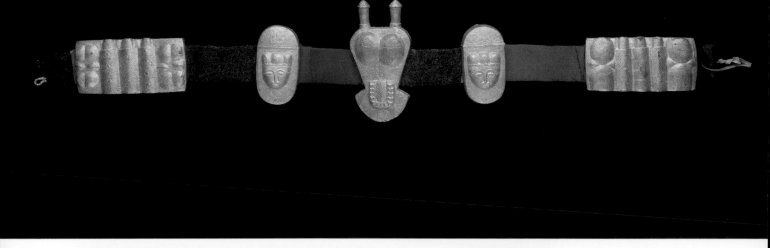

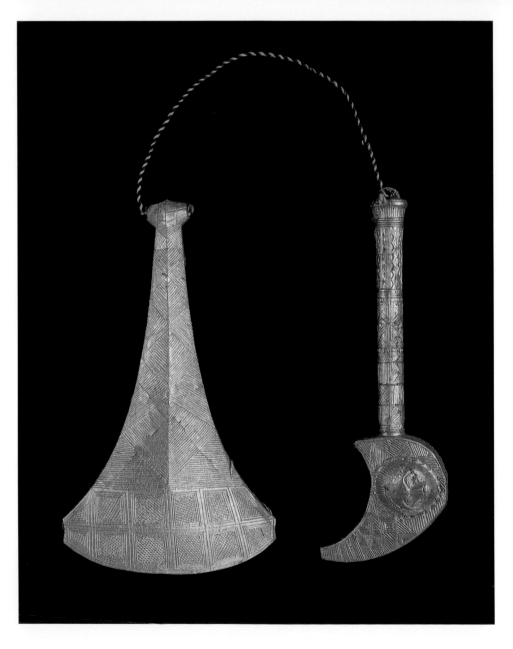

**8.13** Bandolier with ornaments, Baule, Côte d'Ivoire. Gold leaf, wood, leather, fabric. L: 33½ in. 97.752.

**8.14** Gong and beater, Baule, Côte d'Ivoire. Gold leaf, wood. Largest dimension: 7½ in. 97.872.A,B.

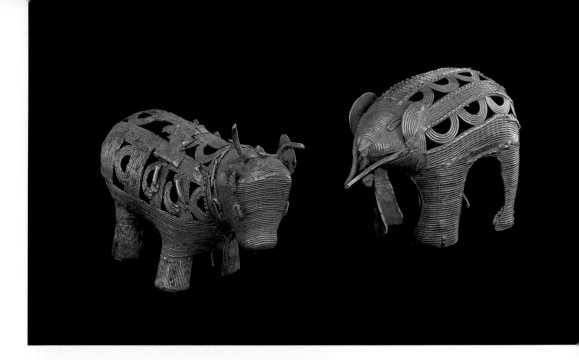

**8.15A,B** Bull and elephant castings, Baule, Côte d'Ivoire. Gold. Largest dimension: 4 in. (A) 97.816; (B) 97.803.

**8.16A–D** Pendants. Baule, Côte d'Ivoire, Gold. L (of largest): 3½ in. Clockwise from top: (A) 97.1051; (B) 97.1063; (C) 97.1482; (D) 97.1046.

The pith helmet and policeman's hat may be among the more cryptic items in the Glassell Collection. As Philip Ravenhill notes, "The colonial pith helmet, one of the most important symbols of raw political power during the early colonial era, became one of the most common accoutrements represented in Baule figurative art of the period" (1996, 22), and one might add in the contents and displays of the *aja*, since these were rarely worn (see fig. 8.10). Similarly, the hat (*képi*) worn by gendarmes in the French colonial police forces appeared in carefully carved versions both with and without gold leaf

**8.17** French colonial policeman's hat, or "*képi*," Baule, Côte d'Ivoire. Wood. L: 9⅝ in. 97.910.

**8.18** Necklace, Baule, Côte d'Ivoire. Gold. L: 14⅞ in. 97.985.

(fig. 8.17). Garrard mistakenly attributes one of these hats worn by an Adiukru elder to a Ghanaian source, but it is unquestionably of Baule origin and of French colonial inspiration (1993a, fig. 390). The existence of these and related genres can be read in at least two ways. On one level they might be seen as embracing the colonial presence, that is, making friends with the enemy to manipulate for political advantage. On another, creating images of nonfunctional headware suggests cooperating with the status quo and also perhaps possessing it.

Baule necklaces and bracelets are easily distinguished from those of the Asante and other Ghanaian Akan and are dominated by varied circular and rectangular beads, with very few beads representing actual objects (figs. 8.18, 8.19). The second of these necklaces actually has some Asante beads mixed in with the Baule. Garrard says that some of these rectangular beads are called

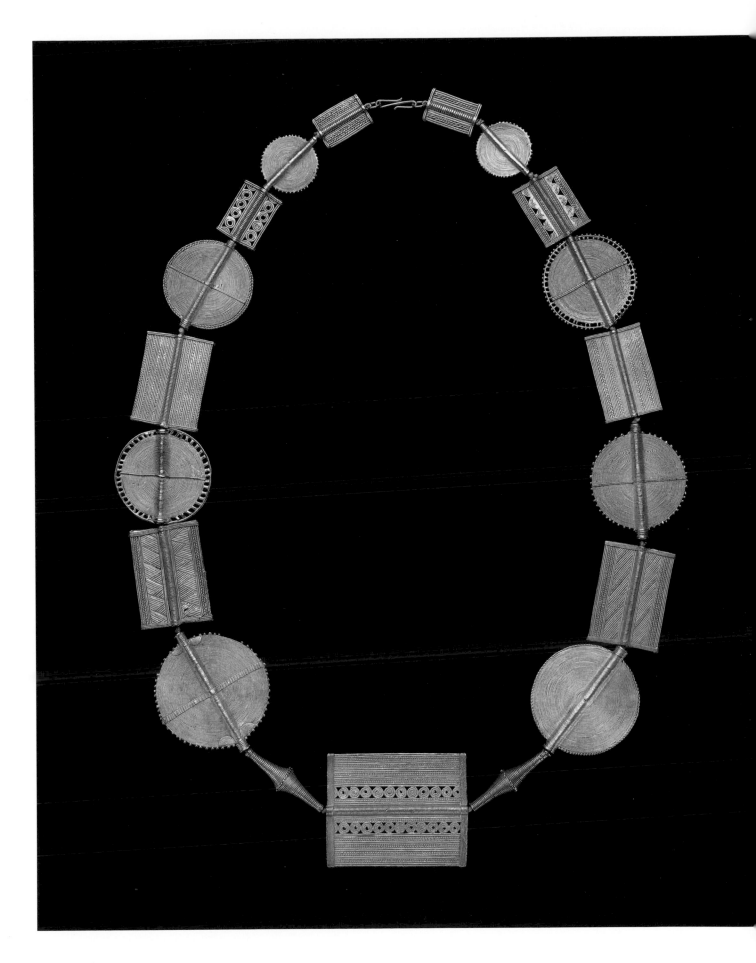

**8.19** Necklace, Baule, Côte d'Ivoire. Gold. L: 18½ in. 97.995.

*srala*, or bamboo door. He notes that "The bamboo door is said to symbolize the chief; it sees what is happening both inside and outside the house, just as the chief knows all that is happening both in his village and outside. Large gold beads of this form are sometimes hung in front of a chief on public occasions, suspended from a string" (1989, 242, fig. 91). Depending on design, other rectangular beads are named "chicken feather," "knife handle," "taro roots" or "back of the tortoise." Disc-shaped beads are called "setting sun" (*senze*) and other names depending on pattern (Garrard 1989, 98–100, 242). According to Garrard, "Disc-shaped beads were sometimes used as a form of marriage payment: in order to obtain the hand of his chosen bride a man would present one of these beads to her family. They formed part of the family 'treasure' handed down from one generation to the next" (1993c, 162).

One of the most interesting and symbolically elusive Baule (or perhaps lagoon) objects in the Glassell Collection is a magnificent disc-shaped "pendant"

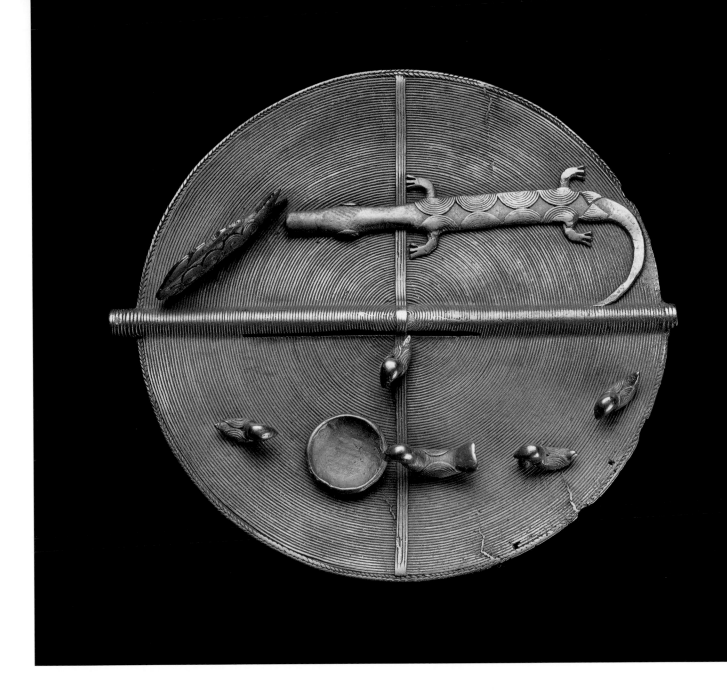

8.20 Pendant, Baule (?),
Côte d'Ivoire. Gold.
DIAM: 3 ⅞ in. 97.1540

that if it were Asante would be called an *akrafokonmu*. The disc is divided in
half with a crocodile attacking a fish on one half and a hen and four chicks
approaching a bowl on the other (fig. 8.20). The Baule were and are more
likely to wear such discs around the wrist or arm rather than suspended from
the neck. The imagery on this disc is clearly more complex than most Baule
examples where an isolated crocodile typically extends across the diameter.
In the latter case some say that this represents the reptilian bridge upon which
Queen Poku crossed the Comoé. In the Glassell example one can only marvel
at the artistry and wonder about what appears to be a combination of predatory
and nurturing imagery.

Perhaps the most distinctively Baule items of regalia are the gold-covered
horse-tail fly whisks (*nandwa blawa*; figs. 8.21, 8.22). The handles of these symbols of authority are artistically elaborated far beyond anything the Ghanaian
Akan produced. They exist in large numbers throughout the Baule area and

**8.21** Baule chief with
entourage from Golikro,
Aitu Region. Photograph
by Susan M. Vogel, 1982.

Himmelheber reported seeing "not hundreds, but thousands of these during
my trips to Baule country" (1972, 191, 192). A lineage head or "chief" may have
five to ten or more whisks. Garrard cites a Baule proverb that helps explain the
whisks, "'money (gold) is like a fly-whisk, a single person cannot catch it.'
Today you may have money, but tomorrow you will be poor again" (1993c,
156). According to some, their function is less to drive away flies than to dispel
evil spirits or "witchcraft." The king is kept pure and protected from harmful
forces through soft stroking by the whisk bearers. The whisks were also apparently used as collateral, and a debtor deposited his whisks with a creditor until
a debt was repaid (Fischer and Himmelheber 1975, 15). And, of course, they
also served as a vital component of the *aja* and as such were crucial items in
funerary displays honoring recently deceased elders (figs. 8.23, 8.24).

The chalice-shaped handles of the whisks may have representational
imagery on the sides, frequently a low relief human face, and are almost always
surmounted by a human or animal figure. The Glassell examples have a human
head (fig. 8.25), two figures playing a game called *awale* (*oware*; fig. 8.26),
a chicken with a grasshopper (see fig. 8.1), a hen (fig. 8.27), parrot (fig. 8.28),
elephant (fig. 8.29), and two fish (figs. 8.30, 8.31). The meaning of these motifs
has not been studied extensively, but Garrard provides a telling explication of
the parrot, "Informants named the main motif as *anyi ako*, 'talking parrot,'
explaining that the parrot, like the chief, knows everything and says whatever
he likes" (1993c, 157).

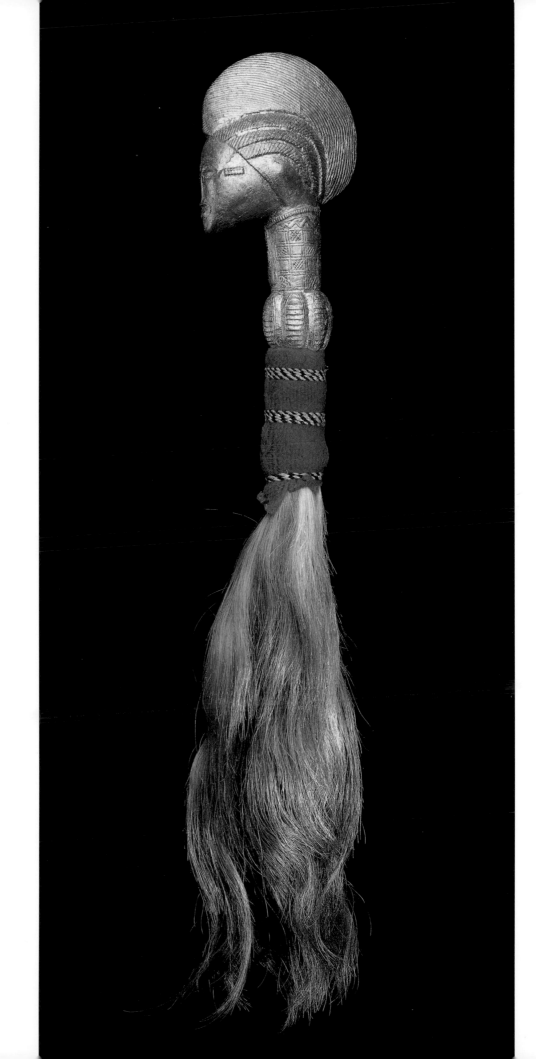

**8.22** Fly whisk, Baule, Côte d'Ivoire. Gold leaf, wood, fabric, fiber cord. L: 23 in. 97.852.

**8.25** (OPPOSITE, LEFT)
Detail of fly whisk, Baule,
Côte d'Ivoire. Gold leaf,
wood, horse tail, fabric,
fiber cord. L: 23 in. 97.852.

**8.26** (OPPOSITE, RIGHT)
Fly whisk with two figures
on handle, Baule, Côte
d'Ivoire. Gold leaf, wood,
horse tail, fabric, fiber cord.
L: 40 in. 97.870.

**8.23** Baule funeral display
at Kongonou, Aitu Region.
Photograph by Susan M.
Vogel, 1982.

**8.24** Funeral bed with dis-
play of fly whisks at Morofe,
Akwe Region. Photograph by
Susan M. Vogel, 1993.

Among the most accomplished display items of the Baule are the freestanding gold-leafed figurative sculptures, generally less than a foot tall (figs.
8.32–8.34). These are covered with the same vocabulary of relief surface decoration
as the representations of inanimate objects and stand in sharp contrast to the
more famous Baule tradition of figurative sculpture, which lacks both the surface
patterning and gold foil (fig. 8.35). The latter figures represent otherworldly
lovers or spirit mates (*blolo bian* for male figures and *blolo bla* for female). These
are carved at the instigation of a diviner to resolve problems (most frequently
infertility) thought to have been caused by one's lover from the otherworld.
Typically, these figures are kept in the bedroom of their owners, are given
periodic sacrifices and offerings, and sleep with their owners on a designated

**8.27** Fly whisk with bird on handle, Baule, Côte d'Ivoire. Gold leaf, wood, horse tail, fabric, fiber cord. L: 37¼ in. 97.854.

**8.28** Fly whisk with bird on handle, Baule, Côte d'Ivoire. Gold leaf, wood, horse tail, fabric, fiber cord. L: 40 in. 97.851.

**8.29** (OPPOSITE, LEFT) Fly whisk with elephant on handle, Baule, Côte d'Ivoire. Gold leaf, wood, horse tail, fabric, fiber cord. L: 46 in. 97.853.

**8.30** (RIGHT, ABOVE) Detail of handle end of figure 8.31, Baule, Côte d'Ivoire. Gold leaf, wood, horse tail, fabric, fiber cord. L: 40 in. 97.849.

**8.31** (RIGHT) Fly whisk, Côte d'Ivoire Gold leaf, wood, horse tail, fabric, fiber cord. L: 40 in. 97.849.

8.32 Standing female figure, Baule, Côte d'Ivoire. Gold leaf, wood. H: 11½ in. 98.723.

8.33 Standing female figure, Baule, Côte d'Ivoire. Gold leaf, wood. H: 8¾ in. 97.823.

8.34 Standing female figure, Baule, Côte d'Ivoire. Gold leaf, wood. H: 7⅜ in. 97.833.

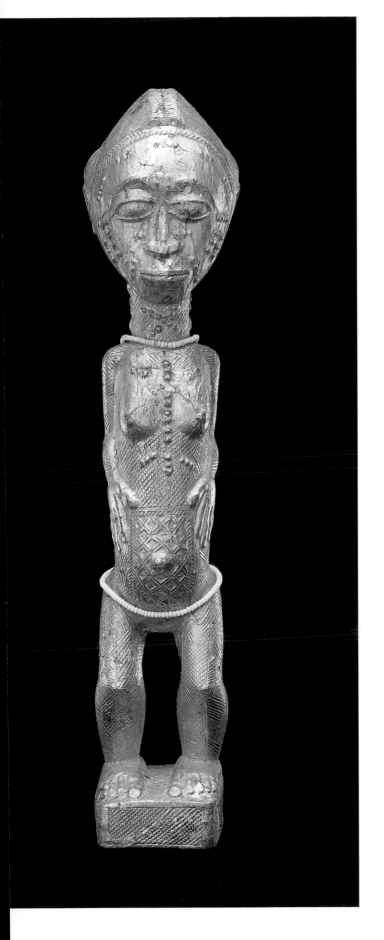

8.35 Seated male figure,
Baule, Côte d'Ivoire. Wood.
H: 16½ in. 91.237. Museum
purchase with funds provided
by the Alice Pratt Brown
Museum Fund.

night each week to appease the spirit of the
otherworld mate and thus eliminate the problem
(see Ravenhill 1996; Vogel 1997, 246–67). Both
Ravenhill and Vogel deny that gold-covered Baule
figures ever served as spirit lovers (personal communications), but both Garrard (1989, 90) and
Alain-Michel Boyer (1993, 348) suggest that they
occasionally functioned in these contexts. Regardless, Boyer states that the ubiquitous gesture of
the hands on the belly "signifies first and foremost
peace and unity" and is a gesture "made by certain
spirits to show their respect or deference when
they meet humans" (1993, 345).

### The Lagoon Peoples of Southeast Côte d'Ivoire

The dozen or so peoples living around the lagoons
of southeastern Côte d'Ivoire speak languages only
distantly related to each other and even further
removed from the Baule to the north and the
Twi-speaking groups to the east. They do not
have a centralized hereditary political structure
like the Akan but are organized in a variety of
age-grades. Most of the groups have a migration
story similar to the Baule, although varying in the
details, but nevertheless pointing to the Akan of
Ghana. Yet, as with the Baule, they must have
been relatively small populations that joined
already existing groups living around the lagoons
(see Visoná 1987; 1993).

In the absence of hereditary chieftaincies,
it is wealthy individuals who through their own
initiative and personal achievement become village
heads and age-grade leaders. As community leaders
they assume the familiar adornment of Akan chiefs
and surround themselves with swords, staffs, and
fly whisks (fig. 8.36). The attainment of wealth
is most visibly manifest in the accumulation and

**8.36** Ebrie chiefs and notables from Anna, Côte d'Ivoire. Photograph by Eliot Elisofon, 1972. National Museum of African Art. Eliot Elisofon Photographic Archives, Smithsonian Institution. EEPA 1546.

**8.37** Akye display of gold ornaments. Photograph by Monica Blackmun Visoná, 1981.

**8.38** Ebrie women wearing gold hair ornaments, Anna, Côte d'Ivoire. Photograph by Eliot Elisofon, 1972. National Museum of African Art. Eliot Elisofon Photographic Archives, Smithsonian Institution. EEPA 2723.

display of gold ornaments—both cast and gold foil over wood—at expensive feasts where the assembled wealth is laid out on tables for the community to see (fig. 8.37).

Timothy Garrard has succinctly described a gold display festival:

Such a ceremony was not lightly undertaken. A man would not attempt it until, after making discreet enquiries, he was certain that his self-acquired gold ornaments were sufficient in number and quality to meet with general approval. If they were not, he would risk public scorn and ridicule. He also needed sufficient means to provide a feast for the community.

On the appointed day the festivities would begin. Amidst singing, dancing and drumming, punctuated with musket fire, the owner of the gold exposed his wealth to public view. His accumulated treasure of gold pendants was set out on a table in the street, where the whole world could examine them. While the display was in progress, those who had already established their status as "big man" could exhibit their gold in the same way. This increased the interest

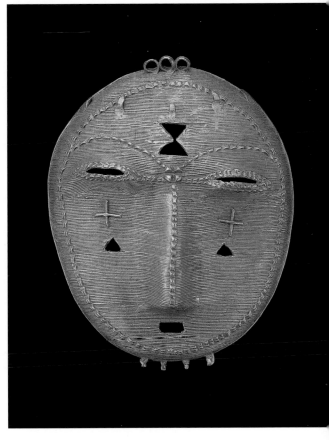

8.39 Ebrie woman wearing gold hair ornaments, Anna, Côte d'Ivoire. Photograph by Eliot Elisofon, 1972. National Museum of African Art. Eliot Elisofon Photographic Archives, Smithsonian Institution. EEPA 2734.

8.40 Pendant. Gold. H: 2¼ in. 97.1032.

of the occasion and no doubt provided a standard by which the efforts of the new aspirant could be judged. [Garrard 1989, 106]

As many as sixty to seventy ornaments might be shown and of course the participants are dressed in their finest cloth and wear some of the most stunning of the ornaments (figs. 8.38, 8.39).

The most common ornaments represent human heads (fig. 8.40), crescent moons (fig. 8.41), and rams' heads (fig. 8.42). Visoná considers the human heads (fig. 8.43) to be, "the faces of the ancestors, whose spiritual powers protect the family treasure and simple gold discs [fig. 8.44A] are believed to deflect jealousy and witchcraft" (1993, 1: 372). For the crescent moon motif Garrard cites a proverb provided by a Baule goldsmith, "When the moon comes out, all can see it. (Secrets will one day be revealed, so it is better to be open in your behavior)" (1989, 236). He also relies on Baule goldsmiths to explain the wonderful variety of abstract rams' heads (see fig. 8.42) citing the saying, "'My strength is in my horns.' Here the ram signifies the chief, for it is powerful, intelligent and wise" (1989, 237). He goes on to say that he received a similar explanation in the lagoons area. For a catfish ornament (fig. 8.44B) he received two different

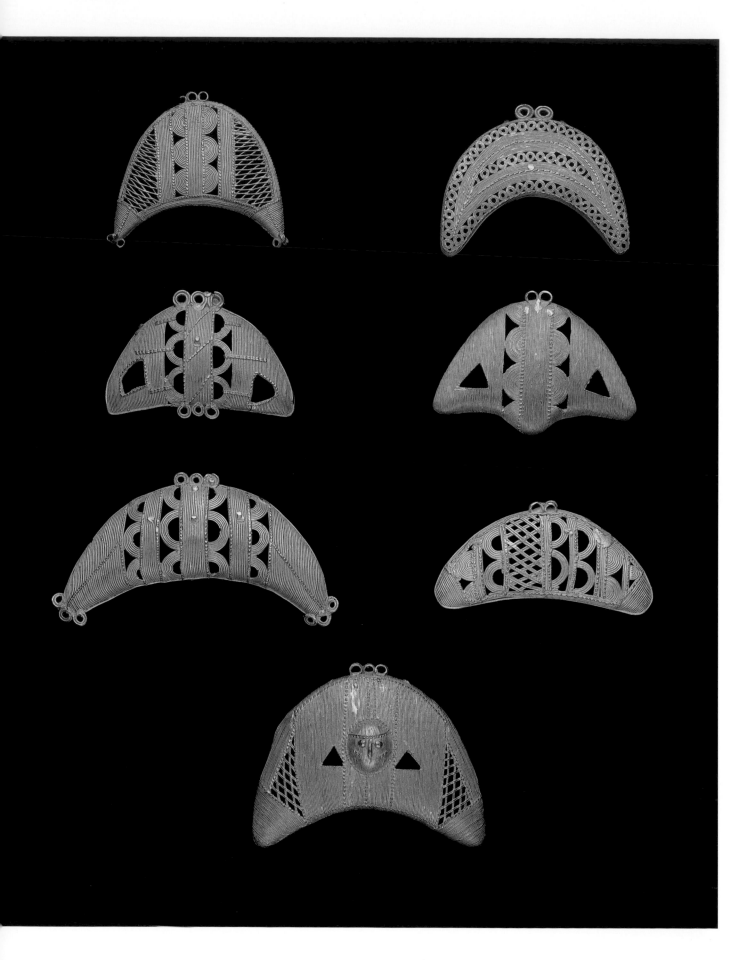

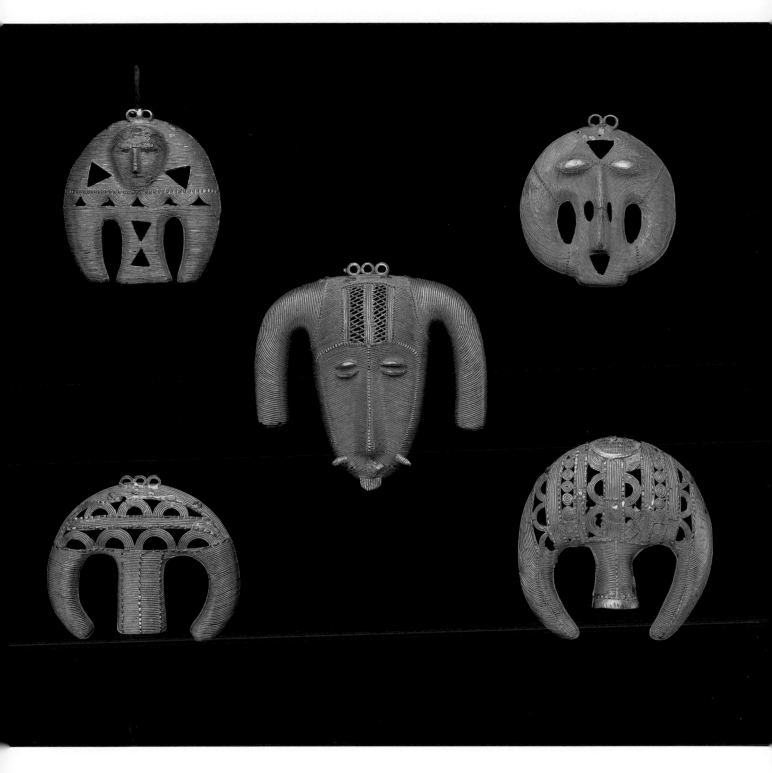

**8.41A–G** Pendants. Gold.
Largest dimension: 4¾ in.
Left to right, top to bottom:
(A) 97.1055; (B) 97.1073;
(C). 97.1031; (D) 97.1034;
(E) 97.1085; (F) 97.1071;
(G) 97.1084.

**8.42A–E** Pendants. Gold.
Largest dimension: 4¾ in.
Clockwise from upper
left to corners, to center:
(A) 97.1050; (B) 97.1058;
(C) 97.1044; (D) 97.1069;
(E) 97.880.

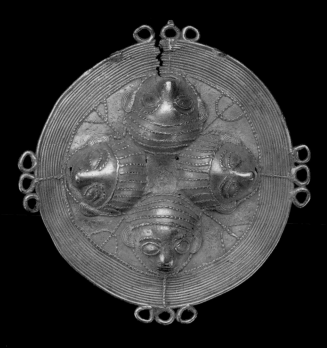

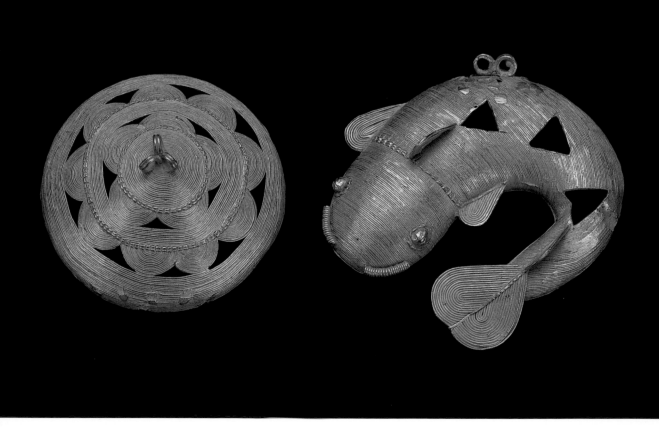

**8.43A,B** Ornaments. Gold. Largest dimension: 3½ in. (A) 97.1539; (B) 97.1319.

**8.45** Standing figure, southern Anyi (?), Côte d'Ivoire. Wood, gold leaf. H: 11½ in. 97.830.

**8.44A,B** Ornaments. Gold. w (of largest): 3¼ in. (A) 97.1045; (B) 97.1039.

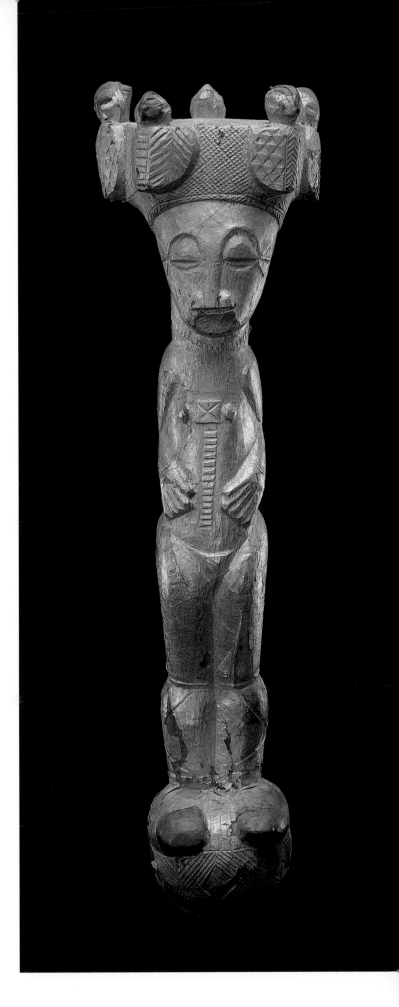

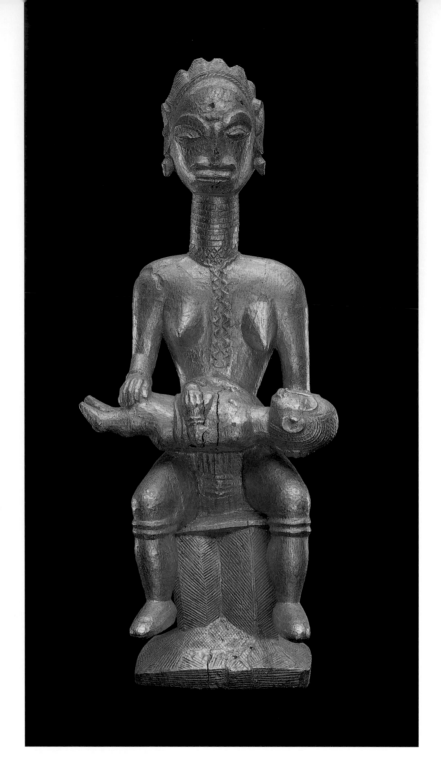

**8.46** Female figure with child, lagoon peoples or Anyi, Côte d'Ivoire. Wood, gold leaf. H: 13 in. 97.814.

explanations: "At Grand Bassam it was said that 'the catfish always hides and doesn't show itself since it is very intelligent. Even when it is killed and put in the pot it wants to see the bottom of the pot.' An Ebrie man interpreted it as meaning: 'When you fish some people say you fish for nothing, but one day you will make a catch'" (1989, 239). Duplicating Baule practice, the lagoon groups also incorporate gold-leaf figurative sculpture into their displays of wealth (figs. 8.45–8.47). Wood sculpture without the gold serves a variety of purposes among the lagoon groups including the representation of spirit spouses and twins, but the gold-adorned figures apparently serve primarily as statements of financial achievement (Visoná 1993, 377–79).[4] ●

**8.47** Figural group, Ebrie, Côte d'Ivoire. Wood, gold leaf. H: 15⅜ in. 97.837.

# 9 Festivals of Arts

The displays of wealth that characterize some Baule and lagoon ritual events have their Ghanaian counterparts in the great variety of Akan festivals where most of the regalia discussed previously appears in processions of chiefs (figs. 9.1–9.4) and the subsequent and slightly more static displays of chiefs sitting in state with their respective entourages—occasions conventionally called durbars by the Akan (figs. 9.5, 9.6). A basic understanding of Akan festivals is critical to the appreciation of both the artistic and political roles that various items of regalia play in expressive culture. The names and ritual functions of the festivals vary from state to state.[1] Some honor the founding of the state, others celebrate the harvest and firstfruits, still others focus on the deities of the state. And all Akan festivals in one way or another pay homage to the ancestors. Regardless, the durbars are the most public face of the vast majority of Akan royal festivals.

The best-documented and most thoroughly analyzed festivals of the Akan are the nineteenth-century Odwira celebrations of the Asante held at Kumase and the late twentieth-century Odwiras of the Akuapem at Akuropon. Odwira is typically translated as "purification," and it is a complex annual festival, although the Asante have largely abandoned it in the twentieth century in favor of Akwasidae Kɛseɛ celebrations held about every five years, the latter nevertheless share most of the same formal public elements as the Odwira.

T. C. McCaskie in an extended and brilliant analysis of the Asante Odwira begins with a concise summary of its purpose:

> By its primary definition, *odwira* was a festival of cleansing and purification orientated towards a ritual meditation on the seamless unity of dead, living and unborn. The eating of new-season yam was an obviously appropriate analogue of this project. The ancestors

9.1 Fante chief being "cooled" by his subjects at annual Fetu Afahye in Cape Coast. Photograph by Doran H. Ross, 1997.

**9.2** Newly installed Fante chief carried through the streets of Saltpond. Photograph by Doran H. Ross, 1975.

**9.3** Fante queen mother in procession following the enstoolment of a new chief at Saltpond. Photograph by Doran H. Ross, 1975.

**9.4** (OPPOSITE, TOP) Asantehene Otumfuo Opoku Ware II riding a in palanquin during the celebration of the twenty-fifth anniversary of his reign. Photograph by Frank Fournier, 1995.

**9.5** (OPPOSITE, BOTTOM) Asantehene Otumfuo Opoku Ware II seated next to the Golden Stool of Asante during the celebration of the twenty-fifth anniversary of his reign. Photograph by Frank Fournier, 1995.

**9.6** Durbar during Odwira celebrations at Akuropon, Akuapem. Photograph by Herbert M. Cole, 1972.

were thanked for the harvest, and offerings were made to symbolize and to underscore the concept of unity with them; and eating the new crop itself—a cyclical, recurrent opening to futurity—was a marker on the road that led onwards to succeeding generations of the unborn. [McCaskie 1995,145]

McCaskie goes on to articulate meticulously the chronological progression of ritual events that ensured the successful functioning of the Asante state from year to year. The timing of the Odwira was driven by the readiness of the new yam crop, the first consumption of which was reserved for the Asantehene during the festival. Preliminary events include a visit to the ancestral black stools at Bantama to inform them of the forthcoming activities and to sacrifice a sheep to feed the ancestors. Also preceding the core events was the restoration or repair of regalia in need of attention. Bowdich suggested even more dramatic changes. "The royal gold ornaments are melted down every Yam Custom, and fashioned into new patterns, as novel as possible. This is a piece of state policy very imposing on the populace, and the tributary chiefs who pay but an annual visit" (1819 [1966], 279). The passage is sometimes interpreted to mean *all* "royal gold ornaments," but this is highly unlikely since the Asante take great pride in tracing certain swords, sandals, headdresses, etc., back to particular Asantehenes. Nevertheless, for other ornaments it provides convincing evidence

for the Asante pursuit of innovative imagery. In addition to the regalia important public spaces around Kumase were refurbished.

On a Thursday of what is seen as the first official day of Odwira, the Asantehene toured the main streets of the town inspecting preparations and offering rum to the principal *abosom* and at important crossroads. He was accompanied by the Golden Stool and "His route was firmly prescribed, and it took him to a succession of ideologically and historically potent sites" (McCaskie 1995, 165). On this day "it was incumbent upon the reigning Asantehene to participate in the ritualistic defilement of his own *ntɔrɔ* as a necessary prelude to its subsequent purification, the latter one of the most important agenda items of the festival itself" (McCaskie 1995, 199).

The next day marked the arrival of chiefs and their retinues from the outlying states with the population of Kumase more than doubling during this period. For the Asantehene and his immediate court, most of this day was spent in preparations. Saturday is the time of the formal state reception and where public display is maximized with the finest of personal adornment (figs. 9.7–9.10). McCaskie variously refers to this event as "a supreme occasion, a quintessential moment"; "dazzled astonishment"; and a "zenith of opulent extravagance" (1995, 203, 205, 206). At this time the various ranks of chiefs renewed their allegiance to the Asantehene and to the Golden Stool. We will return to this day in greater detail below.

9.7 Asante chief at the celebration of the twenty-fifth anniversary of the reign of Asantehene Otumfuo Opoku Ware II. Photographs by Frank Fournier, Kumase, 1995.

**9.8** Asante chief at the celebration of the twenty-fifth anniversary of the reign of Asantehene Otumfuo Opoku Ware II. Photographs by Frank Fournier, Kumase, 1995.

**9.9** (OPPOSITE) Attendees at the twenty-fifth anniversary of the reign of Asantehene Otumfuo Opoku Ware II in Kumase. Photograph by Frank Fournier, 1995.

After the grand public display, the next day was "devoted to a ritualized mourning for the dead," sacrifices of sheep in the palace to strengthen and protect the Asantehene; and human victims were offered to the ancestral spirits (McCaskie 1995, 213). The skulls of past enemies of the state as well as those of major Asante criminals were paraded through the city in part as a history lesson and in part as an opportunity for derision (McCaskie 1995, 218).

The next four days (Monday to Thursday) were devoted to state business. Policy was decided, disputes settled, and judicial proceedings resolved especially in relation to chiefly fidelity. During this period the ritual defilement of the preceding week was rectified through the purification of the chief's *ntɔrɔ* (McCaskie 1995, 227–34). Friday saw the comprehensive purification of the populace and of important items of regalia. The Golden Stool, the blackened ancestral stools, select swords, and many other items of regalia, along with the Asantehene's household objects, were carried down to the Nsuben River where they were sprinkled with water. On this day the Asantehene also ate the first of the new yam.

A few days later there was a final procession to Bantama and a farewell to all the visiting chiefs. The Odwira concluded a day or two later with the purification of the Bosommuru or Bosompra shrines (as opposed to the swords, which were cleansed earlier) in a final procession to the Nsuben River. This very brief sketch of Odwira events provides only a glimpse at the ceremonial contexts for the use and display of regalia but nevertheless suggests the thorough integration of object and ritual in Asante culture.

**9.11** (FOLD OUT) Drawing by Thomas Edward Bowdich of the Asante Odwira of 1817 in Kumase. Photograph courtesy Division of Rare and Manuscript Collections, Cornell University Library.

**9.10** (ABOVE) The queen mother of the Asante, Asantehemaa Nana Afia Kobia Serwaa Ampem II, at the twenty-fifth anniversary of the reign of Asantehene Otumfuo Opoku Ware II. Photograph by Frank Fournier, Kumase, 1995.

Returning to the visually climactic day of Odwira where all the chiefs paraded to the grounds where they sat in state, McCaskie summarized this display in vivid terms: "The odwira *fomemene* reception was characterized by very dense masses of people, intense noise—drumming, firing, cheering, singing, yelling, crying, debating—and a seemingly chaotic, highly fragmented, and relentlessly sustained assault on all of the human senses" (1995, 204). One of the most famous and frequently quoted observations of African cultural history is Bowdich's 1817 account of this renowned event. It was accompanied by a fold-out drawing of this part of the festival (misleadingly called the "First Day" by Bowdich) that along with his description just begins to suggest the theatrical and political complexity of the festival (fig. 9.11).[2]

*"The First Day of the Yam Custom"*
*6 September 1817*
***Drawing and Description by Thomas Edward Bowdich***
On the left side of the drawing is a group of captains dancing and firing, as described in our entré. Immediately above the encircling soldiery, is a young caboceer under his umbrella, borne on the shoulders of his chief slave; he salutes as he passes along, and is preceded and surrounded by boys (with elephants tails, feathers, &c.) and his captains, who, lifting their swords in the air, halloo out the deeds of his fore-fathers; his stool is born close to him, ornamented with a large brass bell. Above is the fanciful standard of a chief, who is preceded and followed by numerous attendants; he is supported round the waist by a confidential slave, and one wrist is so heavily laden with gold, that it is supported on the head of a small boy; with the other hand he is saluting a seated caboceer, sawing the air by a motion from the wrist. His umbrella is sprung up and down to increase the breeze, and large grass fans are also playing; his handsomest slave girl follows, bearing on her head a small red leather trunk, full of gold ornaments, and rich cloths; behind are soldiers and drummers, who throw their white-washed drums in the air, and catch them again, with much agility and grimace, as they walk along. Boys are in the front, bearing elephants tails, fly flappers, &c. and his captains with uplifted swords, are hastening forward the musicians and soldiers. Amongst the latter is the stool, so stained with blood that it is thought decent to cover it with red silk. Behind the musicians is Odumata, coming round to join the procession in his state hammock lined with red taffeta, and smoking under his umbrella, at the top of which is a stuffed leopard. In the area below is an unfortunate victim, tortured in the manner described in the entré, and two of the King's messengers clearing the way for him. The King's four linguists are seen next; two, Otee and Quancum, are seated in conversation under an umbrella; the chief, Adoosey, is swearing a royal messenger, (to fetch an absent caboceer,) by putting a gold handled sword between his teeth, whilst Agay delivers the charge, and exhorts him to be resolute. The criers, all deformed and with monkey skin caps, are seated in the front. Under the next umbrella is the royal stool, thickly cased in gold. Gold pipes, fans of ostrich wing feathers, captains seated with gold swords, wolves heads and snakes as large as life of the

same metal, depending from the handles, girls bearing silver bowls, body guards, &c. &c. are mingled together till we come to the King, seated in a chair of ebony and gold, and dressed much in the same way as described at the first interview. He is holding up his two fingers to receive the oath of the captain to the right, who, pointing to a distant country, vows to conquer it. On the right and left of the state umbrella are the flags of Great Britain, Holland, and Denmark. A group of painted figures are dancing up to the King, in the most extravagant attitudes, beating time with their long knives on the skulls stuck full of thyme. On the right of the King is the eunuch, who superintends the group of small boys, the children of the nobility, waving elephants tails, (spangled with gold,) feathers, &c.: behind him is the above mentioned captain and other chiefs dressed as in the left end of the drawing. Musicians, seated and standing, are playing on instruments cased or plated with gold. The officers of the Mission are next seen, their linguists in front, their soldiers, servants, and flag behind, at the back of whom is placed the King's state hammock, under its own umbrella. Adjoining the officers is old Quatchie Quofie and his followers; at the top of his umbrella is stuck a small black wooden image, with a bunch of rusty hair on the head, intending to represent the famous Akim caboceer who was killed by him; vain of the action, he is seen according to his usual custom, dancing before and deriding his fallen enemy, whilst his captains bawl out the deed, and halloo their acclamations. The manner of drinking palm wine is exhibited in the next group, a boy kneels beneath with a second bowl to catch the droppings, (it being a great luxury to suffer the liquor to run over the beard,) whilst the horns flourish, and the captains halloo the strong names. The Moors are easily distinguished by their caps, and preposterous turbans. One is blessing a Dagwumba caboceer, who is passing on horseback, (the animal covered with fetishes and bells,) escorted by his men in tunics, bearing lances, and his musicians with rude violins, distinct from the sanko. The back of the whole assembly is lined with royal soldiers, and the commoner ones are ranged in front, with here and there a captain and a group of musicians, who, some with an old cocked hat, some with a soldier's jacket, &c. &c. afford a ludicrous appearance. This description will be rendered more illustrative of the drawing, by referring to that of our entré. [Bowdich 1819 (1966), 275–78]

The processional list of the Asantehene's regalia in Appendix A includes all of the regalia mentioned by Bowdich and is a relatively complete inventory of royal arts in the Asantehene's treasury. It also presents each item's prescribed order of presentation. Other Akan states preserve less-oppulent and different combinations of regalia. Regardless, the parading of state stools and swords is a key element in almost all festival processions (figs. 9.12–9.16).

From Bowdich's description it is obvious that the arts of dance, music, sculpture, and adornment coalesce in this spectacular form of ritual theater. And of course it is dance and music that activate the regalia turning the objects into kinetic works of art. Albert Mawere Opoku has analyzed Asante court dances and describes the movements of a chief as he is carried in procession riding in a palanquin:

> The chief is preceded by various attendants, with the shield-bearers shaking, spinning, and tossing their (now obsolescent) decorative shields into the air to the rhythm of the drums. In the palanquin, the chief's head moves to the challenging rhythmic throb of the *fontomfrom atopretia* dance. He holds a musket in his left hand and a state sword in the other. He crosses the sword over the gun, swaying from side to side, like a king cobra, searching for an imaginary foe. He leans to his left, then to his right; he leans forward and points his sword forward. With a studied smile on his lips, he flings himself back onto the cushions behind him. He may twirl the gun with his left hand while making attacking feints with the sword; all the while, he is being rocked and tossed up and down [in the palanquin] to the rhythm of the *fontomfrom* sounds, in a re-enactment of a historic routing of a powerful adversary. [Opoku 1987, 196, 197]

**9.12** Fante stool carried in procession at annual Fetu Afahye. Photograph by Doran H. Ross, Cape Coast, 1979.

**9.13** (OPPOSITE, TOP LEFT) Stools carried in procession at annual Awubia festival. Photograph by Doran H. Ross, Awutu, 1979.

**9.14** (OPPOSITE, TOP RIGHT) Akuapem queen mother's stool at the annual Odwira festival. Photograph by Doran H. Ross, Akuropon, 1976.

**9.15** (OPPOSITE, BOTTOM) Bearers of sandals, swords, and fly whisks of a Fante chief at the annual Fetu Afahye. Photograph by Doran H. Ross, Cape Coast, 1997.

**9.16** Asantehene Otumfuo Opoku Ware II. Photograph by Eliot Elisofon, 1971. National Museum of African Art. Eliot Elisofon Archive, Smithsonian Institution. EEPA 1470.

**9.17** Nana Yamfo Ababio, Paramount chief of Enyan Abaasa dancing in his palanquin at the annual Yam festival. Photograph by Doran H. Ross, Abaasa, 1974.

Overhead two or more umbrellas of a paramount chief are simultaneously twirled and pumped up and down, looking very much like a kaleidoscope when viewed from above. On either side of the chief, sword bearers rest the golden hilts of the state swords gently on the sides of the palanquins, further accentuating the movement of the litter. The *fɔntɔmfrɔm* drum ensemble follows immediately behind the chief with both a monumental visual, as well as musical, presence (see fig. 9.2). Women press close to the palanquin waving cloths, sometimes small pieces of kente, to honor and cool the leader (see fig. 9.1). Periodically the chief precariously stands and dances in the palanquin to honor his subjects (figs. 9.17, 9.18). Later while the chief is seated in state, his subjects will dance for him (fig. 9.19).

One dance gesture, in particular, may find several counterparts in the regalia on display. The placing of the closed right hand on top of the left is an

**9.18** Nana Kwabu Ewusi VI, paramount chief of Abeadze Dominase, dancing for his subjects at the annual Yam festival. Photograph by Doran H. Ross, 1974.

explicit reference to issues of hierarchy and states that everyone has his superior (Opoku 1987, 196). This theme is found on the double umbrella of paramount chiefs prompting the phrase "some umbrellas are higher than other umbrellas" (figs. 9.20, 9.21), and on select state swords with a miniature sword attached to the hilt illustrating "some swords are stronger than others."[3] The same idea is also found on double stools where one stool sits on top of another. These explicit statements of rank and status join the more encrypted proverbial images found on sword ornaments, staff and umbrella finials, and the chief's own personal adornment.

On festival occasions umbrellas are the most visible and monumental of all regalia. As mentioned earlier, the size and number of umbrellas are strictly determined as a measure of status by the paramount chiefs of each state. Drumming ensembles aside, the two most kinetic components of any festival

**9.19** Woman dancing at the twenty-fifth anniversary of the reign of Asantehene Otumfuo Opoku Ware II. Photograph by Frank Fournier, Kumase, 1995.

procession are the umbrella and palanquin, which are "danced" in concert while spatially framing the chief and queen mother above their subjects. Expanding on the importance of the umbrella as both object and concept, McCaskie noted that one courtyard of the Asantehene's palace, used as a place of assembly "was called *kyinihyiamu* (the place of the 'whirling' or 'turning around'). The symbolism invoked here, as in analogous ritual contexts, was protective. The meaning expressed in this courtyard was cognate with ideas of circulation, and of the actual coolness and metaphorical shade or 'defense' afforded by the enveloping shape and agitated motion of the Asantehene's great state umbrellas (*nkyinie*)… in an…environment connoting protection, security and calm (1995, 160).

Themes of rank and status also dominate much of the drum language produced by the state orchestras. Nketia recorded the following drum text at Kokofu played by the *atumpan* talking drums at the beginning of a state assembly:

Chief, you are about to sit down
Sit down, great one.
Sit down, gracious one.
Chief, you have plenty of seating space.
Like the great branch, you have spread all over this place.
Let us crouch before him with swords of state.
Ruler, the mention of whose name causes great stir,

Chief, you are like the moon about to emerge.
Noble ruler to whom we are indebted,
You are like the moon:
Your appearance disperses famine. [Nketia 1963, 147]

Similar praises and eulogies are played on the various elephant tusk trumpets
For example, the *nkofe* might assert:

Opoku the Tall, Aprɛku Atɛ
Opoku to whom the back belongs

Opoku who fights with the gun
and the sword. [Sarpong 1990, 32]

Other sets of horns, the *amoakwa* and *nkrawobɛn*, might proclaim:

The male antelope
When he walks, he walks majestically
We give you a gun, we give you a shield
Osei Tutu the Warrior who has been fighting wars
He walks majestically. [Sarpong, 1990, 22–23]

9.20 Paramount chief of
Oguaa state under a double
umbrella at the annual Fetu
Afahye. Photograph by Doran
H. Ross, Cape Coast, 1997.

These examples of drum and horn language could be multiplied many times throughout a major festival providing verbal and musical support for the chief and his entourage.

The twentieth-century Akuropon Odwira serves many of the same ritual and display functions of its nineteenth-century Asante counterpart. Herbert Cole has analyzed this festival as a "total work of art" using the Wagnerian operatic term *gesamtkunstwerke* as inspiration for his discussion. Cole considers the spatial and temporal composition of the festival in terms of a number of formal structural elements including artistic principles dealing with contrast, hierarchy, repetition, variation, and elaboration with regalia serving as both theatrical and ritual props throughout (1975).[4]

Michelle Gilbert has examined this same festival over a number of years paying special attention to differences between the annual events. In particular she has noted how the presence or absence of certain regalia has reflected shifting political realities within the state:

> In seeking to understand the 1987 Odwira performance the importance of regalia, both old and new, and its public display cannot be over-stated. The king displays his wealth, his power, and his ancestor's war achievements through them, and this in turn represents the wealth of the kingdom. The alleged desecration of the [Akuapem] Golden Stool (symbol of the kingdom's glory) and the theft of the ancient drums (associated with the king's power) were symbolic means of showing political discontent. For regalia to be missing, stolen, or sold is grounds for destoolment, as it implies both mis-management and a threat to the security of the kingdom. [Gilbert 1994, 115–16]

Gilbert concludes, "ritual and symbolic artifacts are good for making political statements because in ritual the structure is visible for all to see, yet the in-built ambiguity of ritual symbols makes the performance a 'safe' medium for the brinksmanship of political aggression" (1994, 119).

Odwira and other Akan festivals present theatrically galvanizing constellations of regalia that proclaim the wealth of the state, the power of the chief, and the honor and continuity of the ancestors. Each item of regalia plays a functional role, sometimes in isolation and at other times in varied ensembles. And each item of regalia as an expression of proverbial wisdom helps codify

9.21 Procession of chief
under umbrellas at the
annual Fetu Afahye.
Photograph by Doran H.
Ross, Cape Coast, 1979

modes of behavior that shape and indeed govern social and political relationships. In addition many items actively participate in re-presenting segments
of Akan history that validate the structures of good citizenship and good
governance. Indeed, it could be argued that the state could not function or
even exist without the presence of select objects.

While the institution of chieftaincy is still clearly valued by many, there are
also a substantial number of Akan (and other peoples with a chief, queen, or
king for that matter) who question the relevance of hereditary monarchs within
a vibrant democracy. One's view of the trappings of royalty is undoubtedly
skewed by whether they are seen as social, political, and economic assets or
indeed liabilities. Contemporary debates aside, the vast majority of objects in
the Glassell Collection were created to buttress the structure of chieftaincy.
Depending on artistic genre, there is a delicate balance in the "conventional
wisdom" conveyed by these objects between those that promote the powers
of chieftaincy on the one hand and those that assert the rights of the chief's
subjects on the other. This is probably the same balance that exists between
the institution of chieftaincy and the national government of Ghana especially
as it stands as representative of the citizens of the country. ●

# APPENDIX A

# Regalia of the Asantehene

An itemized procession order of the regalia of the Asantehene has been published at least four times. The first instance was upon the restoration of the Asante Confederacy in 1935 (Wallace-Johnson 1935). The second appeared on the occasion of the visit of Queen Elizabeth II in 1961 (Kyerematen 1961). Kyerematen's list of 1961 was used with some variations in number and order—but employing almost all of his text without credit—for the publication of the durbar of 1977 in honor of the Prince of Wales (anon. 1977). A fourth list appeared as an account of the Akwasidae Kɛseɛ of 1991 (Boaten I 1993). The last two publications are illustrated. While there is a general consistency across the four publications, there are also a number of discrepancies, the significance of which remains to be analyzed.

The list below largely follows Boaten I with additions from the earlier lists and modifications for clarity. Illustrations feature actual items from the Asantehene's regalia or analogous objects from the regalia of the Mamponhene.

1. *Samanka*, a brass container with medicinal herbs.
2. *Prɛmpɛ* drum, announces presence of the Asantehene.
3. *Sika mpaboa*, multiple pairs of gold-covered sandals (see fig. 6.5).
4. *Nkwontwewa* horn, elephant-tusk trumpet emphasizing the need to keep the time.
5. *Nsafoa*, iron, silver and gold keys (see fig. 6.30).
6. *Nkotokwa*, pair of leather bags, symbolic containers of the Asantehene's wealth (fig. A.2).
7. *Nwakwrannya* horns, seven elephant-tusk horns played to awaken the Asantehene on important festival days.
8. *Ntahera* horns, share responsibilities with number 7, above.
9. *Sanaa* and *fotoɔ*, elephant-hide bags containing gold weights and gold dust.
10. *Nseniefoɔ*, court criers or heralds (see fig. 5.11).
11. *Kete* drums, ensemble that attracts good spirits (fig. A.3).
12. *Nkofɛ* horns, seven ivory trumpets that "sing" the praises of the Asantehene.
13. *Krokrowa*, footstool with leather-covered amulets (see figs. 2.4, 6.4).
14. *Banwoma*, elephant skin that covers the ground under the Golden Stool.
15. *Hwedɔm-tea*, chair for the Golden Stool (see fig. 2.4).
16. *Asipim*, another chair type.
17. *Hwedɔm* (fig. A.1).
18. *Kɔdeɛdwa* (*akonkromfi*) chair, named after eagle finials.

**A.2** Leather treasury bags (*nkotokwa*) from the regalia of the Mamponhene. Photograph by Doran H. Ross, 1976.

**A.3** *Kete* drum ensemble from the regalia of the Mamponhene. Photograph by Doran H. Ross, 1976.

19. *Fotoɔbadwa*, treasury stools.
20. *Nyansapɔdwa*, stool with square-knot support.
21. *Kɔtɔkɔdwa*, stool with support called "porcupine."
22. *Taa-hyefuo*, gold and silver tobacco pipes (fig. A.6).
23. *Dwɛtɛ kuduo*, literally "silver kuduo," carried on top of a cast-brass *kuduo* (fig. A.4).
24. *Asomfofena*, five courier swords with cast-gold ornaments.
25. *Sika akua*, gold-covered drum seen in background of figure 2.5.
26. *Apemsantan*, war shield of elephant skin.
27. *Sika sankuo*, pair of gold-covered harp-lutes.
28. Asikadwa or Sika Dwa Kofi, the Golden Stool of the Asante, under the state umbrellas (figs. 2.4, 2.5).

29. *Apirede, mpedi, nkrawiri,* and *etwie* drums, the latter mimics the growl
    of a leopard.
30. *Adumfoɔ* and *abrafoɔ,* guards and executioners.
31. *Kwatinpomuta,* two drums announcing the Asantehene.
32. *Ekyɛmfoɔ,* bearers of wickerwork shields (fig. A.5).
33. *Kokosesefoɔ,* bearers of ostrich-feather whisks.
34. *Ahoprafoɔ,* carriers of elephant-tail whisks (see fig. 5.21).
35. *Nfenatene,* another set of swords with cast-gold ornaments and including
    the Afenata with two blades.
36. *Bankyiniie,* seven massive umbrellas named Boaman, Oyokoman,
    Nyankonton, Akokɔbaatan, Nankanini, Nfoanfoa, and Prɛkɛsɛ, some
    named after their cloth and some after their finials.

**A.6** Silver tobacco pipe from the regalia of the Mamponhene. Photograph by Doran H. Ross, 1976.

**A.7** *Fɔntɔmfrɔm* drums from the regalia of the Mamponhene. Photograph by Doran H. Ross, 1976.

37. Asantehene riding in a palanquin underneath umbrellas.
38. *Keteanofena*, principal swords of state divided into two groups of six.
38A. *Akrafena*, includes the most important state sword, Mponponsuo with a gold ornament of a viper and hornbill and other swords with cast-gold ornaments of a defeated warrior, a shield and sword, a bunch of plantains, a bird's nest, and bunch of palm kernels. These are all displayed on the Asantehene's right side.
38B. *Abosomfena*, includes one of the two most important swords, the Bosommuru, with the skull of a mangabey as a cast-gold ornament, along with swords featuring ornaments of a crocodile, a ritual container (*kuduo*), an antelope, a hen with her chicks, and a small antelope called a duiker. These are all displayed on the Asantehene's left side.
39. *Kwadomfoɔ*, minstrels who perform grave songs.
40. *Drugyafoɔ*, players of bamboo flutes.
41. *Mmɛntiafoɔ*, performers with a set of elephant-tusk trumpets.
42. *Asɔkɔbenfoɔ*, musicians with a set of long elephant-tusk trumpets.
43. *Tatwea*, a single ivory trumpet that imitates the bark of a dog, reporting or foretelling an execution.

44. *Mpintin*, processional drums.
45. *Fɔntɔmfrɔm* drums, the largest of Akan drums representing only the most important chiefs (fig. A.7).
46. *Mprakyire*, two young girls representing the wealth and beauty of the Asante nation.
47. *Apem adaka*, pair of boxes carrying silver and gold dust.
48. *Atumtufoɔ*, the Asantehene's personal bodyguard, carrying muskets and bandolier bags (see fig. 5.12).
49. *Manwerehene* and followers, officials who guard the palace.
50. *Akomfoɔ*, traditional priests and mediums.
51. Stool of the queen mother (figs. 2.8, 2.9).
52. Queen mother in her palanquin.
53. Large fans shielding queen mother (fig. A.8).
54. *Akwodum* drums of the queen mother.

A.8 Fans of the queen mother of Mampon. Photograph by Doran H. Ross, 1976.

# Akan Figures from Popular Bands

Three wood carvings in the Glassell Collection are painted gold rather than covered with gold leaf. All three were probably either part of drum stands used by traditional Akan popular bands or freestanding performance props for these bands. J. H. K. Nketia was the first to document these voluntary musical associations, noting that they functioned quite independently of the various royal ensembles that served the court, although they might be engaged to perform for the chief on select occasions. Similar to contemporary popular bands everywhere, each band is associated with a particular style of music and dance that is fashionable for a certain period of time before being replaced by more current and popular styles. Groups may perform for a wide variety of occasions including naming ceremonies, puberty celebrations, weddings, and local and national festivals. Funerals are perhaps the most frequent occasion for performance, and it is often said that individuals join these groups to ensure a successful send-off (Nketia 1963, 67–74).

Many groups center their instrumentation around a large "master" drum that is anthropomorphized as a female. It features between one and eight prominent breasts and extensive relief carving (fig. B.2; see Ross 1988; 1989), which reference many of the same proverbs discussed throughout this volume. In lieu of breasts some drums have a nursing female figure, although more often than not the child becomes detached from the main figure and is lost. Figure B.1 is readily identifiable as being by the same hand as a drum stand in the National Museum of Ghana, Accra, and another drum in a private collection (fig. B.3). The National Museum's drum stand was accessioned in 1953 and according to museum records was "made by Kwedwo Awire (popularly known as Robert), a native of Ashanti who settled at Ekutuase near Krobo (Sekondi area) in 1920." The place names referenced create some confusion since Krobo is not near Sekondi, but an Asante attribution with some Fante influence seems likely. Traces of gold paint can still be seen on the drum in the private collection (fig. B.3), and it seems apparent that the Glassell piece served in a similar context.

Another Glassell figure with gold paint can be attributed to the Brong people (fig. B.6; cf. a related piece by the same hand in Kan and Sieber 1995, 75). The third figure in the Glassell Collection was carved by an as yet unidentified carver active in the Fante area from the 1950s to the late 1970s (fig. B.7). He was especially well known for his drums with attached figures (fig. B.4), and numerous shrine carvings by him or his workshop are still in existence. Both the Brong and Fante pieces apparently were never attached to drums but were intended to be displayed near them during performances either on small stages

**B.1** Nursing female figure (child is missing) from a drum ensemble carved by Kwedwo Awire, circa 1950. Wood, pigment, glass, metal. H: 17 5/8 in. 97.805.

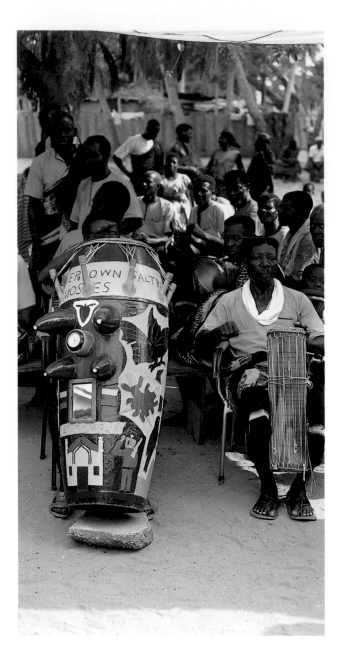

**B.2** Fante drumming group called Moses. Photograph by Doran H. Ross, Saltpond, 1975.

**B.3** Anthropomorphic drum carved by Kwedwo Awire before 1953. Wood, pigment, metal, cloth, glass. H: 35 in. Private collection.

or tables or sometimes just standing on the ground of the venue. Asante *ntan* groups are especially well known for these figurative ensembles, and the Asante carver Osei Bonsu (see pp. 98–100) is recognized as a master of the genre (fig. B.5; Bonsu is seated on the far right). His groups often include a chief, queen mother, district commissioner, policemen, and prisoners. Members of the *ntan* groups frequently said the figures were "just for fancy sake," but two group leaders said that they were sometimes used as the focus of skits making fun of authority figures.

A fourth figurative carving is covered with gold leaf and was clearly intended to be a freestanding sculpture rather than a staff or umbrella finial (fig. B.8). The gold leaf is relatively thick and embossed with very subtle rosettes created by a stamp, both suggesting a date before or about 1930. The figurative style is consistent with shrine sculpture from the Asante, but gold-leafed shrine

figures have not been documented to my knowledge, although gold-leafed regalia is not uncommon in the shrines for important deities (fig. 1.22). It is possible that the work was created by an Asante carver as a display piece for a Baule or lagoon leader (see chapter 8).

**B.4** Fante drum from popular band, said to be near Anomabu. Photograph by Doran H. Ross, 1976.

**B.5** *Ntan* ensemble carved in 1933 with group leaders from the Asante town of Adumoa. The carver Osei Bonsu is seated on the right. Photograph by Doran H. Ross, 1976.

**B.6** Seated male figure
from the Brong area. Wood,
pigment. H: 18 in. 97.808.

**B.7** Standing female figure
holding a rattle (?) from the
Fante area. Wood, pigment.
H: 13¾ in. 97.827.

**B.8** Seated nursing female
from the Asante area. Before
1930. Wood, gold leaf.
H: 14¼ inches. 97.810.

APPENDIX C

# African Gold from
# Senegal, Mali, and Kenya

Although the Akan have the most extensive and varied ensembles of gold jewelry and regalia in all of sub-Saharan Africa, there are nevertheless other significant African gold-working traditions represented in the Glassell Collection. Among the most impressive gold pendants in Africa are those produced by the Tukulor (sedentary Peul or Fulani) of Senegal and Mali and by some of their neighbors. In the form of a massive biconical bead, the *corval* or *korval* (fig. c.1) serves as a centerpiece of a necklace strung on a gold chain and worn on special occasions, often in conjunction with the monumental earrings discussed below (figs. B.2, B.3). Translating the unpublished notes of Dominique Zahan, Marian Johnson writes, "According to Zahan, this form represents the weaver's bobbin. The bobbin symbolizes woman, and the leather cord from which 'she' hangs represents her husband, who has control over his wife: 'A woman, even if she were Queen, is under the power of her husband, just as the weaver's bobbin is under the control of the artisan and the shuttle'" (1994, 42). Johnson calls the globular pendant in figure c.1 "*goubé* (*goubo*) or *san u bara*" and considers it a "spherical variation on the *corval* that originated near Timbucktu" (1994, 42).

The massive hammered and twisted gold earrings (*kwotɛnɛ lange*) worn by women around the inland Niger Delta of Mali are still being produced in Jenne, Mopti, and other towns by Peul goldsmiths (figs. c.2, c.3). Typically the form has four lobes and features stamped or incised designs on the surface. Some examples are gilt brass. The loops intended to pass through the earlobe are usually wrapped with a bright red thread to help protect the ear while at the same time providing a dramatic visual contrast with the gold. Each earring might weigh up to ten ounces, and they are sometimes supported by a strap crossing the head to provide extra support.

Also impressively ornamenting the side of the head are the tear drop-shaped ornaments (*khoulalat*) of the Wolof and Tukulor (figs. c.4, c.5), worn in clusters of two or three and secured to the hair above the ear. They are sometimes worn with equally ornate hemispherical ornaments (fig. c.5, top; see Garrard 1989, 34, 146, 147, 220). Both forms, along with the large biconical bead discussed above, can frequently be seen in the images of the famous Bamako photographer Seydou Keita (Magnin 1997, 21, 116, 123, 127, 165, 191).

The pair of gold earplugs designed to fit within the earlobes of Swahili women (figs. c.6, c.7) are from Paté Island, now part of Kenya. These very discs were photographed Angela Fisher when they were being worn (1984, 289). Called *kuta* by Fisher and *majasi* by James de Vere Allen (n.d., 21), these earlobe ornaments are the most distinctive of Swahili gold jewelry. Swahili women

c.1A,B Tukulor pendants, Senegal or Mali. Gold. H (of round bead): 4 in. (A) 97.1312; (B) Necklace 97.1318.

C.2 Peul woman from Mopti. Photograph by M. Renaudeau, Agence Hoa-Qui, n.d.

C.4 Wolof woman from Senegal. Photograph by M. Renaudeau, Agence Hoa-Qui, n.d.

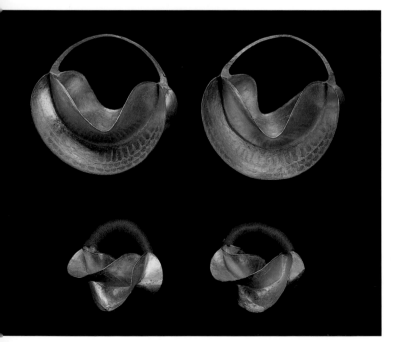

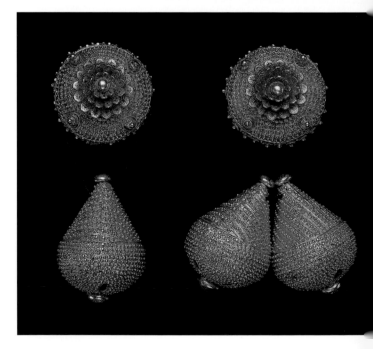

C.3A,B Two pairs of Peul earrings, Mali. Gold, fiber. w: 4¾ in. (A) 97.967A,B; (B) 97.971A,B.

C.5 Hair ornaments from the Wolof or Tukulor, Senegal or Mali. Gold. H: 2½ in. (A) Top 97.879A,B; (B) Bottom 97.878A–C.

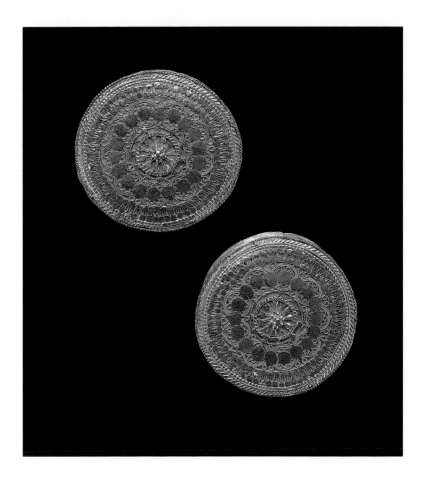

stretch the holes in the lobes of their ears over time by inserting increasingly larger discs of horn or wood. The gold plugs are worn only on festive occasions. Although de Vere Allen refers to, but does not cite, a source that relates these ornaments to those found in southeast India near Madras, he argues that they are of indigenous Paté origin. They are typically worn with "*mabambao,* which are smaller crescent-shaped earrings, or others that are marginally larger with tiny pendants (one of each type sometimes being worn on each ear), as well as with smaller, plain rings running round the upper ear rim" (de Vere Allen n.d., 21). Fisher's photographs show the discs being worn with thirteen of the latter.

These ornaments are only part of a substantial ensemble of jewelry worn by Swahili women including wedding belts, rings, bracelets, necklaces, and Koranic amulet cases—almost all made of silver. Writing about the Swahili town of Lamu to the south of Paté, de Vere Allen notes that "There is a social reason for the survival of so much women's jewelry. Divorce in Lamu remains easy and frequent, and the divorced woman has little chance of taking money with her… but her jewelry she can take. From the first day of marriage, therefore, she tries to get as much jewelry out of him as she can as an insurance for the future.… For the same reason coins are often incorporated into jewelry" (n.d. 18).

**c.6** Pair of Swahili ear spools from Paté, Kenya. Gold. DIAM: 1¾ in. 97.974A,B.

**c.7** Woman from Paté, Kenya, wearing the ear spools in figure c.6. Photograph by Angela Fisher, n.d.

# Notes to the Text

**CHAPTER 1**

1. The history of gold production and of various issues involved with its exploitation is discussed in Garrard (1980), Anquandah (1982), Anin (1994), Ayensu (1997), and Dumett (1998), among many others.

2. The most insightful analysis of Asante architecture is Prussin (1986, 232–54) who convincingly argues for substantial Islamic influence. See Swithenbank (1969) and Debrah (n.d.) for a discussion of still-existing structures.

3. An exception to this model was a stone palace (*aban*), called the "Palace of Culture" by Wilks (1975, 178), completed by stone masons from the coast in 1822 and based upon European architectural principles. It served until its destruction by the British in 1874 as the primary repository of the Asantehene's regalia. The contents of this palace were discussed in some detail by T. B. Freeman (1844 [1968], 141, 142) and especially by Boyle who called it a "museum" and itemized much of its contents (1874, 354, 355, 347–49); cf. Brackenbury (1874 2: 234, 235, 240, 241); Henty (1874, 409–11); Maurice (1874, 377–79); Reade (1874, 357, 358); Stanley (1874, 232–34); and appendix A in this volume.

4. R. S. Rattray itemizes and discusses the sixty-three spaces and rooms of the Kumawuhene's palace and provides a plan as it existed in the early 1920s (1929, 56-61), which makes an instructive comparison with Kyerematen's documentation.

5. "*Ti kɔrɔ nkɔ agyina.*" Recorded during an interview with Kumawuhene Nana Barima Asumadu Sakyi II and his elders, Kumawu, 31 October 1976.

6. The court officials and the household of the Asantehene are discussed in some detail in Wilks (1975, 414–31) and Kyerematen (1961; 1970).

7. Herbert M. Cole coined the phrase "the verbal-visual nexus of Akan arts" (Cole and Ross 1977, 9–12). The verbal arts of the Akan and their intersection with the visual have been the subject of numerous studies, see especially Agyakwa (1979), McCaskie (1989; 1992); McLeod (1984; 1987); Ross (1982b); and Yankah (1995).

8. McLeod (1978) discusses the objects (village house, three-stone hearth) and animals (cat, dog, sheep, pig, and certain birds including vultures and crows) that are not found in the gold-weight corpus and relates their exclusion to an Asante sense of "village/bush dichotomy" and to indigenous concepts of pollution.

9. The largest compendium of Akan proverbs (3,670) was compiled by Johann Christaller and published in 1879. In 1916 R. S. Rattray published a translation and explication of 830 proverbs from Christaller. In 1990 Kofi Ron Lange published a translation of Christaller's work in its entirety, but without any additional elucidation.

10. "*Ɛsono a ɔatu abɛ ase tua n'ano*" (lit., "An elephant that is holding in its mouth a palm tree"). This was recorded during an interview with Kokofuhene Nana Osei Assibey III and his elders, Kokofu, 29 August 1976.

11. "*Ɛsono tia afidie so a ɛnhwan.*" This was recorded during an interview with Adansehene Nana Kwantwi Barima II and his elders, Adanse Fomena, 16 November 1976; also Akyeamehene Nana Nsuase Poku, Kumase, 21 August 1980.

12. "*Ɛsono kokrɔɔ adowa ne panyin*" (lit., "Though the elephant is huge the antelope is the elder"). This was recorded during an interview with Agonahene Nana Boakye Yiadom II and his elders, Agona, 23 August 1980.

**CHAPTER 2**

1. I would like to thank Agbenyega Adedze for considerable help in deciphering this inscription.

2. The Akan are not generally known for traditions of ivory sculpture. There are a number of side-blown ivory trumpets with accomplished relief carving found among the Ewe. (See Ghana Information Service photographs R/8616/19 and R/8616/23 from Peki). The Ewe also have counselors' staffs with figurative ivory finials.

3. *Adinkra* cloths are created with stamps carved from the shells of gourds and were originally worn as mourning cloths. The *adinkra* visual vocabulary is more abstract than most Akan arts. Nevertheless, select *adinkra* motifs are occasionally found on most Akan regalia. See Cole and Ross (1977, 44–47); Mato (1987); and Willis (1998).

4. This was related during an interview with Kumawuhene Barima Asumadu Sakyi II and his elders, Kumawu, 31 October 1976.

5. This is one of the most commonly found of all *adinkra* motifs (see note 3 this chapter) and is discussed in some detail in Willis (1998, 96, 97). See also discussion of figures 3.33, 3.34 this volume.

6.  See OED (1971, s.v. "palanquin"). Christaller also lists *bonkara* as a "wicker-hammock, traveling basket" (1933, 38); "*denkyedenkye* as a hammock, presumably because it is shaken" (1933, 75); and "*ahamankaa* a cognate with the English hammock" (1933, 166).

7.  Based on records at the UCLA Fowler Museum of Cultural History, two distinct litters were mistakenly identified as Akan palanquins based on auction records that indicated one of them was taken from Kumase in 1896 (Cole and Ross, 1977, 144, fig. 304). Both in fact were created out of parts of Indian camel saddles and were probably an invention of British colonial officials whose families lost track of the history of these works (FMCH x65.1613, x65.1614).

8.  In 1994 the Zanzibar Museum had a virtually identical example of this type of palanquin on display and indicated that it was used by the sultan in the late nineteenth century.

## CHAPTER 3

1.  This was related in an interview with Mamponhene Nana Atakora Amaniampong II and his elders, Mampon, 17 November 1976.

2.  This was related in an interview with Offinsohene Nana Wiafe Akenten II and his elders, Offinso, 3 September 1976.

3.  "*Aboa nya wo na ɔnnkye wo a, ɔnnwene ne sɛ nkyeyɛ wo.*" This was recorded in an interview with Edwesohene Nana Diko Pim III and his elders, Edweso, 2 September 1976.

4.  "*Ɔsebɔ, oso nsa fufu a hena na obetumi ato gyese gyata.*" This was recorded in an interview with Kokofuhene Nana Osei Assibey III and his elders, Kokofu, 29 August 1976. "*Awinadze a oewu ye dzen sen ɔsebɔ a otse ase.*" This was recorded in an interview with Supi Kwamina Amoaku, Anomabu, 2 September 1978.

5.  Not all sword ornaments are cast gold, as seen in the gold leaf over wood example in figure 3.12. Another crocodile ornament by the same carver adorns one of the state swords of Denkyira as seen in Ghana Information Services photograph R/8288/6.

6.  "*Denkyɛmniampa a ɛduru afeɛ a ɔmene boɔ.*" This was recorded in an interview with Mamponhene Nana Atakora Amaniampong II and his elders, Mampon, 17 November 1976.

7.  "*Opitire mene adeɛ a ɔmene ma owura.*" This was recorded in an interview with Kumawuhene Barima Asumadu Sakyi II, Kumawu, 31 October 1976.

8.  This was recorded in English in an interview with Edwesohene Nana Diko Pim III and his elders, Edweso, 2 September 1976.

9.  "*Ɔhene te sɛ bemu woto tuo bɔ no a wosee w'akorabɔɔ.*" This was recorded in an interview with Kumawuhene Barima Asumadu Sakyi II, Kumawu, 31 October 1976.

10. "*Ɔhene bi wu na mana rekɔ ayie ase a na ɔde kɔ kyerɛ sɛ n'ani abere enti ɔrewe bese.*" This was recorded in an interview with Kumawuhene Barima Asumadu Sakyi II, Kumawu, 31 October 1976.

11. "*Ɔbanin Tweneboa a ne ho bɔn atuduro.*" This was recorded in an interview with Kumawuhene Barima Asumadu Sakyi II and his elders, Kumawu, 31 October 1976.

12. The wisdom knot (*nyansapɔ*) as a motif by itself is also a common image in gold weights (Menzel 1968, figs 1159–67), jewelry (figs. 6.43, 7.24 this volume), and on the shafts of counselors' staffs.

13. "*Adwetakyi anoma werɛmfoɔ a ɔso aprɛmo ne atuduro nam.*" This was recorded in an interview with Edwesohene Nana Diko Pim III and his elders, Edweso, 2 September 1976. This sword ornament is also found at Offinso.

14. "*Ti korɔ nkɔ agyina.*" This was recorded in an interview with Kumawuhene Barima Asumadu Sakyi II, Kumawu, 31 October 1976.

15. "*Ɛsono kuntaan gyan, adowa na ɔdze ne man.*" This was recorded in an interview with Agonahene Nana Boakye Yiadom II, 4 September 1980 (cf. Yankah 1995, 42; this volume, p. 40).

16. "*Wosɔ ɔwɔ ti a, nea aka nyinaa yɛ ahoma.*" This was recorded in an interview with Edwesohene Nana Diko Pim III and his elders, Edweso, 2 September 1976 (cf. Yankah 1995, 42).

17. This was recorded in an interview with Edwesohene Nana Diko Pim III and his elders, Edweso, 2 September 1976.

18. This was recorded in English in an interview with the paramount chief of Awutu, Nai Wyetey Agyeman Larbie II, and his elders, Awutu, 30 September 1979 (see Ross 1984, fig. 18). Although not generally considered an Akan state, the regalia of Awutu is heavily influenced by the Akan.

19. "*Sɛ wo bɛto gyata tuo na wanwuo deɛ fanyinam.*" This was recorded in an interview with Nana Kwabu Ewusi VI and his elders, Abeadze Dominase, 19 August 1975.

20. This was recorded in English in an interview with Offinsohene Nana Wiafe Akenten II, Offinso, 3 September 1976. Quarcoo (1975, 18) recorded a different saying at Offinso, "'*Ohene ye se abrobɛ*' (The ruler is as resplendent as the pineapple)."

21. "*Tɔ wakyi a fa.*" This was recorded in an interview with Adansehene Nana Kwantwi Barima II, Adanse Fomena, 16 November 1976, among many other recordings of this most common image.

22. I have not recorded this motif on any regalia I have studied, but it is found on several Fante *asafo* shrines (*posuban*) including number two company, Mankesim, as related in an interview with Tufohene Nana Kodwo Baiden, Mankesim, 8 September 1978.

23. "*Ɔsrane ne nsoroma, kyɛkyɛ pɛ awareɛ.*" This was recorded in an interview with Kokofuhene Nana Osei Assibey III, Kokofu, 29 August 1976.

24. "*Sɛ afafantɔ mpɛ nsa a, anka adɛn na ɔte nsa kwan so*" (personal communication, Peggy Appiah, 1976).

25. *"Odwenini sisi a ɔde ne korona ɛnyɛ ne mmɛn."* This was recorded by Quarcoo (1975, 35).

26. *"Dupɔn kesee si afuo so a yɛnwo abe ngu ahaharata."* This was recorded in an interview with Dwabenhene Nana Kofi Siriboe II and his elders, Dwaben, 27 October 1976.

27. *"Nnua nyinaa bɛwoso a eka abɛ."* This was recorded in an interview with Akyeamehene Nana Nsuase Poku, chief counselor of the Asantehene, Kumase, 21 August 1980. See note 28 below.

28. *"Nnua nyinaa woso ɛbɛka abɛ."* This was recorded in an interview with Adansehene Nana Kwantwi Barima II, Adanse Fomena, 16 November 1976. Although the Twi for note 27 above and this note are essentially the same, the English translations are presented as recorded at the time.

29. See note 9, this chapter.

30. This was recorded in English in an interview with Dwabenhene Nana Kofi Siriboe II and his elders, Dwaben, 27 October 1976 (see also fig. 4.39 second from left).

## CHAPTER 4

1. In an interview master carver Osei Bonsu (see Ross 1984) recited that the first *ɔkyeame* was an old woman named Nana Amoah who intervened on behalf of select individuals who came before the Asantehene. Bonsu said the first *ɔkyeame poma* was used by her son Adoku based on her walking stick and in her honor (Cole and Ross 1977, 160).

2. Two other nineteenth-century staffs based on European prototypes are in the British Museum (McLeod 1981, 99).

3. The individuals in question were: Nana Nsuase Poku, Akyeamehene for the Asantehene, Kumase, 21 August 1980; Osei Bonsu, Kumase, 28 October 1976.

4. This was recorded in English in an interview with Asumegyahene Odeneho Oduro Numapau II and his elders, Asumegya, 28 August 1979.

5. For images and interpretations of counselors' staffs, see Beckwith and Fischer (1999, 372–75); Glover (1971); Odoi (1985, 134–77); Ross (1982b); and Yankah (1995, 33–44).

6. *"Dee adee wɔ no na ɔdie na ɛnyɛ dee ɛkɔm de no."* This was recorded in an interview with the Asantehene's Akyeamehene Nana Nsuase Poku, Kumase, 21 August 1980 (cf. Yankah 1995, 35).

7. *"Ɔkɔtɔ nwo anoma."* This was recorded in an interview with an unidentified *ɔkyeame*, Mankesim, 8 September 1979.

8. This was related in an interview at Cape Coast, 3 September 2001. The *ɔmanhene* has an isolated crab on one of his present staffs. At the Asante state of Bekwai an isolated crab adorns one of the state swords and illustrates the saying *"Ɔkɔtɔ kesee a ɔwere abura"* (The great crab that scratches [digs] the well). This was

recorded in an interview with Bekwaihene Nana Osei Kwadwo II and his elders, Bekwai, 14 November 1976.

9. *"Anomaa nua ne nea ɔne no da korɔ."* This was recorded in an interview with Nana Yamfo Ababio II and his elders, Enyan Abaasa, 4 September 1974.

10. *"Kontronfi se odene ho kotwitwi etwie na one ofroterɛ aye pe."* This was recorded in an interview with Dwabenhene Nana Kofi Siriboe II and his elders, Dwaben, 27 October 1976.

11. *"Wo foro dua pa a, na yepia wo."* This was recorded in an interview with an unidentified divisional chief, Cape Coast, 1 September 1979 (see Ross 1982b, fig. 24).

12. *"Baako werɛ aduro a ɛgu."* This was recorded in an interview with Osei Bonsu, Kumase, 20 November 1976 (cf. Yankah 1995, 40, fig. 3.7 and appendix B, fig. B.5, p. 283 of this volume).

13. This was related in an interview in Kumase, 20 November 1976.

14. See Ghana Information Services, photograph R/8343/5.

15. This was related in an interview at Busua, 2 September 2001; see also Sutherland (1954, 9).

16. For a history of land claims and stool disputes in Ahanta see Welman (1969, part II).

17. *"Akokɔberɛ nim se adeɛ bɛkye nso ɔhwɛ akokɔnini ano."* This was recorded in an interview with Nana Yamfo Ababio II and his elders, Enyan Abaasa, 4 September 1974 (cf. Ross 1982b, fig. 14).

18. *"Akokɔ nan tia ba na nkum ba."* This was recorded in an interview with Osei Bonsu, Kumase, 20 November 1976.

19. *"Wosɔ owɔ ti a, nea aka nyinaa yɛ ahoma."* This was recorded in an interview with Edwesohene Nana Diko Pim III and his elders, Edweso, 8 September 1980, in relation to a staff finial of a man holding the head of a snake (cf. Yankah 1995, 42, fig. 5.2)

20. *"Ɔbosomaketerɛ, onim ntama dane a, ɔdan nea efira yɛn, ɔnnane nea ɛhyɛ adaka mu."* This is depicted on an *ntan* drum and documented in an interview with Osei Bonsu, Kumase, 10 September 1976.

21. This was provided by Ernest Yeboah, assistant to the Asantehene's private secretary A. S. Y. Andoh, Kumase, 5 September 2001.

22. This was related in an interview at Busua, 2 September 2001.

23. This was related in an interview at Cape Coast, 3 September 2001.

24. This was related by an unidentified member of the chief's family, Butre, 2 September 2001.

25. *"Obi ntɔ ananseesɛm kyerɛ Ntikuma."* This was recorded in Twi in an interview with Nai Wyetey Agyeman Larbie II and his elders, Awutu, 30 September 1979.

26. This is Osei Bonsu's emphatic statement in English of what is usually translated as "When elephant steps on trap, it does not spring," Kumase, 23 September 1976, see fig. 1.27.

27. McLeod reports that an umbrella finial still preserved by the Bantama stool is a "model of an elephant" covered in animal skin (1981, 111). Another practice no longer followed is the creation of finials as effigies of defeated enemies. Bowdich documents an Asante general who had a finial representing a defeated Akyem chief "before which he dances with every insulting gesture and vaunt" (1819 [1966], 237).

28. "*Wo kum apim a apim bɛba.*" This was recorded in relation to a porcupine sword ornament at an interview with Offinsohene Nana Wiafe Akenten II and his elders, Offinso, 3 September 1976 (Ross 1977, fig. 5). Yankah provides three different expressions in relation to porcupines on counselors' staffs (1995, 41).

29. "*Apese yɛ kɛseɛ a ɔyɛ ma dufɔkyeɛ.*" This was recorded in an interview with an unidentified divisional chief, Mankesim, 8 September 1979 (see Ross 1982b, fig. 20; cf Yankah 1995, 38, 39, fig. 3.5).

30. Rattray lists eight for the Asante and discusses the issue of "clans" at some length (1929, 62–71).

31. At Asumegya the expression associated with this staff is "*Aduana otwa ba*" or "The Aduana carried it." This was recorded in an interview with Asumegyahene Odeneho Oduro Numapau II, Asumegya, 28 August 1979.

## CHAPTER 5

1. Although Nana Kwadwo Nyantakyi III, Sanaahene, and Nana Akwasi Asafo Agyei II, Abanasehene, indicated that sword bearers' regalia was specific to each of the Asantehene's swords (Kumase, 5 September 2001), this pendant was photographed with two different swords in the references cited here. Another pendant of the same design is in the British Museum (1900. 4–27).

2. Interview with the Asantehene's court officials Nana Kwadwo Nyantakyi III, Sanaahene, and Nana Akwasi Asafo Agyei II, Abanasehene, Kumase, 5 September 2001. Both officials agreed that this remarkable disc was unlikely to be of Asante manufacture, and it is possible that it was not produced by the Fante either. The technique of very fine spirally wound threads forming the disc and the crocodile motif itself are more typical of Baule workmanship than Ghanaian Akan.

3. The largest *akrafokonmu* known to me is a repoussé disc in the British Museum (1925.10.24.1), which is 8⅜ inches in diameter. This same disc or a nearly identical one was photographed by Edouard Foa between 1886 and 1890, apparently in Accra, Album 1, #90, in *Views of Africa*, seven albums in the library of the J. Paul Getty Museum (Archival #93.R.114; Id #94-F156).

4. "*Sɛ nea fofoo pɛ ne sɛ gyinatwi abɔ bidie.*" This was recorded in an interview with the Asantehene's court officials Nana Kwadwo Nyantakyi III, Sanaahene, and Nana Akwasi Asafo Agyei II,

Abanasehene, Kumase, 5 September 2001 (cf. Willis 1998, 108, 109; Menzel 1968, 176, figs. 540, 541).

5. This was related in an interview with the Asantehene's court officials Nana Kwadwo Nyantakyi III, Sanaahene, and Nana Akwasi Asafo Agyei II, Abanasehene, Kumase, 5 September 2001.

6. This was related in an interview with Mamponhene Nana Atakora Amaniampong II, Mampon, 17 November 1976.

7. It is Ghana Information Services photograph R/9914/8.

## CHAPTER 6

1. "*Asantrofie anomaa, wofa no a w'afa mmusuo, wogyae no a w'agyae sadeɛ.*" This was recorded in an interview with Edwesohene Nana Diko Pim III and his elders, Edweso, 2 September 1976. This ornament /expression is also found at Kamawu and Nsuta.

2. This motif does not occur on the two earliest known cloths, the first collected by Thomas Edward Bowdich in 1817 and the second accessioned by the Rijksmuseum voor Volkenkunden, Leiden, before 1826. It *is* found in a late nineteenth-century Basel Mission Archive photograph (Cole and Ross 1977, fig. 72) of the production process and on a cloth collected from Asantehene Agyeman Prempe I while in exile in Sierra Leone in 1897 (*Fortune* 1997, cover). See also Maro (1987, fig. 131) and Willis (1998, 138, 139).

3. "*Ɔsrane bewu agya nsoroma*"; "*Nsoroma pe awareɛ.*" This was recorded in an interview with Kumawuhene Barima Asumadu Sakyi II and his elders, Kumawu, 31 October 1976.

4. This association was made by the Asante carver Osei Bonsu, Kumase, 19 November 1976, while carving a wood crown like the work in figure 6.18, and by Nana Yamfo Ababio, paramount chief of Enyan Abaasa, who can be seen wearing a crown of this type in figure 9.17, 4 September 1976.

5. This was related in an interview with Nana Abrafi Mansah, Kumase, 29 August 2001. The proverb "*Ɔhene nsuro ayeye*" was also recorded in relation to an umbrella top (fig. 4.39 second from left), in an interview with Dwabenhene Nana Kofi Siriboe II, Dwaben, 27 October 1976.

6. Gold beads recovered in excavations at Elmina included cold-hammered examples dating to the seventeenth century, as well as perforated nuggets, leading Christopher DeCorse to conclude that "Cold hammering, drawing, bending, folding, cutting, and stamping may have initially been the predominant methods of working gold, but they were increasingly supplanted by casting technology in the seventeenth century" (2001, 127, fig. 4.8).

7. Garrard attributes these cruciform pendants to the Maure or Tukulor of Mali and Mauritania (1989, 153, 154).

8. The multicolored cordage to which the amulets are attached is named after kente patterns, e.g., red, yellow, and green cordage is called Oyokoman; blue and yellow is Fathia Fata Nkrumah. This

was related in an interview with Nana Abrafi Mansah, Kumase, 30 August 2001.

9. Kyerematen identifies this as "the tail of the crow," which became "the totem Akyeneboa, of the royal Oyoko clan" (1966, 10).

10. "*Aponkyerɛneɛ wu a, na yɛhunu ne tenten.*" This was recorded in an interview with Kumawuhene Barima Asumadu Sakyi II and his elders, Kumawu, 31 October 1976 (see fig. 6.53).

11. See note 7, chapter 3.

12. "*Ɛkaa nwa ne akyekyerɛ nko a, anka otuo nnto wɔ kwae mu da.*" This was recorded in relation to a counselor's staff in an interview with the paramount chief of Mankesim Nana Adoku V and his elders, Mankesim, 7 July 1975.

13. "*Ana kɔnkɔnkyea anafia atworodo, ɔka, ɔbaatan ba a, gye sɛ asomrofi adwo.*" This was recorded in an interview with Agonahene Nana Boakye Yiadom II and his elders, Agona, 23 August 1980 (see fig. 6.51).

14. "*Kotoku saa bobe, ɔnnkasa nso ɔhome.*" This was recorded in an interview with Asumegyahene Odeneho Oduro Numapau II and his elders, Asumegya, 28 August 1972 (see fig. 6.52). This cocoon also appears as a direct cast in the gold-weight corpus (Menzel 1968, figs. 585, 586).

15. This was related in an interview with Bekwaihene Nana Osei Kwadwo II, Bekwai, 14 November 1976.

16. "*Pa pa yɛ nkɔ akyiri.*" This was recorded in an interview with weaver Samuel Cophie, Bonwire, 23 August 1998.

## CHAPTER 8

1. Susan M. Vogel is emphatic in stating that "There is no king recognized by the Baule, though the colonial system sought and eventually created leaders who are sometimes referred to as kings" (1997, 30; see also Garrard 1993b).

2. See also the inside front cover of Fischer and Himmelheber 1981. The two Fischer and Himmelheber volumes include a number of photographs of notables at Sakassou with staffs, crowns, fly whisks, and even a double-bladed sword (1975, fig. 10).

3. See Vogel for a discussion of trance diviners and for examples of the actual gongs and mallets (1997, 221–39).

4. I would like to thank Monica Blackmun Visoná for clarifying the attributions of these sculptures.

## CHAPTER 9

1. Most guides to West Africa (e.g., *Lonely Planet* and *Rough Guide*) include a list of Ghanaian festivals dominated by those in Akan areas. There are also several locally produced guides aimed at visitors to Ghana (see especially A. A. Opoku 1970 and Fosu 2001).

2. McCaskie provides an annotated version of Bowdich's famous description and identifies individuals mentioned in the text (1995, 268–71).

3. This use of a miniature sword attached to a full-scale sword is found at most Asante paramountcies, including Bekwai, Mampon, Kumawu, Agona, and on the Asantehene's Mponponsuo sword (Ross 1977, figs. 11, 12, 13, 15, 25, 26). The last figure should be identified as coming from Agona and not Kumase.

4. Cole's provocative analysis (1975) includes diagrams of festival circulation patterns, a "schematic of energy-flow," a graphic itemization of the festival procession, and another diagram of hierarchical groups contrasting procession and durbar. Together these provide considerable insight into the aesthetic structure of Akuropon Odwira.

# References Cited

Abbey, H. Nii
1997   *Kofi Antubam and the Myth around Ghana's Presidential Seat.* Accra: Studio Brian Communications.

Adler, Peter, and Nicholas Barnard
1992   *African Majesty: The Textile Art of the Ashanti and Ewe.* London: Thames and Hudson.

Agyakwa, Kofi O.
1979   *The Educational Wisdom of Our Fathers.* Cape Coast: University of Cape Coast.

Akrofi, C. A.
n.d.   *Twi mmebusɛm (Twi proverbs).* Accra: Waterville Publishing House Division of Presbyterian Book Depot Kumasi.

Allen, James de Vere
n.d.   *Lamu.* Nairobi: The Regal Press, Ltd.

Allman, Jean Marie
1993   *The Quills of the Porcupine: Asante Nationalism in an Emergent Ghana.* Madison: The University of Wisconsin Press.

Anin, T. E.
1994   *Gold in Ghana.* 4th ed. Accra: Selvyn Publishers Ltd.

Anon.
1925   *Visit of His Royal Highness the Prince of Wales to the Gold Coast Colony.* Accra: Govt. Printing Office.

Anon.
1977   *Durbar in Honor of His Royal Highness the Prince of Wales.* Kumasi.

Anon.
1989   *Corps sculptés, corps parés, corps masqués: Chefs-d'oeuvre de Côte-d'Ivoire.* Paris: Galeries Nationales du Grand Palais. Ministère de la Coopération et du Développement.

Anon.
1995   *The Adae Kese Durbar Festival Program,* Kumase Sports Stadium (13 August). Otumfuo Opoku Ware II Asantehene. Kumase, Ghana.

Anon.
1999   *Programme for the Funeral of Otumfuo Opoku Ware II.* Kumase: Otumfuo Opoku Ware Jubilee Foundation.

Anquandah, James
1982   *Rediscovering Ghana's Past.* London: Longman.

Anquandah, James, ed.
1975   *Sankofa: The Legon Journal of Archaeological and Historical Studies* 1. Legon: Legon Archaeological Society.

Antubam, Kofi
1961   *Ghana Arts and Crafts.* Ghana: Ghana National Trading Corporation.
1963   *Ghana's Heritage of Culture.* Leipzig: Koehler & Amelang.

Appiah, Joseph
1996   *The Autobiography of an African Patriot.* Accra: Asempa Publishers.

Appiah, Peggy
1979   "Akan Symbolism." *African Arts* 13 (1): 64–67.

Arens, W., and Ivan Karp
1989   *Creativity of Power: Cosmology and Action in African Societies.* Washington, D.C.: Smithsonian Institution Press.

Arhin, Kwame
1983a   "Peasants in Nineteenth-Century Asante." *Current Anthropology: A World Journal of the Sciences of Man* 24 (4): 471–80.
1983b   "Rank and Class among the Asante and Fante in the Nineteenth Century." *Africa: Journal of the International African Institute* 53 (1): 2–22.
1986   "The Asante Praise Poems." *Paideuma, Mitteilungen zur Kulturkunde* 32: 163–97.
1990   "Trade, Accumulation, and the State in Asante in the Nineteenth Century." *Africa: Journal of the International African Institute* 60 (4): 524–37.

Austin, Dennis
1964   *Politics in Ghana, 1946–1960.* London: Oxford University Press.

Ayensu, Edward S.
1997   *Ashanti Gold: The African Legacy of the World's Most Precious Metal.* London: Marshall Editions Development Ltd.

Barber, Karin, and P. F. de Moraes Farias
1989   *Discourse and Its Disguises: The Interpretation of African Oral Texts.* Birmingham: Centre of West African Studies, Birmingham University.

Barbier, Jean Paul, ed.
1993    *Art of Côte d'Ivoire from the Collections of the Barbier-Mueller Museum.* 2 vols. Geneva: The Barbier-Mueller Museum.

Barbier, Monique
2000    "An Ebrie Goldsmith of Côte d'Ivoire." *Arts and Cultures* (1): 64–70.

Baum, Peter
2001    *Gold aus Afrika.* Linz: Neue Galerie der Stadt.

Beckwith, Carol, and Angela Fisher
1999    *African Ceremonies.* New York: Harry N. Abrams.

Bedu-Addo, Ato
1981    *Sankofa Arts and Culture* I (1). Legon: Arts Council of Ghana and Institute of African Studies, University of Ghana.

Berry, Sara S.
2001    *Chiefs Know Their Boundaries: Essays on Property, Power, and the Past in Asante, 1896–1996.* Portsmouth, N.H.: Heinemann.

Blake, J. W.
1937    *European Beginnings in West Africa, 1454–1578.* London: Longmans, Green and Co.
1942 [1967]  *Europeans in West Africa, 1450–1560.* Vols. 1 and 2. Wiesbaden: Lessing-Druckerei.

Boaten I, Barfuo Akwasi Abayie
1993    *Akwasidae Kese: A Festival of the Asante: People with a Culture.* Accra: National Commission on Culture.

Bosman, William
1704 [1967]  *A New and Accurate Description of the Coast of Guinea: Divided into the Gold, The Slave, and the Ivory Coasts.* London: Frank Cass & Co. Ltd.

Bowdich, Thomas Edward
1819 [1966]  *Mission from Cape Coast Castle to Ashantee.* 1st ed. London: John Murray. 3d ed. London: Frank Cass & Co.

Boyer, Alain-Michel
1993    "Art of the Baule." In *Art of Côte d'Ivoire from the Collections of the Barbier-Mueller Museum.* Vol. I. Edited by Jean Paul Barbier, 302–67. Geneva: The Barbier-Mueller Museum.

Boyle, F.
1874    *Through Fanteeland to Coomassie: A Diary of the Ashantee Expedition.* London.

Brackenbury, Henry
1874    *The Ashanti War: A Narrative.* London: William Blackwood and Sons.

Braffi, Emmanuel Kingsley
1984    *The Esoteric Significance of the Asante Nation.* Kumasi: E. K. Braffi.
1995    *Silver Jubilee of Otumfuo Opoku Ware II Asantehene and Some Aspects of Asante History.* Kumase: University Press.

Bravmann, Rene A.
1968    "The State Sword, A Pre-Ashanti Tradition." *Ghana Notes and Queries* 10 (December): 1–4.

Bravmann, Rene A., and Raymond A. Silverman
1987    "Painted Incantations: The Closeness of Allah and Kings in Nineteenth-Century Asante." In *The Golden Stool: Studies of the Asante Center and Periphery,* edited by Enid Schildkrout, 93–108. Anthropological Papers of the American Museum of Natural History, vol. 65, part 1. New York: American Museum of Natural History.

Brincard, Marie-Thérèse
        *Sounding Forms: African Musical Instruments.* New York: The American Federation of Arts, 1989.

Brun, Samuel
1611 [1983]  "Samuel Brun's Voyages of 1611–20." In *German Sources for West African History, 1599–1669,* edited by Adam Jones, 44–96. Wiesbaden: Franz Steiner Verlag GMBH.

Bury, Shirley
1985    *An Introduction to Sentimental Jewellery.* London: Her Majesty's Stationery Office.
1991    *Jewellery: The International Era, 1789–1910.* Vol. 2, *1861–1910.* Woodbridge: Antique Collector's Club.

Busia, K. A.
1951    *The Position of the Chief in the Modern Political System of Ashanti: A Study of the Influence of Contemporary Social Changes on Ashanti Political Institutions.* London: Frank Cass & Co. Ltd.

Cameron, Elisabeth
1996    *Isn't S/He a Doll? Play and Ritual in African Sculpture.* Los Angeles: UCLA Fowler Museum of Cultural History.

Carter, William Grandvil
1971    "The Ntahera Horn Ensemble of the Dwaben Court: An Ashanti Surrogating Medium." Master's thesis, UCLA.

Christaller, Johann Gottlieb
1874    *A Dictionary, English, Tshi (Ashante), Akra.* Basel: Basel Evangelical Missionary Society.
1879 [1990]  *Three Thousand Six Hundred Ghanaian Proverbs (From the Asante and Fante Language).* Translated by Kofi Ron Lange. Studies in African Literatures, vol. 2. Lewiston: The Edwin Mellen Press.
1933    *Dictionary of the Asante and Fante Language Called Tshi (Twi).* 2nd ed. Basel: Basel Evangelical Missionary Society.

Christensen, James Boyd
1954    *Double Descent among the Fanti.* New Haven: Human Relations Area File.

Cohen, Abner
1974     *Two-Dimensional Man: An Essay on the Anthropology of Power and Symbolism in Complex Society.* Berkeley and Los Angeles: University of California Press.

Cole, Herbert M.
1975     "The Art of Festival in Ghana," *African Arts* 8 (3): 12–22, 60–62, 90.

Cole, Herbert M., and Doran H. Ross
1977     *The Arts of Ghana.* Los Angeles: UCLA Museum of Cultural History.

Dalton, George, ed.
1983     *Research in Economic Anthropology.* Vol. 5. London: Jai Press Inc.

Danquah, J. B.
1944     *The Akan Doctrine of God.* African Modern Library, no 2. London: Frank Cass & Co. Ltd.

Davies, O.
1971     "A West African Stool with Gold Overlay." *Annals of the Natal Museum* 20 (3): 467–77.

Debrah, I. N., et al.
n.d.     *Asante Traditional Buildings.* Accra: Ghana Museum and Monuments Board.

Debrunner, H.
1959     *Witchcraft in Ghana: A Study on the Belief in Destructive Witches and Its Effect on the Akan Tribes.* Accra: Presbyterian Book Depot, Ltd.

DeCorse, Christopher R.
2001     *An Archaeology of Elmina.* Washington, D.C.: Smithsonian Institution Press.

De Marees, Pieter
1602 [1987]  *Description and Historical Account of the Gold Kingdom of Guinea.* Translated and edited by Albert Van Dantzig and Adam Jones. New York: Oxford University Press.

De Moraes, Farias, and Karin Barber
1990     *Self-Assertion and Brokerage: Early Cultural Nationalism in West Africa.* Birmingham: Centre of West African Studies, Birmingham University.

Dickson, Kwamina B.
1971     *A Historical Geography of Ghana.* London: Cambridge University Press.

Dickson, Kwamina B., and George Benneh
1988     *A New Geography of Ghana.* London: Longman Group Limited.

Donne, J. B.
1977     "West African Goldwork," *Connoisseur* (February): 100–106.

Drewal, Margaret Thompson
1988     "Ritual Performance in Africa Today." *TDR The Drama Review* 32 (2, T188): 25–30.
1992     *Yoruba Ritual: Performers, Play, Agency.* Bloomington: Indiana University Press.

Dumett, Raymond E.
1998     *El Dorado in West Africa.* Athens: Ohio University Press.

Dupuis, Joseph
1824 [1966]  *Journal of a Residence in Ashantee.* London: Frank Cass & Co. Ltd.

Ehrlich, Martha A.
1981     *A Catalogue of Ashanti Art Taken from Kumasi in the Anglo-Ashanti War of 1874, Pt. 1 and 2.* Ph.D. diss., Indiana University.
1989     "Early Akan Gold from the Wreck of the Whydah." *African Arts* 22 (4): 52–57, 86–87.

Fagg, William
1974     "Ashanti Gold." *Connoisseur* 185 (743): 41–48.

Fagg, William, and Margaret Plass
1964     *African Sculpture.* London: Studio Vista Limited.

Field, Margaret J.
1960     *Search for Security: An Ethno-Psychiatric Study of Rural Ghana.* Reprint. New York: W. W. Norton & Co., 1970.

Fischer, Eberhard, and Hans Himmelheber
1975     *Gold aus West Afrika.* Zurich: Museum Rietberg.
1981     *Das Gold in der Kunst Westafrikas.* Zurich: Museum Rietberg.

Fisher, Angela
1984     *Africa Adorned.* New York: Harry N. Abrams, Inc.

Fisher, Carol Garrett
1991     *Brocade of the Pen: The Art of Islamic Writing.* East Lansing: Kresge Art Museum, Michigan State University.

Flower, Margaret
1973     *Victorian Jewellery.* New York: A. S. Barnes and Company.

Fortune, Lesa Farrar
1997     *Adinkra: The Cloth That Speaks.* Washington, D.C.: National Museum of African Art.

Fosu, Kwaku Amoako-Attah
2001     *Festivals in Ghana.* Kumase: N.p.

Fraser, Douglas, and Herbert M. Cole
1972     *African Art and Leadership.* Madison: The University of Wisconsin Press.

Freeman, Richard Austin
1898 [1967]  *Travels and Life in Ashanti and Jaman.* Westminster: Archibald Constable & Co.

Freeman, Thomas B.
1844 [1968] *Journal of Various Visits to the Kingdoms of Ashanti, Aku, and Dahomi in Western Africa.* London: Frank Cass & Co. Ltd.

Frenee, Okyeame Awuku (Akuapem State Linguist)
1976 *1976 Odwira Handbook: Some Historical Facts, Figures, Record of Events and Programmes.* Accra: Liberty Press Limited.

Fynn, John Kofi
1971 *Asante and Its Neighbours, 1700–1807.* Evanston: Northwestern University Press.

Garrard, Timothy F.
1980 *Akan Weights and the Gold Trade.* London: Longman and Group Limited.
1984 "Akan Silver." *African Arts* 17 (2): 48–53, 89.
1989 *Gold of Africa.* Munich: The Barbier-Mueller Museum, Geneva, and Prestel-Verlag.
1993a "The Arts of Metal in Côte d'Ivoire." In *Art of Côte d'Ivoire from the Collections of the Barbier-Mueller Museum.* Vol. I. Edited by Jean Paul Barbier, 384–401. Geneva: The Barbier-Mueller Museum.
1993b "The Baule: An Introduction." In *Art of Côte d'Ivoire from the Collections of the Barbier-Mueller Museum.* Vol. 1. Edited by Jean Paul Barbier, 290–301. Geneva: The Barbier-Mueller Museum.
1993c "Catalogue Entries." In *Art of Côte d'Ivoire from the Collections of the Barbier-Mueller Museum.* Vol. 2. Edited by Jean Paul Barbier, 153–58. Geneva: The Barbier-Mueller Museum.
1995 "Pectoral Disc." In *Africa: The Art of a Continent*, edited by Tom Phillips. London: Royal Academy of Arts.

Gilbert, Michelle
1989 "Sources of Power in Akuropon-Akuapem: Ambiguity in Classification." In *Creativity of Power: Cosmology and Action in African Societies*, edited by W. Arens and Ivan Karp. Washington, D.C.: Smithsonian Institution Press.
1993 "The Leopard Who Sleeps in a Basket: Akuapem Secrecy in Everyday Life and in Royal Metaphor." In *Secrecy: African Art that Conceals and Reveals*, edited by Polly Nooter Roberts, 122–39. New York: The Museum for African Art.
1994a "Aesthetic Strategies: The Politics of a Royal Ritual." *Africa: Journal of the International African Institute* 64 (1): 99–125.
1994b "Vengeance as Illusion and Reality: The Case of the Battered Wife." *Man: The Journal of the Royal Anthropological Institute* 29 (4): 853–73.
1997 "'No Condition Is Permanent': Ethnic Construction and the Use of History in Akuapem." *Africa* 67 (4): 501–33.
1998 "Concert Parties: Paintings and Performance." *Journal of Religion in Africa* 28 (1): 62–92.

Glanville, Philippa, and Jennifer Faulds Goldsborough
1990 *Women Silversmiths, 1685–1845.* Washington, D.C.: National Museum of Women in the Arts.

Gloag, John
1972 *Guide to Furniture Styles: English and French, 1450–1850.* New York.

Glover, E. Ablade
1971 "Linguist Staff Symbolism" (poster/chart). Labadi: Art-Gallery.

Goody, Jack
1963 "Feudalism in Africa?" *Journal of African History* 4 (1): 1–18.
1969 "Economy and Feudalism in Africa." *The Economic History Review*, 2d ser., 22 (3): 393–405.

Gott, Suzanne
Forthcoming "Golden Emblems of Maternal Benevolence: Transformations of Form and Meaning in Akan Regalia." *African Arts.*

Gros, J.
1884 *Voyages, aventures et captivité de J. Bonnat chez les Achantis.* Paris.

Gyekye, Kwame
1995 *An Essay on African Philosophical Thought: The Akan Conceptual Scheme.* Rev. ed. Philadelphia: Temple University Press.

Hair, P. E. H., Adam Jones, and Robin Law, eds.
1992 *Barbot on Guinea: The Writings of Jean Barbot on West Africa, 1678–1712.* 2 vols. London: The Hakluyt Society.

Henige, David, and T. C. McCaskie
1990 *West African Economic and Social History.* Madison: African Studies Program, University of Wisconsin–Madison.

Henty, G. A.
1874 *The March to Coomassie.* London: Tinsley Brothers.

Himmelheber, Hans
1972 "Gold-Plated Objects of Baule Notables." In *African Art and Leadership*, edited by Douglas Fraser and Herbert M. Cole, 185–208. Wisconsin: The University of Wisconsin Press.

Hinks, Peter
1991 *Victorian Jewelry: A Complete Compendium of Over Four Thousand Pieces of Jewelry.* London: Studio Editions.

Hunwick, John, and Nancy Lawler, eds.
1980 *The Cloth of Many Colored Silks: Papers on History and Society Ghanaian and Islamic in Honor of Ivor Wilks.* Evanston: Northwestern University Press.

Hutchinson, William
1819 [1966] "Diary." In *Mission from Cape Coast Castle to Ashantee*, by Thomas Edward Bowdich, 381–421. 1st ed. London: Johan Murray; 3rd ed. London: Frank Cass & Co., Ltd.

Huydecoper, W.
1816–17 [1962]  *Huydecoper's Diary: Journal from Elmina to Kumasi 28th April 1816–18th May 1817,* translated by Graham Irvine. Legon: Department of History, Legon

Isert, Paul Erdmann
1788 [1992]  *Letters on West Africa and the Slave Trade: Paul Erdmann Isert's Journey to Guinea and the Caribbean Islands in Columbia.* Translated by Selena Axelrod Winsnes. Union Académique Internationale, Fontes Historiae Africanae, serie varia 7. Oxford: Oxford University Press.

Johnson, Marian Ashby
1994  "Gold Jewelry of the Wolof and the Tukulor of Senegal." *African Arts* 27 (1): 36–49, 94.

Johnson, Marion
1937  "Wood-Carving by the Wood Carver to the Asantehene." *The Teacher's Journal* 10 (3): 269–71.
1979a  "Ashanti Craft Organization." *African Arts* 13 (1): 60–63, 78–82, 97.
1979b  "Ekyem, the State Shield." In *Akan-Asante Studies,* 6–10. British Museum Occasional Paper, no 3. London: British Museum.

Johnson, Marion, and M. D. McLeod
1979  *Akan-Asante Studies.* British Museum Occasional Paper, no 3. London: British Museum.

Jones, Adam
1983  *German Sources for West African History, 1599–1669.* Wiesbaden: Franz Steiner Verlag GMBH.
1993  "'My Arse for Okou': A Wartime Ritual of Women on the Nineteenth-Century Gold Coast." *Cahiers d'études africaines,* 132 (23–24): 545–66.
1994  "Drink Deep, or Taste Not: Thoughts on the Use of Early European Records in the Study of African Material Culture." *History in Africa: A Journal of Method* 21: 349–70.

Kahlenberg, Mary Hunt, ed.
1988  *The Extraordinary in the Ordinary: Textiles and Objects from Lloyd Cotsen and the Neutrogena Corporation.* New York: Harry N. Abrams.

Kan, Michael, and Roy Sieber
1995  *African Masterworks in the Detroit Institute of Arts.* Washington, D.C.: Smithsonian Institution Press.

Kemp, Dennis
1898 [1982]  *Nine Years at the Gold Coast.* London: Macmillan and Co. Limited.

Klein, A. Norman
1981  "The Two Asantes: Competing Interpretations of 'Slavery' in Akan-Asante Culture and Society." In *The Ideology of Slavery in Africa,* edited by Paul E. Lovejoy, 149–67. Beverly Hills: Sage Publications.

Kyerematen, A. A. Y.
1961  *Regalia for an Ashanti Durbar.* Ghana: Kwame Nkrumah University of Science and Technology.
1964  *Panoply of Ghana: Ornamental Art in Ghanaian Tradition and Culture.* New York: Praeger.
1966  "Ashanti Royal Regalia: Their History and Functions." Ph. D. diss., Oxford University.
1969  "The Royal Stools of Ashanti." *Africa: The Journal of the International African Institute* 39 (1): 1–13.
1970  *Kingship and Ceremony in Ashanti: Dedicated to the Memory of Otumfuo Sir Osei Agyeman Prempeh II, Asantehene.* Kumase: UST Press.

Lainé, Daniel
1991  *African Kings.* Berkeley: Ten Speed Press.

Lamb, Venice
1975  *West African Weaving.* London: Duckworth.

Law, Robin
1985  "Human Sacrifice in Pre-Colonial West Africa." *African Affairs Journal of the Royal African Society* 84 (334): 53–88.
1989  "'My Head Belongs to the King': On the Political and Ritual Significance of Decapitation in Pre-Colonial Dahomey." *Journal of African History* 30: 399–415.

Lee, R. (formerly Mrs. T. Edward Bowdich)
1835  *Stories of Strange Lands; and Fragments from the Notes of a Traveller.* London: Edward Moxon.

Loucou, Jean-Noël
1993  "Peoples and Cultures of Côte d'Ivoire." In *Art of Côte d'Ivoire from the Collections of the Barbier-Mueller Museum.* Vol. I. Edited by Jean Paul Barbier, 10–29. Geneva: The Barbier-Mueller Museum.

Lovejoy, Paul E., ed.
1981  *The Ideology of Slavery in Africa.* Beverly Hills: Sage Publications.

Loyer, Godefroy
1714 [1935]  "Relation du voyage du Royaume d'Issiny." In *L'Establissement d'Issiny, 1687–1702.,* edited by Paul Roussier, 109–235. Paris: Librairie Larose.

Magnin, Andre, ed.
1997  *Seydou Keita.* Zurich: Scalo Edition.

Maier, D. J. E.
1990  "Military Acquisition of Slaves in Asante." In *West African Economic and Social History,* edited by David Henige and T. C. McCaskie, 119–32. Madison: African Studies Program, University of Wisconsin Madison.

Mato, Daniel
1987  *Clothed in Symbol—The Art of Adinkra among the Akan of Ghana.* Ph.D. diss., Indiana University.

Maurice, J. P.
1874    *The Ashantee War: A Popular Narrative*. London: Henry S. King and Co.

McCaskie, T. C.
1981    "Anti-Witchcraft Cults in Asante: An Essay in the Social History of an African People." *History in Africa: A Journal of Method* 8: 125–54.
1983    "Accumulation, Wealth, and Belief in Asante History: 1. To the Close of the Nineteenth Century." *Africa: Journal of the International African Institute* 53 (1): 23–43.
1985    "Power and Dynastic Conflict in Mampon." *History in Africa* 12: 167–85.
1986a   "Accumulation: Wealth and Belief in Asante History: 2. The Twentieth Century." *Africa: Journal of the International African Institute* 56 (1): 3–23.
1986b   "Komfo Anokye of Asante: Meaning, History, and Philosophy in an African Society." *Journal of African History* 27 (2): 315–40.
1989a   "Asantesεm: Reflections on Discourse and Text in Africa." In *Discourse and Its Disguises*, 70–86. Birmingham University African Studies Series, no. 1. Birmingham: Centre of West African Studies.
1989b   "Death and the *Asantehene*: a Historical Meditation." *Journal of African History* 30 (3): 417–44.
1990    "Inventing Asante." In *Self-Assertion and Brokerage*, edited by P. F. de Moraes Farias and Karin Barber, 55–67. Birmingham: Centre of West African Studies, Birmingham University.
1992    "People and Animals: Constru(ct)ing the Asante Experience." *Africa: Journal of the International African Institute* 62 (2): 221–47.
1995    *State and Society in Pre-Colonial Asante*. Cambridge: Cambridge: University Press.
2000    *Asante Identities: History and Modernity in an African Village, 1850–1950*. International African Library, 25. Edinburgh: Edinburgh University Press.

McLeod, Malcolm D.
1976    "Verbal Elements in West African Art." *Quaderni Poro* 1: 85–102.
1978    "Aspects of Asante Images." In *Art and Society*, edited by Michael Greenhalgh and Vincent Megan, 305–16. London: Duckworth.
1979    "Asante Spokesmen's Staffs: Their Probable Origin and Development." In *Akan-Asante Studies*, 11–20. British Museum Occasional Paper, no. 3. London: British Museum.
1981    *The Asante*. London: British Museum Publications.
1984    "The Golden Ax of Asante." *Natural History* 10: 62–72.
1987a   "Gifts and Attitudes." In *The Golden Stool: Studies of the Asante Center and Periphery*, edited by Enid Schildkrout, 184–91. Anthropological Papers of the American Museum of Natural History, vol. 65, part 1. New York: American Museum of Natural History.
1987b   "Asante Gold-weights: Images and Words." *Word and Image* 3 (3): 289–95.

Menzel, Brigitte
1968    *Goldgewichte*. Berlin: Museum für Volkerkunde.
1972    *Textilien Aus Westafrica*. Vols. 1 and 2. Berlin: Museum für Volkerkunde.
1973    *Textilien Aus Westafrica*. Vol. 3. Berlin: Museum für Volkerkunde.

Meyerowitz, Eva Lewin-Richter
1960    *The Divine Kingship in Ghana and Ancient Egypt*. London: Faber and Faber.

Müller, Wilhelm Johann
1673 [1983]   "Wilhelm Johann Muller's Description of the Fetu Country, 1662–1669." In *German Sources for West African History, 1599–1669*, edited by Adam Jones, 134–258. Weisbaden: Franz Steiner Verlag GMBH.

Nketia, J. H.
1963    *Drumming in Akan Communities of Ghana*. Legon: Thomas Nelson and Sons, Ltd.

Odoi, Oykeameba
1970    "The Traditional African Secretary of State." Ph.D. diss., University of Pennsylvania.

OED
1971    *The Compact Edition of the Oxford English Dictionary*, s.v. "palanquin."

Ofori-Ansa
1993    *Kente Is More than a Cloth* (poster). Hyattsville, Md.: Sankofa Publications.

Ohene, I. B.
1971    "Gesture—Language of the Hand." Senior thesis, University of Science and Technology, Kumase.

Opoku, A. A.
1970    *Festivals of Ghana*. Accra: Ghana Publishing Corporation.

Opoku, Albert Mawere
1987    "Asante Dance Art and the Court." In *The Golden Stool: Studies of the Asante Center and Periphery*, edited by Enid Schildkrout, 192–99. Anthropological Papers of the American Museum of Natural History, vol. 65, part 1. New York: American Museum of Natural History.

Owusu, Francis Kwame
1978    "The Importance of the Linguist and His Staff in the Sefwi Wiawso Traditional Area." Student thesis, Winneba Specialist Training College.

Owusu-Ansah, David
1983    "Islamic Influence in a Forest Kingdom: The Role of Protective Amulets in Early Nineteenth-Century Asante." *Transafrican Journal of History* 12: 100–33.
1987    "Islamization Reconsidered: An Examination of Asante Responses to Muslim Influence in the Nineteenth Century." *Asian and African Studies* 21: 145–63.

1991 *Islamic Talismanic Tradition in Nineteenth-Century Asante.* African Studies, vol. 21. Lewiston: The Edwin Mellen Press.

Patton, Sharon F.
1984 "The Asante Umbrella." *African Arts* 17 (4): 64–73.
1987 "The Stool and Asante Chieftaincy." *African Arts* 13 (1): 74–77, 98–99.

Phillips, Tom, ed.
1995 *Africa: The Art of a Continent.* London and Munich: Royal Academy of Arts and Prestel Verlag.

Plass, Margaret Webster
1967 *African Miniatures: The Goldweights of the Ashanti.* London: Lund Humphries.

Posnansky, Merrick
1987 "Prelude to Akan Civilization." In *The Golden Stool: Studies of the Asante Center and Periphery,* edited by Enid Schildkrout, 14–22. Anthropological Papers of the American Museum of Natural History, vol. 65, part 1. New York: American Museum of Natural History.

Preston, George
1972 *Twifo-Heman and the Akan Leadership Complex.* Ph.D. diss., Columbia University.

Prussin, Labelle
1986 *Hatumere: Islamic Design in West Africa.* Berkeley: University of California Press.

Quarcoo, A. K.
1970 *The Language of Adinkra Patterns.* Legon: Institute of African Studies, University of Ghana.
1975 "Leadership Art: Exhibition on the Occasion of the Intergovernmental Conference on Cultural Policies in Africa, 27th October–6th November 1975." Legon: Institute of African Studies, University of Ghana.
1990 "The Sacred Asessedwa and Mission." *International Review of Missions* 79 (316): 493–98.

Ramseyer, Friedrich August, and Johannes Kühne
1875 *Four Years in Ashantee.* New York: Robert Carter and Brothers.

Rattray, Robert S.
1916 *Ashanti Proverbs.* Oxford: Clarendon Press.
1923 *Ashanti.* Oxford: Clarendon Press.
1927 *Religion and Art in Ashanti.* Oxford: Clarendon Press.
1929 *Ashanti Law and Constitution.* Oxford: Clarendon Press.
1930 *Akan-Ashanti Folk-Tales.* Oxford: Clarendon Press

Ravenhill, Philip L.
1996 *Dreams and Reverie: Images of Otherworld Mates among the Baule, West Africa.* Washington, D.C.: Smithsonian Institution Press.

Reade, Winwood
1874 *The Story of the Ashantee Campaign.* London: Smith, Elder and Co.

Reindorf, Rev. Carl Christian
1895 [1966] *The History of the Gold Coast and Asante.* Accra: Ghana Universities Press.

Roberts, Polly Nooter, ed.
1993 *Secrecy: African Art That Conceals and Reveals.* New York: The Museum for African Art.

Rømer, Ludewig Ferdinand
2000 *A Reliable Account of the Coast of Guinea (1760).* Translated and edited by Selena Axelrod Winsnes. Oxford: Oxford University Press.

Ross, Doran H.
1974 "Ghanaian Forowa." *African Arts* 8 (1): 40–49, 88–89.
1977 "The Iconography of Asante Sword Ornaments." *African Arts* 11 (1): 16–25, 90–91.
1978 "Apropos: Snakebit." *African Arts* 11 (4): 10–11, 13.
1979 *Fighting with Art: Appliquéd Flags of the Fante Asafo.* Los Angeles: UCLA Museum of Cultural History.
1980 "Cement Lions and Cloth Elephants: Asafo Arts in Southern Ghana." In *5000 Years of Popular Culture: Popular Culture before Printing,* edited by Fred E. H. Schroeder, 287–317. Bowling Green: Bowling Green University Popular Press.
1982a "The Heraldic Lion in Akan Art: A Study of Motif Assimilation in Southern Ghana." *Metropolitan Museum Journal* 16: 165–80
1982b "The Verbal Art of Akan Linguist Staffs." *African Arts* 16 (1): 56–67, 95.
1983a "Four Unusual *Forowa* from the Museum of Cultural History." In *Akan Transformations: Problems in Ghanaian Art History,* edited by Doran H. Ross and Timothy F. Garrard, 54–59. Los Angeles: UCLA Museum of Cultural History.
1983b "The Akan Double-Bladed Sword: A Case of Islamic Origins." In *Akan Transformations: Problems in Ghanaian Art History,* edited by Doran H. Ross and Timothy F. Garrard, 60–69. Los Angeles: UCLA Museum of Cultural History.
1984 "The Art of Osei Bonsu." *African Arts* 17 (2): 28–40, 95.
1986 "Akan Gold Rings." In *Bulletin,* no. 30. Geneva: The Barbier Mueller Museum.
1988 "Queen Victoria for £25: The Iconography of a Breasted Drum from Southern Ghana." *College Art Journal* 47 (2): 114–20.
1989 "Drums of Akan Popular Bands." In *African Musical Instruments,* edited by Marie-Thérèse Brincard, 78–81. New York: American Federation of Arts
1992a *Elephant: The Animal and Its Ivory in African Culture* (ed.). Los Angeles: UCLA Fowler Museum of Cultural History.
1992b "More than Meets the Eye: Elephant Memories among the Akan." In *Elephant: Elephant and its Ivory in African Culture,* edited by Doran H. Ross, 137–59. Los Angeles: UCLA Fowler Museum of Cultural History.
1994 *Visions of Africa: The Jerome L. Joss Collection of African Art at ucla* (ed.) Los Angeles: UCLA Fowler Museum of Cultural History.

1996a   "Akua's Child and Other Relatives: New Mythologies for Old Dolls." In *Isn't S/He a Doll? Play and Ritual in African Sculpture*, edited by Elisabeth Cameron, 42–57. Los Angeles: UCLA Fowler Museum of Cultural History.

1996b   "Asante." In *The Dictionary of Art*, edited by Jane Turner, 584–90. New York: Macmillan Publishers Ltd.

1997   "Ashanti Leadership Arts." In *Art and Life in Africa*, edited by Christopher Roy, developed by L. Lee McIntyre. Iowa City: University of Iowa. (Twenty-eight-screen chapter in interactive CD-ROM.)

1998a   *Wrapped in Pride: Ghanaian Kente and African American Identity* (ed.). Los Angeles: UCLA Fowler Museum of Cultural History.

1998b   "Hammock?" In *The Extraordinary in the Ordinary: Textiles and Objects from Lloyd Cotsen and the Neutrogena Corporation*, edited by Mary Hunt Kahlenberg, 180. New York: Harry N. Abrams.

2002   "Misplaced Souls: Reflections on Gold, Chiefs, Slaves, and Death among the Akan." *The Bulletin of the Detroit Institute of Arts* 76 (1/2): 22–39.

Ross, Doran H., and Timothy F. Garrard, eds.

1983   *Akan Transformations: Problems in Ghanaian Art History.* Los Angeles: UCLA Museum of Cultural History.

Roussier, Paul, ed.

1714 [1935]  *L'Establissement d'Issiny, 1687–1702.* Paris: Librairie Larose.

Sarpong, Peter Kwasi

1967   "The Sacred Stools of Ashanti." *Anthropos* 62 (1/2): 1–60.

1971   *The Sacred Stools of the Akan.* Accra-Tema: Ghana Publishing Corporation.

1974   *Ghana in Retrospect: Some Aspects of Ghanaian Culture.* Tema: Ghana Publishing Corporation.

1990   *The Ceremonial Horns of the Ashanti.* Accra: Sedco Publishing Limited.

Schildkrout, Enid, ed.

1987   *The Golden Stool: Studies of the Asante Center and Periphery.* Anthropological Papers of the American Museum of Natural History, vol. 65, part 1. New York: American Museum of Natural History.

Schildkrout, Enid, and Frank Fournier (photographer)

1996   "Kingdom of Gold." *Natural History* 105 (2): 36–47.

Schroeder, Fred E. H., ed.

1980   *5000 Years of Popular Culture: Popular Culture before Printing.* Bowling Green: Bowling Green University Popular Press.

Shinnie, Peter

1996   "Early Asante: Is Wilks Right?" In *The Cloth of Many Colored Silks: Papers on History and Society Ghanaian and Islamic in Honor of Ivor Wilks*, edited by J. Hunwick and N. Lawler, 195–203. Evanston: Northwestern University.

Silverman, Raymond

1982–83   "Fourteenth–Fifteenth Century Syrio-Egyptian Brassware in Ghana." *Nyame Akuma* 20: 13–16.

1987   "Historical Dimensions of Tano Worship among the Asante and Bono." In *The Golden Stool: Studies of the Asante Center and Periphery*, edited by E. Schildkrout, 272–88. Anthropological Papers of the American Museum of Natural History, vol. 65, part 1. New York: American Museum of Natural History.

1990   "All That's Gold Does Not Glitter: Review of *Gold of Africa*," *African Arts* 23 (2): 71–80, 103.

1998   "The Gods Wear Kente." In *Wrapped in Pride: Ghanaian Kente and African American Identity*, edited by Doran H. Ross. Los Angeles: UCLA Fowler Museum of Cultural History.

Stanley, Henry M.

1874   *Coomasie and Magdala: The Story of Two British Campaigns in Africa.* New York: Harper and Brothers.

Sutherland, D. A.

1954   *State Emblems of the Gold Coast.* Cape Coast: G. B. Pound.

Swithenbank, Michael

1969   *Ashanti Fetish Houses.* Accra: Ghana Universities Press.

Terray, E.

1983   "Gold Production, Slave Labor, and State Intervention in Precolonial Akan Societies: A Reply to Raymond Dumett." In *Research in Economic Anthropology, A Research Annual,* edited by George Dalton, 95–129. London: Jai Press Inc.

Thompson, Robert Farris

1974   *African Art in Motion.* Berkeley: University of California Press.

Tilleman, Erick

1697 [1994]  *A Short and Simple Account of the Country Guinea and Its Nature.* Translated and edited by Selena Axelrod Winsnes. Madison: African Studies Program, University of Wisconsin.

Tooley, Sarah

1897   *The Personal Life of Queen Victoria.* London: Hodder and Stoughton.

Turner, Jane, ed.

1996   *The Dictionary of Art.* New York: Macmillan Publishers.

Van Dantzig, Albert

1970   "A Note on 'The State Sword—A Pre-Ashanti Tradition.'" *Ghana Notes and Queries* 11 (June): 47–48.

Van Dantzig, Albert, and Adam Jones, trans. and eds.

1978   *The Dutch and the Guinea Coast, 1674–1742: A Collection of Documents from the General Archive at the Hague.* Accra: GAAS.

1987   *Description and Historical Account of the Gold Kingdom of Guinea (1602), by Pieter de Marees.* New York: Oxford University Press.

Visoná, Monica Blackmun
1987 "The Asante Origins of the Lagoon Peoples as an Art Historical Problem." In *The Golden Stool: Studies of the Asante Center and Periphery*, edited by Enid Schildkrout, 298–309. Anthropological Papers of the American Museum of Natural History, vol. 65, part 1. New York: American Museum of Natural History.
1993 "The Lagoons Peoples." In *Art of Côte d"Ivoire from the Collections of the Barbier-Mueller Museum.* Vol. 1. Edited by Jean Paul Barbier, 368–83. Geneva: The Barbier-Mueller Museum.

Vogel, Susan Mullin
1997 *Baule: African Art Western Eyes.* New Haven: Yale University Press.

Wallace-Johnson, Isaac T. A.
1935 "A Full and Illustrated Report of the Proceedings of the Restoration of the Ashanti Confederacy." Supplement to *The West African Sentinel.* Accra.

Warren, Dennis Michael
1975 *The Techiman-Bono of Ghana: An Ethnography of an Akan Society.* Dubuque: Kendall/Hunt Publishing Company.
1976a *Bibliography and Vocabulary of the Akan (Twi-Fante) Language of Ghana,* Indiana University Publications, African Series, vol. 6. Bloomington: Indiana University.
1976b "Bono Shrine Art." *African Arts* 9 (2): 28–34.

Warren, Dennis Michael, and J. Kweku Andrews
1977 "An Ethnoscientific Approach to Akan Arts and Aesthetics." In *Working Papers in the Traditional Arts, no. 3.* Philadelphia: Institute for the Study of Human Issues.

Warren, Dennis Michael, and K. Owusu Brempong
1971 *Techiman Traditional State, Part I: Stool and Town Histories.* Legon, Ghana.

Weiskel, Timothy C.
1987 "Asante and the Akan Periphery: The Baule on the Western Akan Frontier." In *The Golden Stool: Studies of the Asante Center and Periphery*, edited by Enid Schildkrout, 260–71. Anthropological Papers of the American Museum of Natural History, vol. 65, part 1. New York: American Museum of Natural History.

Welman, C. W.
1969 *The Native States of the Gold Coast.* London: Dawsons of Pall Mall.

Wilks, Ivor
1961 *The Northern Factor in Ashanti History.* University College of Ghana.
1975 *Asante in the Nineteenth Century: The Structure and Evolution of a Political Order.* London: Cambridge University Press.
1976 "A Photograph of the Asantehene Kwaku Dua II." *Asante Seminar '76: The Asante Collective Biography Project Bulletin* 4 (February): 39–40.

1988 "Asante: Human Sacrifice or Capital Punishment: A Rejoinder." *The International Journal of African Historical Studies.* 21 (3): 443–52.
1993 *Forests of Gold: Essays on the Akan and the Kingdom of Asante.* Athens: Ohio University Press.

Williams, Clifford
1988 "Asante: Human Sacrifice or Capital Punishment? An Assessment of the Period, 1807–1874." *The International Journal of African Historical Studies* 21 (3): 433–42.

Willis, W. Bruce
1998 *The Adinkra Dictionary.* Washington, D.C.: The Pyramid Complex.

Wiredu, Kwasi
1983 "The Akan Concept of Mind." *Ibadan Journal of Humanistic Studies,* no. 3 (October): 113–34.

Wright, Dudley
1936 *Gould's History of Freemasonry throughout the World.* Vol. 4. Revised by the author. New York: Charles Scribner's Sons.

Yankah, Kwesi
1985 "The Proverb in the Context of Akan Rhetoric," Ph. D. diss., Indiana University.
1995 *Speaking for the Chief: Okyeame and the Politics of Akan Royal Oratory.* Bloomington: Indiana University Press.

Yarak, Larry W.
1990 *Asante and the Dutch, 1744–1873.* Oxford: Clarendon Press.
1996 "Slavery and the State in Asante History." In *The Cloth of Many Colored Silks: Papers on History and Society Ghanaian and Islamic in Honor of Ivor Wilks*, edited by J. Hunwick and N. Lawler, 223–240. Evanston: Northwestern University Press.